Digital Collage and Painting

Using Photoshop and Painter to Create Fine Art

Susan Ruddick Bloom

ELSEVIER

AMSTERDAM • BOSTON • HEIDELBERG • LONDON
NEW YORK • OXFORD • PARIS • SAN DIEGO
SAN FRANCISCO • SINGAPORE • SYDNEY • TOKYO

Focal Press is an imprint of Elsevier

Focal
Press

Acquisitions Editor: Diane Heppner
Project Manager: Paul Gottehrer
Assistant Editor: Cara Anderson
Marketing Manager: Christine Degon Veroulis
Cover Design: Gary Regalia
Interior Design: Julio Esperas

Focal Press is an imprint of Elsevier
30 Corporate Drive, Suite 400, Burlington, MA 01803, USA
Linacre House, Jordan Hill, Oxford OX2 8DP, UK

 Recognizing the importance of preserving what has been written, Elsevier prints its
books on acid-free paper whenever possible.

Library of Congress Cataloging-in-Publication Data
Application submitted

British Library Cataloguing-in-Publication Data
A catalogue record for this book is available from the British Library.

ISBN 13: 978-0-240-80705-8
ISBN 10: 0-240-80705-7

For information on all Focal Press publications
visit our website at www.books.elsevier.com

Printed in Canada

06 07 08 09 10   10 9 8 7 6 5 4 3 2 1

Contents

Part II *Step-by-Step Painting*

Dedication

Many people have been invaluable to me as I wrote this book. My Editor at Focal Press, Diane Heppner, who asked me to consider writing this book and then held my hand through the whole 2-year process, was a joy to work with. The 21 digital artists that participated in Chapter Three were wonderful digital pioneers, willing to share their skills with all. My colleagues at McDaniel College were supportive and patient throughout the writing process. My friends, that cheered me on through times when the words didn't flow well were a great boon to my spirit. But foremost in my heart, is my family. My parents, Earvin and Dorothy Ruddick, who instilled the love of art in my life at an early age and nurtured it throughout my life. My children, Sara and Emily, who have posed for me throughout their entire lives, have been a constant source of joy and pride. Most special thanks go to my husband, Calvin, who single-handedly built my artist's studio that is such a pleasure to work in. He took on the chores of laundry and cooking as I spent untold hours creating art and writing about it. Sincere and loving thanks to all.

Susan Ruddick Bloom
April 2006

I

Planning and Inspiration

1 Concept

Where does that kernel of inspiration come from? Does it hit you when you are in the shower or when you are driving on the turnpike? Wherever it takes hold of you, it marks the beginning of the process of making a piece of art. Some artists agonize step-by-step in the creation process. For some people the work flows seamlessly from an inner fountain of inspiration.

There is an endless array of possible starting points. The *ah-ha* moment can be when you look at the texture of an old wall with peeling paint, the detail contained on a moth's wing, or the sweep of the landscape contours on a hillside. As artists, we can be surprised by almost anything as we explore our world. Anything and everything is at our disposal as possible elements for inspiration.

OPPOSITE PAGE: *"Autumn Vista"*

Often we are taken by surprise, as a particular element "suggests" itself to us. The making of art is very intuitive and the artist learns to follow his nose. The actual making of the art is seldom a smooth ride. Instead, I would compare it to a roller-coaster ride. The process involves many unexpected twists, turns, and bumps. It is full of thrills and can be harrowing at times. But we wouldn't miss it for the world!

Once the seed of thought begins, where do you go with it? It is important to think this thing through before you begin. What is the total concept? How can you integrate images into the completed work that might enhance that beginning concept? What additional imagery do you need? How do you see it coming together?

Visually there are many things to consider. If you are using several images, as in a collage, how will you make them read as a whole? There needs to be a uniformity that unites the piece. You need to create a cohesive feel or mood. What will accomplish that for you? There are many unifying factors. Color can be the tie-in for you, or it might be scale, contrast, directionality, or more. We will cover some of these unifying factors in Chapter 2.

We will assume that the creative bug has gotten hold of you and you are now compelled to make a piece of art. So hold on to your socks and here we go.

What is a Collage, Montage, or Assemblage?

What form will the imagery take? Of course, artists throughout time have used marble and stone for sculpture, canvas and panels for paintings, paper for drawing and printmaking, and photographic paper for photography, to mention only a few formats. But, there is a dawning of a new age in art materials. We are fortunate to be living in the beginning of the digital age. For the artist, this introduces a whole new range of artistic tools and possibilities. The computer can be used to make imagery and is yet another tool in the imaginary tool belt that artists have at their disposal.

I attended a superb art college, where I was grounded in all the basics: strong drawing and painting skills, intense study of art history, and a good exposure to a variety of different artistic pursuits, from ceramics to fiber art, from lithography to photography. Mastery of the tools and techniques was a must in every field of endeavor. The artist needs to become so well acquainted with the materials and equipment that creative applications become second nature. Once some mastery of the materials is in place, the work flows more easily. When a more complete understanding of the tools and techniques is in place, the inquisitive mind of the artist often explores variations on the techniques. So it is with the field of computer imagery. The artist needs to prepare by obtaining a basic body of knowledge about the computer, software, and printing devices. Once these elements are in place, the artist can begin to fluidly make art using the digital tools at hand.

In this book, I have chosen to concentrate on two digital applications in the field of art: Digital Collage and Digital Painting. There are endless possibilities in this arena and I will attempt to explore the pos-

Art is an affirmation of life.
—ALFRED STEIGLITZ, *Photographs and Writings*, ed. by Sarah Greenhough and Juan Hamilton (1983)

The role of the artist is to hold up a vision of spiritual reality.
—JOSEPH CAMPBELL, *Hero with a Thousand Faces* (1949)

sibilities with you. How does the dictionary define assembled imagery? *The Merriam-Webster* definitions include the following concepts:

Collage
An artistic composition of fragments (as of printed matter) pasted on a surface

Montage
A composite photograph made by combining several separate pictures
An artistic composition made up of several different types of elements
A varied mixture: jumble

Assemblage
A collection of persons or things: gathering
The act of assembling
An artistic composition made from scraps, junk, and odds and ends
The art of making assemblages

For the sake of consistency in this book, I will refer to assembled images as collages, keeping in mind that in the field of art, assembled images could mean many different things, in both two and three dimensions. Traditional collage materials might vary in form, from magazine photos to flattened chewing gum wrappers, from dried plant materials to beach pebbles. Everything is fair game if it can be used for a purpose that enhances the imagery. Our imagery will be digital in nature, but as you will see later, that won't stop us from making artwork that has a more three-dimensional quality. There aren't any digital police that will stop you from pushing the artistic envelope. I would encourage you to experiment and explore where these digital tools might take you with your artistic expressions.

All art is at once surface and symbol.
—OSCAR WILDE,
The Picture of Dorian Gray (1891)

Figure 1-1
Scottish Cottage painting

What is a Digital Painting?

Digital painting, for me, usually involves just one image. I start with a photograph that I would like to transform into a painting. I use both a photo manipulation program (Adobe Photoshop) and a painting program (Corel Painter). I will show you in Chapters 4 and 5 how I approach creating a painting digitally. We will use tools that truly mimic real art materials, such as charcoal, colored pencils, airbrushes, pencils, and paint. But first a word on photography and its impact on the creation of artwork.

Let's put photography's contribution to making art in perspective. Since the announcement of the invention of the daguerreotype in 1839, artists have seized on the artistic possibilities that photography offers. Artists were the leaders in exploring this new medium. Itinerant portrait painters often converted to the craft of photography and emerged as the first traveling photographers. Samuel Morse, the Father of American photography, was present in Paris for the announcement of Daguerre's process to the French Academy of Sciences. Most of us know Morse for his invention of the telegraph and other scientific endeavors, but he was also an accomplished painter. Morse brought the techniques of photography to America and later trained one of the most acclaimed photographers of the nineteenth century, Matthew Brady.

The list of artists that have used photography as an aid in the creation of their paintings is long indeed, incorporating such esteemed names as Degas, Duchamp, and Eakins. For some artists the camera was used to stop-action the positioning of the body in motion. This was a task easily captured by the camera but not possible for the human eye.

One of the certainties in the art world, that seems to transcend time, is the dialogue that emerges as soon as a new type of medium is explored. We see that discussion currently, with the advent of digital fine art. Is it "really" art, if it came from the computer? It is as if the computer has somehow mechanically stained or lessened the artistic output. This cry is an old and recurrent one. Ansel Adams, Alfred Steiglitz, and Edward Steichen are a few of the prominent names in photography that fought that artistic battle in the 1940s and 1950s. They fought to create Departments of Photography in major museums.

Shortly after the announcement of Daguerre's photographic process was made in Paris, the painters in the French Academy declared "Painting is dead." If the camera could capture in a few seconds what a painter would take months to paint, what was to happen to the painter? What did the artist have to offer that the camera did not? I think it is no coincidence that painting starts to take a new path in the years that followed. Artists began to paint the essence of a moment in time, creating the impression of the moment rather than a strictly realistic rendition. The movement of Impressionism became dominant in painting in the years that followed the mass acceptance of the new technology of photography.

In the works of Michelangelo the creative force seems to rumble.
—AUGUSTE RODIN,
  in *Art*, trans. by Paul Gsell (1912)

What I do is the result of reflection and study of the great masters: of inspiration, spontaneity, temperament . . . I know nothing.
—EDGAR DEGAS,
  in *The Notebooks of Edgar Degas*, trans. by T. Reff (1976)

New technology has the force to propel art in new and unexpected directions. Change and growth always seem to come with controversy. I'm reminded of the quote that "Only babies with a wet diaper want a change." The rest of us usually find reasons why we don't want to change. Change often requires retooling ourselves and a large chunk of time to learn the new methods. It is easier to impugn the new methods than to learn from them. So beware! If you start to create art with the methods contained in this book, you may indeed be criticized and classified as a lesser artist. Wear the banner proudly—you are a pioneer! You come from a fine tradition of artists that have dared to explore new materials and methods and see what those new technologies have to offer in the making of their art.

A word of caution should be extended early in this book. Using the computer to create art doesn't make you an artist, just as using pastels doesn't make you an artist. Ultimately, over time, the artwork will be judged on its own merits artistically. Your challenge will be to learn the techniques that this new form of expression offers to you. Once the vocabulary of the digital art world is well known to you and you can understand and practice the techniques, your artistic vision will be what separates you from others in the field.

Ultimately, the tools really don't matter. They are quite simply the tools that allow the art to emerge. Picasso could use a discarded bicycle seat to make art; Jackson Pollock could fling paint onto a canvas to make his paintings. Both artists were strongly criticized as to whether their work deserved the title of art. Over time, their vision has come through and the work is seen in context.

Expect to incur some flack as a digital artist. Some art shows do not allow the inclusion of digitally produced art. Lack of knowledge about this field is the primary culprit, but some of the fault lies with ill-conceived and poorly executed artwork, produced without much consideration to basic art and design concepts. Educate yourself as an artist. Continue to explore opportunities to learn more. Sign up for workshops and courses. Go to museums regularly, to study at the feet of the masters. Get together with other artists to work, talk, and critique. The myth of the artist, tucked away in an attic garret making masterpieces, is just that, myth. Art is both a visual and an intellectual endeavor. You can never be too knowledgeable. Art is not made in a vacuum, but is created in context with our society and current events. It should be no surprise that the art world is being transformed in the digital age, as the rest of society and commerce is undergoing enormous upheavals in this new digital world we live in.

> Study the past, if you would divine the future.
> —CONFUCIUS,
>   *Analects* (c. 50 B.C.)

. . . .

Think it Out First, Assembling the Needed Images

It is very important to think through the intended project. What tools will you need? What imagery will be required? Try to extend the project out in your mind. Brainstorm a bit around your idea. Keep notes and draw thumbnail sketches. Maybe try a few little painting and sketching exercises around the concept. One of the things I have discovered in teaching, and in life as a whole, is that most people often pursue their first thought. Given a choice, most people will select the easiest and fastest track. It is easier to go with that first idea, than to take the time to think it through more thoroughly. It is often the case that the fifth or twelfth idea would really work better. But, most people never allow that possibility to occur. Take the time to explore your initial concept in depth.

What do you want to communicate? Are you trying to go for a mood or evoke an emotion? Are you trying to create a political satire? What is your intended message? What would be the best method to convey that concept? These are the moments when the course of the project is determined. Take the necessary time to let the idea germinate well.

Will you need to initiate an artistic scavenger hunt to find the necessary imagery for this project? In these litigious times we live in, I think it is always wise to rely solely on your own imagery. Use your scanner as a camera. It is a cheap and very effective tool. Use your digital camera as a collection device. Freed from the consumption of costly film and processing, digital photography has transformed our willingness to gather a vast array of imagery.

On a recent trip to Italy, I took over 4000 photos digitally. On my return home, those images were burned onto two digital video discs (DVDs) for a real fraction of the cost that film and processing would have incurred. Digital photography frees you to explore nuances of things. Did that scrap of paper in the gutter hold some appeal for you? Did that light beam outlining your toothbrush look interesting? Don't hesitate. Take the photo! Become a pack rat of imagery. Begin to create large files of photos to use later. This will result in a digital mountain of subject matter that will need to be cataloged and archived in some systematic manner. Be sure to spend some time with these issues.

> Paintings have a life of their own that derives entirely from the painter's soul.
> —Vincent van Gogh, in *The Complete van Gogh*, by Jan Hulsker (1977)

Are You Drowning in Digital Files?

I recommend that you immediately burn a compact disc (CD) or DVD of your downloaded images, before you alter them at all. This is your digital negative. Treat it as such. You will never have more pixels than you have at that moment, especially if you are shooting RAW. Burn a duplicate of this CD or DVD and store it in another location, in case of fire or a hurricane. Get in the practice of writing on the container or envelope but not directly on the disc (this can harm your files over time). Develop a system of cataloging and archiving your imagery, for easy retrieval. I know many digital artists that are drowning in their multitude of files and can never lay their hands on the photo they currently are seeking. Give meaningful names to your files and folders. You can batch process a folder of images, giving them new sequential numbers and names, instead of the crazy numbers and letters that come with the metadata from your camera. You can make contact sheets in Photoshop and keep notebooks of thumbnail images contained on each disc. You can purchase a piece of software that will archive your work for easy retrieval. In short, find a system that works for you and how you work and think. This one small piece of advice can really facilitate the ease with which you will work.

What is the Intended Output Size?

This one concept is huge in determining everything else. How big will you ever print this piece? You must match your file size to the requirements of the largest possible usage of your artwork. You can always make an image smaller, without sacrificing quality. The reverse of this is not true. You want to avoid asking the software to create more pixels than were originally captured. Think about medium- and large-format photography. Why did Ansel Adams go to the trouble of carrying big view cameras and heavy tripods up dangerous mountainsides? The answer, of course, is detail. The larger the negative, the more detail it contains. On film, the detail was made by particles of silver. In the digital world, we use pixels. You want as many pixels as you will need to output your image at the largest size you will ever intend to print out. Err on the side of caution if you are uncertain and go for a larger file. The flip side of this, of course, is that a large file takes longer to manipulate and is a storage hog. Seldom, however, have I regretted making a file size large at the outset. I can always create a smaller file of the same image for a project requiring less detail and resolution. With those housekeeping notes aside, we will proceed to some basic design considerations.

When I see a tree . . . I can feel that tree talking to me.
—JOAN MIRO,
Art News Magazine
(January 1980)

2 *Important Considerations Before You Begin*

Unifying Factors

Unifying factors cannot be underestimated. They are not big and flashy additions but they are frequently the glue that holds a composition together. Ideally you would like to have a cohesive feel throughout a piece. Every item in the piece should appear to be woven from the same cloth. Collage is particularly susceptible to problems with disparate elements. Generally, collages are assembled from items taken from a variety of source materials. The items can come from photographs, magazine clippings, scannings, and more. Frequently the resolution of the items will vary. In order for your completed artwork to present a cohesive feel, we will consider the unifying factors: texture, color, contrast, and noise or grain.

The first truth is form. Put on paper what you know is true rather than what you see.
—KIMON NICOLAIDES,
The Natural Way to Draw
(1941)

Texture

Texture in collage can be handled particularly well with the choice of your background layer. Where can you find a good background? Actually, background layers are all around us. I am constantly photographing textures and compiling CDs full of these images. They become a visual vocabulary that I can pull from, as a source for backgrounds. Where can you begin to find these textures? I'll share some of my favorites—skies, gardens, water, and rocks.

Skies

No bird soars too high if he soars with his own wings.
—WILLIAM BLAKE, *Proverbs of Hell* (1790)

My first suggestion would be to look up! The sky is a fabulous source. The sky is constantly changing and the colors are great, with subtle variances. The scale can be easily manipulated for your needs later. Photographing the sky doesn't require you to travel to exotic locales; you just need to step outside. You can live in a city or the country and still be able to gather good sky images. I find that people don't pay much attention to the sky unless they see a great, colorful sunset or see threatening storm clouds. The ordinary sky of our everyday lives is frequently overlooked, but seldom boring. If you train yourself to be looking at its marvelous variances throughout the day, you will quite simply be amazed at how beautiful it is. Take your digital camera out each day and start to make a catalog of sky images. You can sort the images, if you like, into folders by the type of cloud, color, etc. Begin today!

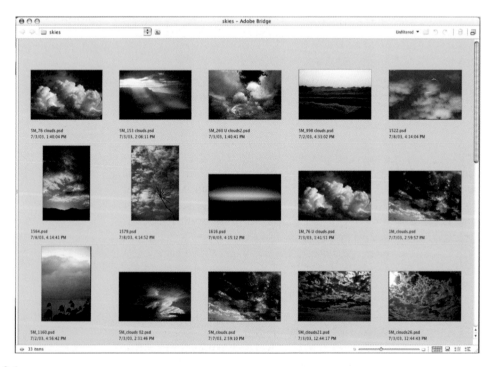

Figure 2-1
Various skies in the Adobe File Browser

Gardens

Another excellent source for backgrounds is the garden. Begin to develop files of images that explore the textures of plant life, from ordinary grasses, to leaves, to exotic flowers. Try some extreme close-ups of the anatomy of a flower or leaf. The colors range across the entire spectrum. You can find shiny surfaces or dull ones, and delicate, transparent petals to thick, waxy cactus leaves.

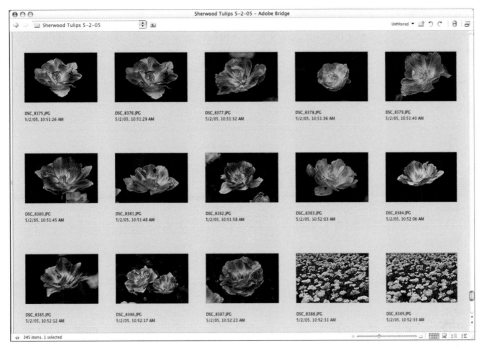

Figure 2-2
Catalog of garden flowers

Water

Take your camera everywhere. Photograph the beach with its rolling and crashing waves. Try some close-ups of the sea as it meets the shore. Photograph lakes and streams. If you can find an underwater housing for your camera, take some shots from under the sea. Another possibility for great water images is a ride on a glass-bottom boat or a visit to a local aquarium. Water, like the sky, can be an element that doesn't have an apparent scale. That can be a useful thing when you are constructing collages.

Rocks

Rocks are wonderful source materials. Rocks are everywhere: there are the smooth stones along Maine's coast, the unique ochre-colored desert rocks, and the ordinary rocks that you find in your driveway or along pathways. In an image, it often is not possible to distinguish between a boulder and a pebble by shape, contour, and color. Digitally it is possible for the boulder and pebble to be interchangeable.

Figures 2-3, 2-4, and 2-5 illustrate the various types of views available in Adobe Bridge (new with Adobe Photoshop CS2). Bridge replaces the File Browser we have grown accustomed to. It is integrated into Photoshop CS2 but is also a stand-alone piece of software.

Figure 2-3
Bridge—Filmstrip view

Figure 2-4
Bridge—Thumbnails view

My artistic center is in my
head and I am strong just
because I am never misled
by others, but make what
is in me to do.
—PAUL GAUGIN,
in *Avant et Apres:
Paul Gaugin's Intimate
Journals*, trans. by Van
Wyck Brooks (1958)

Figure 2-5
Bridge—Details view

Color

What is the predominant color effect you want to achieve in your piece
of artwork? Do you want it to be made with soft pastel tones or vibrant
bright colors? Do you want a monotone or neutral effect?

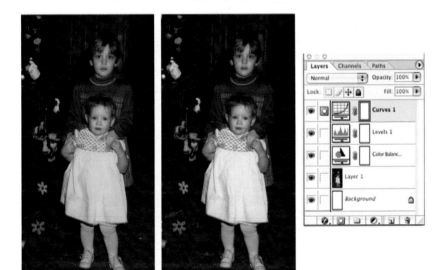

Figure 2-6
*Color-corrected old slide
(that had developed green
tones)*

There is no blue without yellow and orange.
—Vincent van Gogh, in *The Complete van Gogh*, by Jan Hulsker (1977)

If you are combining many photos of people, you will be sure to notice the variance in skin tones and the variety of lighting conditions that the photos were made under. Undoubtedly, you will need to modify the color to achieve a uniformity of tone. If you are using color photographs from 20 or 30 years ago, you will notice extreme color shifts due to time. The dyes in the print migrate and degrade over time, producing color shifts that can tend toward yellow, pink, or green. Photoshop and some current color management programs are capable of "restoring" the original colors of vintage prints. Figure 2-6 illustrates color corrections that can be made in Photoshop to restore the original look and feel of an old photograph or slide. Color correction is often necessary on photos made today. Even photos taken on the same day in similar lighting conditions will vary and may need some color corrections.

Contrast

Contrast deals with the range of tonal values from dark to light. High-contrast images have strong dark and light tones with fewer mid-tones. Low-contrast images are full of lots of mid-tone values, but the tones are not as strong in the extreme ends of the tonal scale. In order to provide continuity in a piece of art you may find it necessary to increase or decrease the contrast in an image, to make it more adaptable to your composition.

Noise and Grain

Black is not a color.
—Edouard Manet, in *The World of Manet*, by Pierre Schneider (1966)

Why black is the queen of colors.
—Auguste Rodin, in *Art*, trans. by Paul Gsell (1912)

Author's note: It appears that even the great artists will disagree from time to time.

In film we are aware of the "grain." These particles are more apparent in higher speed film. I often use infrared film, which has a very noticeable grain. If you scan your negatives or slides, you will be picking up the grain structure of the particular film type. In the digital world, we use the term "noise." Noise is usually an unwanted by-product of low light conditions with digital capture or of images that have been manipulated too much. You will find it necessary to sometimes "match" the effect of noise or grain, in the interest of uniformity.

Figure 2-7
Close-up of infrared film scan with large grain structure

Scale

Scale is an amazing element to use in your work. Reality is not a limitation in this design component. You are free to enlarge a small bird's feather to the size of a skyscraper, or to shrink a giant tree to the size of a toothpick. You are in total control. As the temporary captain of the universe, your only true directive is to make the composition work. It should hold together visually and your choices should be valid ones. There are many different reasons for using an image that is not to scale. You may need a particular texture that the image affords. You may want the literal context of the artwork to be enhanced by the off-scale component. You may want to make your exaggeration a very deliberate showcase of the difference in scale, perhaps for a humorous pun. Whatever your motivation, pause to think about the effect that scale can have on your finished piece of art. Gigantic to miniscule—what's your choice? Let's take a look at an example.

Tree House Exercise

An enjoyable exercise in scale is to find a big, fat tree, to be your base image, and then photograph various items such as windows, doors, steps, etc. to use to turn the tree into a tree house. This exercise will teach you scaling (through the transform tool) and how to match up the colors, contrast, lighting, and noise. Roam your neighborhood with a digital camera to collect component parts.

Figure 2-8
Completed tree house with layers

Figure 2-9
Base photograph of a tree

The base photograph should be of a tree that is sufficiently large in girth to accommodate the imaginary elfin family within. There are no rules. Let your imagination run free. We are not making "fine art" on this one. It is just a wacky exercise to learn about scale. (A tutorial on scaling is included in Chapter 12.) The first element to set the scale of those that follow is the door. The red door that I photographed had plants sitting in front of it. I knew that I could later clone the plants out with the rubber stamp tool.

Figure 2-10
Imported door

Rotating, Distorting, and Transforming

I simply love the transform tool in Photoshop. This is one of my major tools for altering an image. If you don't use it currently, try it out. Take it for a test drive and learn the shortcut of Command + T for Mac (Alt + T for PC). This is a simple exercise for working with layers and the transform tool.

Figure 2-11
Door transformed to proper scale

Using the transform command, the door was scaled down to size. The rubber stamp tool was used to eliminate the plants in front of the door. One by one, other elements were added into the collage. Adjustment layers were used to correct color and contrast. Shadows were added to nestle the elements into place, avoiding a cut-out feel.

Figure 2-12
Close-up of tree house

If you are unaccustomed to using the transform tool, be sure to try the exercise in Chapter 12.

Lighting

The very nature of collage usually requires pulling a multitude of images together from a wide variety of sources. You may sit down and peruse your contact sheets, pages of slides, scanned images, and clippings for inspiration. Once the idea starts to take form, you will begin to select images that you think will work well together. The items might be ideal except for one thing . . . lighting. Perhaps the light was flat when the photo was made and the rest of the images to be used are more contrasty. The flat image stands out as a puzzle piece that doesn't belong with the rest. Maybe the light was coming from the wrong direction. Lighting and the color of the light are very important for believability.

Directionality of Light

Look at the photo and play detective. Where was the sun or light source when the photo was made? Follow the shadows and trace them back to the light source. Was the light overhead or from the side?

Quality of Light

What about the quality and color of the light? Was the photo made in early morning gray light? Was it taken in the direct light of noon? Was it taken in those glorious minutes of golden-colored light before sunset? Was the sun already down and the light had blue tones? A good exercise is to photograph the same object at different times of the day to prove to yourself how the color of an object changes relative to the time of day and the type of light falling on it. Weather and cloud cover also have tremendous influences. Chances are that your collage components will be gathered from sources that are varied in their lighting conditions.

Dramatic vs. Subtle

Full bright sunlight will render an object with sharp edges and deep shadows. Sometimes the highlights will blow out, depending on the range restriction of your film or digital camera. A foggy day may render edges in a soft manner. Shadows may not exist in highly overcast situations. As you assemble your component parts for your collage, you will need to determine the viability of each piece. Can you make the pieces work together? Not all pieces can be made to be successful candidates for your collage. Let's look at a practical situation.

Projects: Places That Never Were

As part of a series, I made several collages depicting spaces that never existed in reality. Sometimes the images were sacred landscapes, like Ayers Rock or the Olgas in the Australian outback, that hold religious meaning to the aboriginal inhabitants. Sometimes they were awe-inspiring waterfalls or canyons. Collages in this series frequently used a man-made piece of art or architecture and incorporated it into a vast landscape, from different parts of the world. Could I make the created scene look like it really existed?

Australian Boulder

Our first example used a relief sculpture from central Turkey (Figure 2-13) and a portion of an Australian boulder that, although it exists in a desert, had at one time been subject to the effects of a flow of water (Figure 2-14). I imported the relief sculpture into the Australian landscape.

Figure 2-13
Turkish carving

Figure 2-14
Ayers Rock, Australia

Turkish relief carving is placed on top of the rock layer and blended with a Layer Mask

Figure 2-15
Turkish relief carving and rock face combined

Canvas extended (Image—Canvas Size)

Figure 2-16
New sky component

All artists, including sculptors, are children of light.
—ALEXANDER ELIOT,
  Sight and Insight (1959)

The sky was a flat pleasant blue but not much of it showed. So, I extended the length of the canvas and imported a punchier sky that I thought would work with the other two images.

Sky added on a separate layer—Layer Mask used to blend

Figure 2-17
Sky area added to the composition

I decided not to use the section of the sky that had birds in it. It was too much. The birds didn't help the composition. Only the lower portion of sky was used.

Image—Adjustment—Color Balance used to add more color to the relief portion

Figure 2-18—*"Sacred Place #1"*
Completed collage

A mask was used to integrate the relief into the existing boulder. The relief sculpture also needed to have a color balance layer adjustment. This layer adjustment brought the gray-toned relief into the warmer colors of the Australian boulder.

Hawaiian Waterfall

Figure 2-19
Hawaiian waterfall

There is no such thing as shadow, merely the absence of light.
—KIMON NICOLAIDES,
The Natural Way to Draw
(1941)

Another collage that was made for the series involved a waterfall photographed in Hawaii. The tones tended toward a magenta cast. What could I integrate into this space?

After several tries with various potential components, I settled on a photograph that I made in underground Istanbul. There is a fabulous world under the streets of Istanbul; the subterranean area is flooded with water and contains columns from ancient times. The photograph was a dark image that I thought might work.

Figure 2-20
Columns under the city of Istanbul

Transform the column image to proper scale

Adjustment Layer—Color Balance to synchronize the color of the columns to the waterfall photo

Layer Mask used to integrate columns into the waterfall setting

Figure 2-21—*"Sacred Place #2"*
Columns added to waterfall image

I sized down the image and tried to match the color tones that existed on the wall of the cliff. For this, I used a color balance layer adjustment. The columns were integrated into the cliff with a layer mask. The lighting on each component was similar enough that the only real adjustment was with balancing the color and masking the image into the cliff. That was pretty simple.

Figure 2-22
Close-up of finished collage

Menace in Venice

Figure 2-23
Florida Everglades alligator

Figure 2-24
Venice canal

The preceding examples were pretty simple. How about a tougher project? This next little collage was just too much fun. We artists tend to be so serious about our art that we can lose our sense of humor. Try doing something outlandish, just for the fun of it. In that vein, I offer up a little piece I call "Menace in Venice." The thought was to make the tranquility of the magical city of Venice a little edgier. Tourists in Venice often contemplate what is really in that canal water. The collage I have created certainly won't be used by the tourist council of Venice, but it was worth a laugh to put together in a realistic manner.

Adjustment Layer of Color Balance was applied to the alligator layer

Layer Mask was applied to integrate the alligator into the Venetian canal water

Figure 2-25
Color Balance applied to just the alligator layer

People always talk about
the different light in
different places. They
say the light is different
in Greece, or in the
Galapagos. But light is
light. It's all the same.
I think it's subjective. I
think it's the emotional
state the person is in.
—Eliot Porter,
 Artlines, vol. 5, no.
 11 (December 1985/
 January 1986)

The canal has a green color cast. The alligator has a magenta color cast. A Color Balance adjustment layer is definitely in order. The mask applied to the alligator took out the leaves and sticks floating near the alligator. The ripples were carefully conserved to show the motion of the alligator.

Eye dropper samples the color of the shadowed water

A new layer was added and the sample color was painted with a light opacity over the back of the alligator

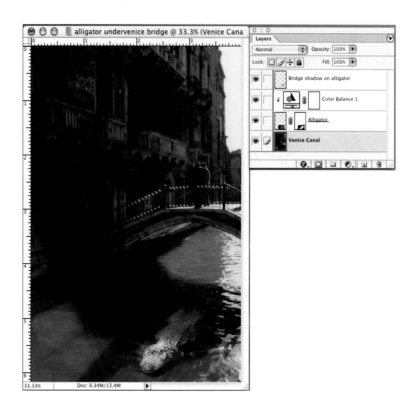

Figure 2-26
Shadow from the bridge was painted onto the alligator's back

It was time to step back and analyze what else would help our deception. The bridge over the canal was casting a shadow onto the water, where our alligator was gliding. Using the eyedropper tool, a sampling was made in the shadowed water area. A new layer was made. With a very light opacity, the shadow was painted onto the new layer. The blending mode was set to darken, instead of normal. This addition helps our menacing alligator to appear to be swimming under the shadow of the bridge, emerging into the sunlight. The shadow on a separate layer is more forgiving, if it needs to be corrected. It hasn't affected the actual alligator image.

In this type of project, try to give yourself some forgiveness, and a way to back out, if you make mistakes. It goes without saying that you should "save" frequently. Mistakes happen, machines crash, power goes out in a storm, and you can lose hours of work very easily. Make it a habit to save your art frequently as you are working on it, not just when your session is finished.

Figure 2-27
Completed—"Menace in Venice"

Although the completed collage is not likely to be used by the Venetian tourist board, it could bring about a new extreme sporting event for the gondoliers.

In short, it is wise to carefully select the component parts for your collages. Assess the feasibility of using the components together. Will the colors work? What is the directionality and quality of the light? How about contrast? Can the scales be adjusted? Does the grain or noise need to be altered? Consideration of all of these elements will ensure the success of your collages.

3 *Inspiration*

Digital Artists and Their Work

As we are thinking about the components that make a collage or painting successful, it would be wise to look at the work of several digital artists working today. I have selected them as stellar examples of how fine art work is being produced around the globe. Their techniques vary widely, and their subject matter and styles are equally diverse.

When looking at a piece of digital art we often want to know "How did they do that?" In this chapter you will find out. Each artist was invited to submit one piece and to detail the steps that were made in the creative process of constructing that piece of art. I also encouraged them to divulge what equipment they use, favorite papers, etc. This allows you a tiny peek at how each artist works. I hope you enjoy their work as much as I do. May their work serve as an inspiration to you as you proceed in your own personal growth as an artist.

Figure 3-1
Paul Biddle

Paul Biddle

Devon, United Kingdom
info@paulbiddle.com
www.paulbiddle.com

Equipment
Computers: Mac 9500 OS 9, 768MB RAM, Dedicated Scratch Disc/A.3 Wacom tablet/22" La Cie Monitor; Mac G4 Dual Processor OS X, 2GB RAM, Dedicated Scratch Disc/A.3 Wacom tablet/23" Cinema Display.
Scanner: Heidelberg Hi Res.
Printers: Epson 1290, Epson 1160, Epson 7600 with UltraChrome pigment inks.
Favorite Papers: Hahnemuhle Photo Rag 308, Somerset Velvet Enhanced, Ilford Galerie Pearl (for a more photographic feel and look), Epson matte paper heavyweight, Epson Premium glossy, Epson Photo paper for Aim Prints from accurately profiled 1160.
Any Color Management Systems: The 1160 and 1290 are both accurately profiled for each paper I use with them. I use the 1160 purely for Aim Prints as it is only a four-color printer, and when accurately profiled produces a print that is achievable with normal four-color CMYK. I use the Epson 7600 for my exhibition and portfolio prints. The seven-color UltraChrome inkset produces wonderful prints. I have experimented with accurate profiles but now use an Imageprint Rip, giving me both accurate color and very neutral B&W prints. I calibrate the monitors once a month on average. I use a GretagMac-

beth Eye-One color instrument coupled with Basic Color calibration and profile software. I get a pretty good monitor to print match.

Cataloging and Archiving: This is an area I have yet to address since entering the digital world. When I shot on film, my system was to store the 4×5 and 10×8 transparencies in transparent and archival suspension files in metal filing cabinets. Now I am surrounded by an ever-growing mountain of CDs. I am very naughty and disorganized about cataloging my work—one day I hope to use something like I View Media Pro or similar software system.

About the Artist: Background, Education, Inspirations

I used to be with various stock agencies. I have since left these stock libraries because of the lack of control of how my images were used. My work has been in exhibitions all over the world but I am not yet represented by any galleries. I have been very lucky in that I have won several awards and so have been invited to exhibit in many solo or group shows. Now I am in the process of finding galleries around the world to represent my work. I must admit I'd like an agent to do this for me, which would leave me more time to be creative.

I went to art school originally with the idea of becoming a painter but I was lousy at drawing and then fortunately was taught the basics of B&W photography. That was it for me—I decided I wanted to become a photographer. Since this introduction I am entirely self-taught. I went into teaching for about 10 years and then finally took the plunge and became a photographer. I was lucky in that I developed a recognizable style quickly. This was as a direct result of my wife Pam telling me to take photos that looked like my rather child-like drawings . . . together with the realization that I could set up images in the studio involving painting and drawing and 3D illustration, instead of wandering around outside desperately searching for "Decisive Moments," which are best left to the Cartier Bressons of this world, who are brilliant at that kind of photography.

Current Job: It is virtually impossible to make a living at fine art photography in the U.K. Consequently I also take commercial commissions. Often I am given free reign creatively so even though these images are for a commercial purpose they still look like my work (not a watered-down version).

I know many photographic galleries frown on so-called art photographers soiling their hands with commercial work. I do not agree with this view. Firstly, I'm much happier not working in a garret. Secondly, artists' work reaches a much greater audience on a billboard than on a gallery wall with a restricted audience. Hopefully these divisions are beginning to blur a little, with work that started life commercially ending up more often on the gallery wall.

Artistic Inspirations: I find it hard to select just one artist or photographer. My inspirations range from Renaissance art to Dadaism and Surrealism, from Picasso to Japanese woodblock prints. As my training was in art rather than photography, my influences often tend to be artists, but there are many wonderfully creative photographers that have also had a great effect on me. To list a few specifics: artists include Brueghel, Bosch, Archimboldo, Morandi, Max Ernst, Hans Bellmer, Sanchez-Cotan, and some of the other 16th- and 17th-century Spanish still-life painters. Some of my favorite photographers are Irving Penn, Josef Sudek, Raoul Ubac, Man Ray, and Joel-Peter Witkin.

Why am I drawn to these artists? That's a little difficult to define, as so much of what one is drawn to seems to be instinctive. I love enigmatic objects—things that make you look a little closer and think or perhaps smile a little. I like the idea that anything can, with the right lighting and composition, become beautiful even if it's decayed or deformed. Of course, color and composition are of prime importance.

Creative Process
The piece of work I have chosen to discuss here is called "Cloudy Island" and is part of a series of fantasy islands that I am working on. They are mostly a mixture of elements shot on 4 × 5 film and digital capture.

Figure 3-2

The initial image of the plaster casts of the nose and the mouth was shot in the studio on glass to give a realistic reflection. It is quicker and better than creating one in Photoshop. The set was lit simply by accurately positioning a side light to graze light across the planes and surfaces and give good 3D modeling. There is also a soft diffused backlight. This was shot on 4 × 5 Polaroid Type 55 positive/negative material. I scanned the neg and altered levels or curves to create more contrast. I like this film very much—it produces a beautifully even tonal transition.

Figure 3-3

First, I captured a shot digitally of a sea and sky, which I gradually blended in Photoshop with the original studio image of the nose and mouth using various layer modes.

Figure 3-4

Then I captured some clouds digitally and cut them out using "Knock Out" software. I then comped these clouds into the image to imply eyes or bushy eyebrows.

Figure 3-5

I captured a shot of the umbrella digitally in the studio and cut it out and comped it into the image, making sure the lighting matched the original shot in both direction and quality. Figure 3-5 is the finished B&W image; sometimes I prefer this monochrome version to the tinted version.

Figure 3-6

I then tinted the B&W version in Photoshop, selecting colors carefully and painting them in with a nice big soft-edged brush in Color Mode. Before beginning tinting I opened the image up a little—i.e., reduced contrast so that the tinting would sit better. For the final image, the umbrella was removed and a Christmas tree and stars were added; this became our Christmas card for that year.

Figure 3-7
Final image—"Christmas Island Variation" (© Paul Biddle)

Figure 3-8
Julieanne Kost

Julieanne Kost

San Jose, California
jkost@adobe.com
www.adobeevangelists.com

Equipment
Computers: Windows running XP and Mac running OS X; each has
2GB of RAM.
Scanners: Imacon Flextight Precision 3, Epson Perfection 3200 Photo.
Printers: Epson 2200, Epson 7600.
Favorite Papers: Varies based on content.
Any Color Management Systems: Sony Artisan Monitor (self-calibrat-
ing monitor, GretagMacbeth Eye-One for printer profiles).
Cataloging and Archiving: Backup to DVD as well as to a 250GB hard
drive for instant access to my entire library.

About the Artist: Background, Education, Inspirations
Julieanne combines a passion for photography, a mastery of digital
imaging techniques, and, with a degree in psychology, finds within
herself the raw components of visual emotion. Her explorations often
contain images she finds disturbing: textures, structures, colors, even
her own skeletal system, are all potential ingredients. These snip-
pets of emotions, reactions, and sensations are later combined into a
single work, hopefully conveying more than any one of the individual
photographs.

Julieanne has worked for Adobe Systems for the past 12 years
and now serves as the Digital Imaging Evangelist. She frequently
teaches courses in Adobe Photoshop at distinguished fine art and
photography workshops, prominent industry events, and conferences

around the world. She is the author behind *Photoshop Fundamentals* and *Advanced Photoshop Techniques* training DVDs published by Software Cinema and cofounder, with her husband, Daniel Brown, of www. adobeevangelists.com.

"John Sexton and Jerry Uelsman were an early inspiration for photography. Steven Johnston made me realize that I couldn't get the most out of digital imaging without truly understanding the tools. Maggie Taylor [inspires] for her compositing work, beautiful color palette, and a certain playfulness that I don't really have in my work. She's also a great example of truly having a vision in your head, and the tools, whether digital or traditional, are just different ways of expressing it."

Creative Process

I find the notion of human flight irresistible, as seen in several of my pieces. I've made wings and flight part of other pieces, but here, wanted to focus singularly on the power one might feel if capable of flight. When people fall, they tend to put their arms out, presumably in an attempt to break a fall. An enticing theory I heard suggests that we don't just raise our arms when we fall, but we are spreading what once were wings. True or not, it was an irresistible notion that with or without wings, we still retain the instincts of flight.

Many people also have "flying dreams" wherein that fantasy is realized. I've had many myself and always recall thinking, "Why haven't I been flying all along? I guess I just didn't realize I could." While waking up dissolves the notion that flight is possible, the idea of not having ever done something simply because you assumed you couldn't still remains. The image, to me focuses on the beauty of flight physically as well as the emotional triggers it would cause . . . the freedom in having managed to "spread your wings." Literally and figuratively. There is a suggestion of "bandages" on the body, hinting that few first flights, or attempts of many kinds, succeed on the first try. This subject has the "scars" of attempts failed, but now revels in success.

A combination of three images comprises the background in Figure 3-9. As is often the case, the subjects are rather surprising, considering the end result. The images are a long exposure of headlights, an underwater shot of small silvery fish in Fiji, and a rock texture with deep vertical scratches in it. Despite their diverse backgrounds, all of the images suggested vertical movement to me. By varying opacity and blend modes, and adding a channel mixer adjustment layer to decrease saturation, what were three very different images were combined into a layer set for organization, and to create the background behind the figure.

The raw figure was combined with other rock textures (which creates the "patchwork" you see in Figure 3-10). In order to mask the rocks to the shape of the figure, a clipping mask (this used to be called a "clipping group" in previous versions of Photoshop) was used to confine multiple rock layers to the shape of the figure. To give the rock texture more depth, I painted on a blank layer with the mode set to "Soft Light," and another channel mixer layer controlled overall tone

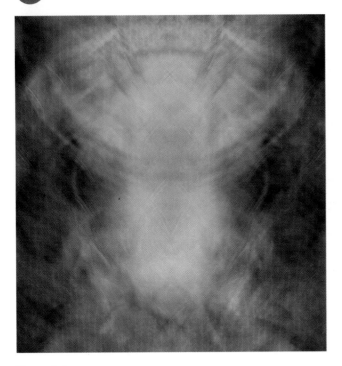

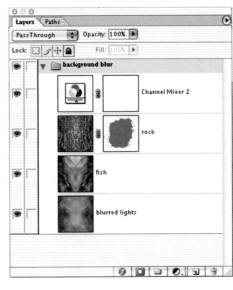

Figure 3-9
Background elements

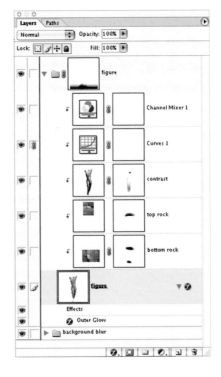

Figure 3-10
Figure introduced

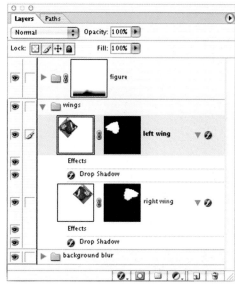

Figure 3-11
Wings added

and color values. All elements comprising the figure were placed in a layer set, and a layer mask was added to the set to fade the legs into the background. An outer glow was added to the entire figure to set it off from the background.

The wings were "sandwiched" between the figure and the background. The wings were from a deceased bird brought to me by a student at a Photoshop class. It was scanned on a flatbed scanner and then isolated from the background with the pen tool. (The placement of the wings into the scanner results in a lighting effect much different than one would get if the wings were photographed. It also yields an incredibly high-resolution image.) Only one wing was scanned, and then flipped horizontally and rotated just slightly to keep it from being perfectly symmetrical and to match the curve of the shoulders. A drop shadow separates the wings from the background.

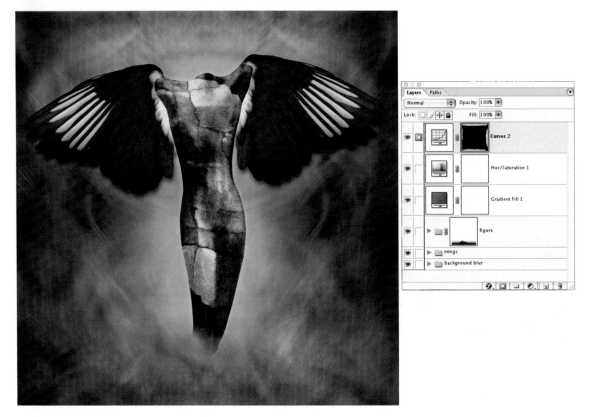

Figure 3-12
Finished piece with Layers

Finally, a Gradient Fill layer was added and a Hue/Saturation Adjustment performed a final tweak on the colors. A curves adjustment layer with a layer mask was added to darken the edges slightly.

Figure 3-13
Completed collage (© Julieanne Kost)

Figure 3-14
Maggie Taylor

Maggie Taylor

Gainesville, Florida
www.maggietaylor.com
jermag@earthlink.com

Equipment
Computer: Macintosh G4, 1.5GB RAM, OS X.
Scanners: Epson and Microtek 9800XL (tabloid size).
Printers: Epson 9600, 1280, 2200.
Favorite Paper: Royal Renaissance by Media Street (mediastreet. com).
Any Color Management Systems: Monaco Optix, GretagMacbeth Eye-One.
Cataloging and Archiving: Burned CDs and a notebook record of all CD "contact sheets."

About the Artist: Background, Education, Inspirations
Educational Background: BA in Philosophy, Yale University; MFA in Photography, University of Florida.
Current job: Self-employed, full-time artist.
Artist or Photographer That Has Inspired You: Jerry Uelsmann (also my spouse), as both a teacher in graduate school and later as my life partner—his work and devotion to image-making are very inspirational.
Gallery Representation: Lawrence Miller in New York City; Bassetti Fine Art in New Orleans; Center of the Earth in Charlotte, NC; Fay Gold in Atlanta.

Creative Process

Figure 3-15

The image "Boy Who Loves Water" was created in 2004, and began with an old tintype photograph of a boy in a photographer's studio. I placed the photograph on my flatbed scanner, and then began by retouching and adding color to the boy's skin and clothing as various layers in Photoshop.

Figure 3-16

Gradually I came up with the idea of having him be a prince, with a crown. The crown was drawn in Photoshop on a layer, with burning and dodging to add dimension. Then I decided to add frog's legs—also drawn in Photoshop. I use a Wacom tablet when I am drawing. Once that was worked out, I realized he might need water in his environment, and gradually I built the background from several digital camera images of clouds and a distant mountainous landscape (vaguely visible in the distance). The water is from a scan of a black and white photograph of a pond. The boy's house is a scan of a toy house, which was placed directly on my scanner. The smoke/clouds are invented in Photoshop.

Figure 3-17

Figure 3-18
Completed collage—"Boy Who Loves Water" (© Maggie Taylor)

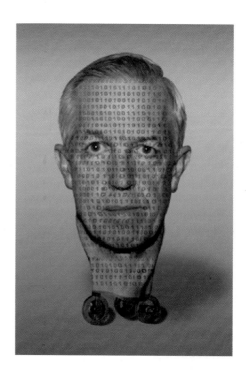

Figure 3-19
Lou Oates

Lou Oates

Mesa, Arizona
louoates@banet.com
www.louoates.com

Equipment
Computer: Mac G5 Dual Processor, OS 10.3, 4GB RAM.
Scanner: Epson 3200 Photo.
Printers: Epson 2200, 1280.
Favorite Paper: Epson Enhanced Matte.
Any Color Management Systems: Monaco EZ Color.
Cataloging and Archiving: I use Photoshop File Manager to name folders and retrieve files from two external hard drive storage systems. I archive finished images and RAW files on the external hard drives and DVD and CDs.

About the Artist: Background, Education, Inspirations
I have photographs in many galleries, retail stores, and on my web site, www.louoates.com. I also sell images on www.istockphoto.com, a stock photo web site. I have an undergraduate degree in communication from the University of Illinois and within the last six years have attended many university and college courses in photography, web design, and digital imaging. I have attended many photography workshops. I am retired from my business career and devote 100% of my time to my photography. It is a full-time job both shooting and keeping up with the latest technologies.

The first artistic influence was Stephen Marc, my digital imaging teacher at Arizona State University, who does great conceptual and intricate magic with photographic images. From him I learned that there really were no rules in bending the photographic image to suit the intent. The other big inspiration has been Maggie Taylor, especially her whimsical conceptual approach and her techniques of using scanned images and objects.

Creative Process

The concept of using old portraits as a base for composite images began with work I saw by Maggie Taylor. I was looking for a realistic starting point (a person) to build fanciful images around. While Maggie uses old portraits as a launching pad for really whimsical work, I wanted to build a more realistic scene where viewers wouldn't immediately see that something strange was going on.

Before creating much of anything I had accumulated dozens of old studio portraits from flea markets and antique stores and set them all around my studio. I was shocked to realize that just by having them there I began to interact with them. Stories of their lives came to me. Their expressions suggested what they must have been like. Their aspirations. Their dreams. Their idiosyncrasies. Suddenly the whole concept came to me. Here were people who were cherished in their lives, but ended up forgotten. Their portraits that once graced mantel-pieces and family albums were discarded like so many buggy whips and butter churns.

So I thought how nice it would be if I could tell a story about them. Give them another shot at fame. Let them be seen one last time as a person before fading into the past. So the "Family Album" 24-image series took shape. "Cousin Sadie Tried to Enlist" was the third in that series. She is a good example of the process that I used.

Figure 3-20

The original studio portrait, from about 1900, was a photograph commemorating her Confirmation. The book on the table I believe was a prayer missal. She seemed to me to be a very direct, very determined person. I thought that something military may have been in her future.

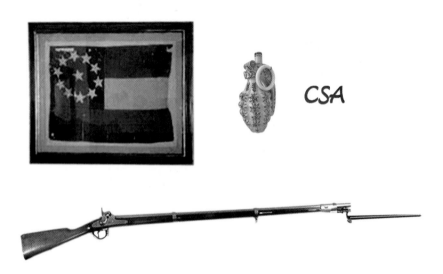

Figure 3-21

I chose the middle 1800s as the setting by adding the CSA (Confederate States of America) insignia to her belt, an 1850s-era musket, a period rug, and a Confederate battle flag to the wall. The two designer grenades were just a whim addition. The missal I changed to "War for Ladies."

Figure 3-22

Figure 3-23

I colorized Sadie's skin, clothes, corsage, plus all the original studio props: the tables, chair, flowers, and vase.

Figure 3-24

The well-worn frame was from a separate 1900-era portrait. The drop shadow behind the frame serves to add dimension to the piece, floating it above the paper. The caption serves as title to this work, much as our ancestors wrote descriptive captions on album pictures.

I used 51 image and adjustment layers in Photoshop to create the final version.

Figure 3-25
Finished collage—"Cousin Sadie Tried to Enlist" (© Lou Oates)

Figure 3-26
Katrin Eismann (photo by Mark Beckelman)

Katrin Eismann

Weehawken, New Jersey
katrin@photoshopdiva.com
www.katrineismann.com
www.photoshopdiva.com

Equipment
Computer: Apple G5/2.5 Dual Processor with 4GB of RAM, OS X 3.8.
Scanner: Imacon Precision 3.
Printer: Epson 2200.
Favorite Papers: The Somerset papers have a wonderful tone and feel that I appreciate a great deal.
Any Color Management Systems: GretagMacbeth Eye-One Pro, and I make my own printer profiles and they work like a charm.
Cataloging and Archiving: Hard drives and DVDs, Extensis Portfolio.

About the Artist: Background, Education, Inspirations
Presently, I am concentrating on writing books and teaching at the School of Visual Arts.

Education: 2002, Masters of Fine Arts in Design, School of Visual Arts, New York City; 1991, Bachelor of Fine Arts in Photography, Rochester Institute of Technology.
Current Job: 1/3 artist, 1/3 author, and 1/3 educator. These three intertwine—the books I author get me invited to speak in interesting places where I can photograph images that I include in artwork. I spend a great deal of time in airports waiting for flights to domes-

tic and international destinations, where I teach and present on a wide variety of digital imaging topics. Most importantly, being an artist challenges me to be curious, honest, and vulnerable . . . in other words, to feel.

Inspiration: Too many to list—from Karl Blossfeldt to John Heartfield to Miles Davis: inspiration is all around us.

Creative Process

"Blatter Andacht" was constructed from photographs made in Tomar, Portugal with a Nikon D100 and a 28–070mm lens.

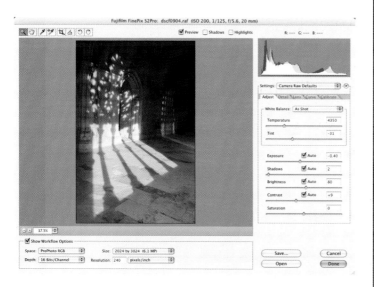

Figure 3-27

Figure 3-28

Using Photomerge I created the background from one file I had duplicated and flipped to create the labyrinth hallway.

Figure 3-29

I added the tree texture to insinuate my faith and deep belief in nature.

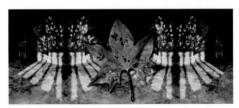

Figure 3-30

The leaf represents the invaluable and overlooked.

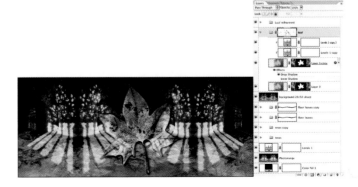

Figure 3-31

Figure 3-32
Completed image—"Blatter Andacht" (© Katrin Eismann)

Figure 3-33
Stephen Burns

Stephen M. Burns

Encinitas, California
chrome@ucsd.edu
www.chromeallusion.com

Equipment

Computer: A PC computer running an Intel P4 3.6GHz Hyper Threaded processor. It has 2GB of RAM. The video card is a Geforce 6800 with 256MB of RAM. The hard drive capacity is currently close to 0.5TB.

Scanner: Nikon Coolscan 8000 ED.

Printers: Epson Stylus Photo 1280 and 2200.

Favorite Papers: Hahnemuhle German Etching, Epson Photo Luster.

Any Color Management Systems: No color management systems used.

Cataloging and Archiving: All of my work is custom cataloged.

About the Artist: Background, Education, Inspirations

I began my education by achieving a Certificate of Photography at Palomar College (San Marcos, CA). From there, I chose to work professionally in commercial products, corporate, portraiture, and fine art. I soon discovered my real passion was for fine art.

I have exhibited in Durban Art Museum in South Africa, Citizens Gallery in Yokohama, Japan, and CECUT Museum of Mexico (Tijuana), to name a few. Part of my exhibiting won me first place in the prestigious Seybold International digital arts contest. I am the author of *Photoshop CS Trickery and FX* published by Charles River Media and a contributing writer to *HDRI 3D* Magazine (www.hdri3d.com).

In addition to the digital workshops that I teach from my studio (www.chromeallusion.com), I am currently instructing courses in digital imaging with Photoshop at Palomar College. In addition, I instruct a course in digital photography at the University of California, San Diego, Craft Center Extension. I am currently the president of both the San Diego Photoshop Users Group (1500 members) and the San Diego LightWave 3D Users Group (150 members).

My influences include the great abstractionists and the surrealists, including Jackson Pollock, Wassily Kandinsky, Pablo Picasso, Franz Kline, Mark Rothko, Mark Tobey, and Lenore Fini, to name a few. Their philosophy, to be unique as well as to follow your own gut instinct, as opposed to creating from nature, has been a major influence on my approach to being creative. The photographers that have influenced my work along a similar approach, to using abstraction as a means to express emotion, include Aaron Siskin, Brett Weston, Laszlo Moholy-Nagy, and Alfred Stieglitz.

Creative Process

Figure 3-34
*Original components—
portrait, leaves, kelp tree,
smoke*

The photograph of the model and the tree bark was shot with the Canon D60 digital camera. This gave me a 6.1-megapixel image. All of the leaves were scanned into my computer at a resolution of 1200 pixels per inch with the Hewlett-Packard ScanJet 6300C and producing file sizes of 30 megabytes and up. The smoke streams are 3D-rendered HyperVoxel objects created in LightWave 8. I chose these objects primarily for their texture; with each one being so unique from the other, it was a challenge to decide how to utilize them to complete the final result. I could have gone into a variety of directions but I chose to envision the textures on more of an abstract level and mold them to become an integral part of the model.

To keep the many layers organized, a series of layer sets were produced. Each one will be introduced along the way, but I started with the Background layer set.

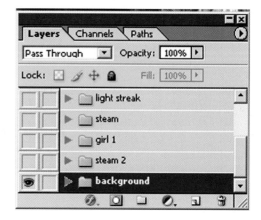

Figure 3-35
Organized layer sets

The tree bark has an interesting biomorphic feel to it, so it was ideal to serve as a background for my human model. After duplicating the

Figure 3-36
Background created

layer (Ctl J) and inversing it horizontally (Edit > Transform > Flip Horizontal) I used a mask to hide the seams where the two images came together. Painting with black on the mask makes the bark go away. Painting with white brings it back. As a result, the two produced an interesting symmetrical array of fluid shapes.

Next, the background is given a sense of depth by allowing the viewer to focus more on the foreground areas. Two techniques are used

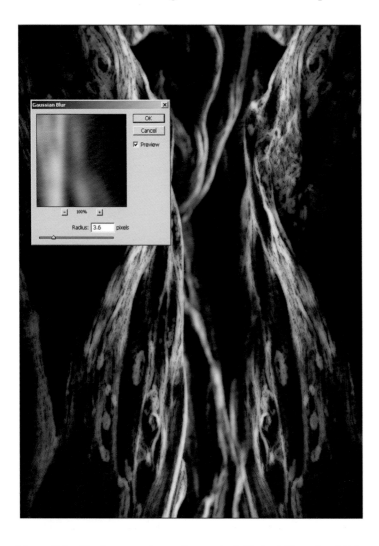

Figure 3-37
Gaussian Blur added to background

to achieve this. First, a new layer is created. By holding the Alt key on the keyboard and selecting the Merge Visible command from the layers submenu, all layers were merged into the new one without merging the original ones. The next step involves applying Gaussian Blur to the new layer, because this will serve to provide the shallow depth of field. Once completed, a mask is added and edited so the blur effect is restricted mostly to the center portion of the background.

The background has a reddish color cast, so using a Hue and Saturation adjustment layer, the Saturation slider is taken all the way to

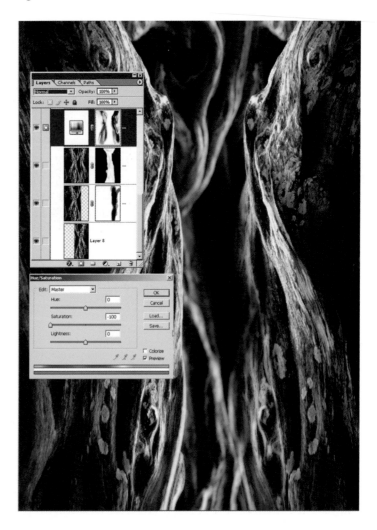

Figure 3-38
*Hue and Saturation mask
edited*

the left, leaving the image B&W. Because I did not want the color completely taken away, the mask is edited to isolate the reddish hue to the foreground areas.

The background still had quite of bit of tonal information that could compete with the main subject matter, so a Curves adjustment layer

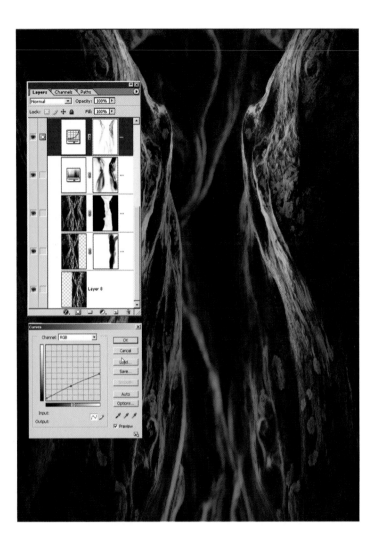

Figure 3-39
Curves adjustment layer is applied

is used to restrict the tonal range to deeper shades of gray. The white points on the curve are dragged down to lower the highlights to a richer tone, as shown.

The Curves layer is duplicated to ensure that the tones are very rich and once again the mask is edited to restrict the tones to the center of the image.

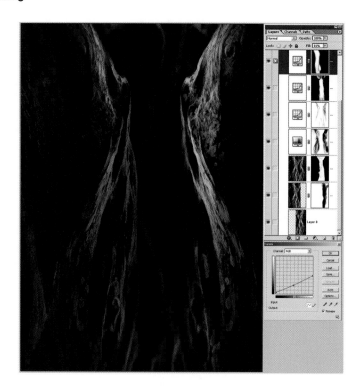

Figure 3-40
Curves adjustment layer was duplicated

Now we are ready to bring the model in. She was placed into the "Girl 1" layer set organized on top of the background and the Distort

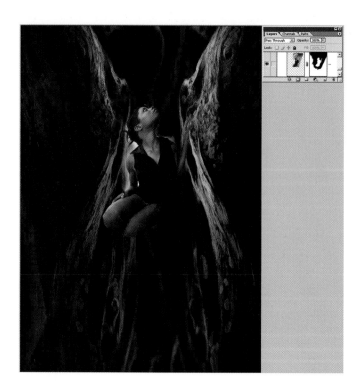

Figure 3-41
Model placed in "Girl 1" layer set

tool (Edit > Transform > Distort) is used to stretch her body up toward the upper right.

To change the lower part of her body into a leaf-like figure, the Shear tool (Filters > Distort > Shear) is used on the red leaf.

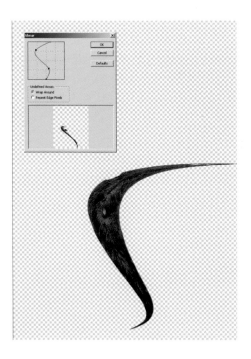

Figure 3-42
Shear applied to red leaf

The tail is positioned with a mask added. The mask is edited to mold the leaf to the model's lower body. It is also duplicated sev-

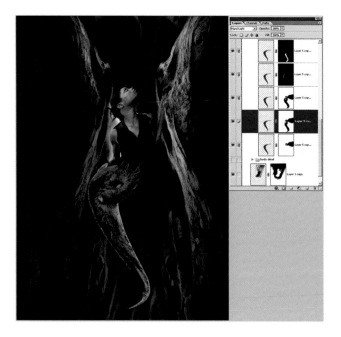

Figure 3-43
Sculpted red leaf

eral times and each layer is edited to sculpt the leaf in the form shown.

Next, the green and yellow leaf and the green leaf are applied to the body. The green and yellow leaf's blend mode is set to Linear Light

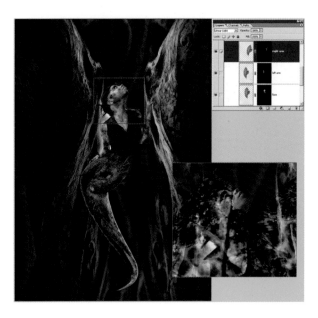

Figure 3-44
Texturing the body

blend mode in one layer example. In the lower layer example the green leaf's blend mode is set to Hue. Both examples blend well with the skin and maintain the model's contour. Let's discover in the next step some details as to how this is initially applied.

Figure 3-45 shows the leaf before a mask is applied as well as the results after the mask is edited. The use of the Wacom tablet for editing

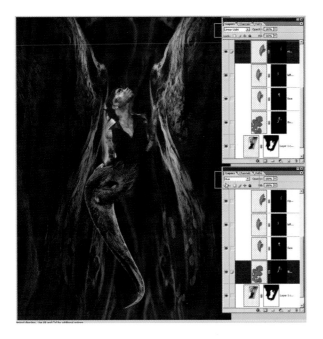

Figure 3-45
Texturing detail of green and yellow leaf

the mask and applying painting techniques is, in my humble opinion, invaluable.

In just the same way, the tail was created in, and the red leaf is added to the head of the model to represent hair. These layers are placed into the Head Set folder.

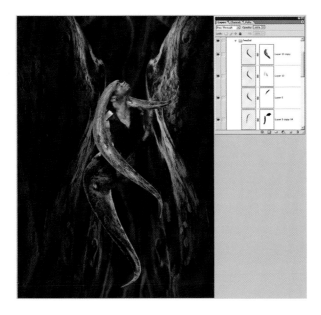

Figure 3-46
Head detail with red leaf

Using the brown leaf, its textures are restricted to the model's upper body to form a type of clothing unique from the original. No blend

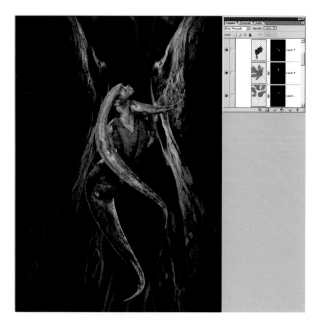

Figure 3-47
*Brown leaf and dried kelp
detail in upper body*

modes were used here. I wanted the original detail of the leaf. Finally, the kelp is used to form the collar.

The brown leaf was so successful for the upper body that I decided to use it as an additional composite for the model's face and neck

Figure 3-48
*Brown leaf applied to face
and neck with mask applied*

region, but this time, the blend mode is changed to Overlay. This is an example with the mask applied.

Now it's time to bring in the smoke streams that were rendered in LightWave 8. Two images were rendered and saved in a tiff format,

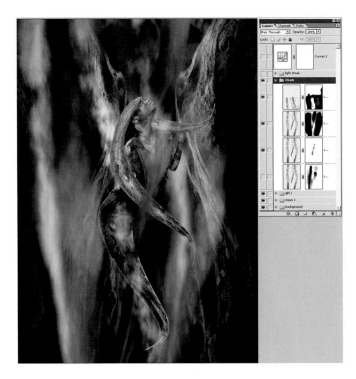

Figure 3-49
Smoke streams with mask applied

so that the smoke would be rendered onto a transparent background. Once the layer is placed, it is resized and duplicated to compose the steamy smoke streams around the model. These images are placed into the "Steam 2" layer set that is positioned just above the "background" layer set but below the "Girl 1" folder.

More of the smoke streams were applied, but this time they were placed into the "Steam" layer set, which is positioned above the "Girl

Figure 3-50
White paint applied over the model's face

1″ folder. These Layers Blend modes are set to Screen to enhance the whites. Now the effect is more steam than smoky. The Light Streak layer set is placed on top of all other layers. Within it is a layer with a small swatch of white paint applied and positioned over the model's face.

Once its blend mode is changed to overlay, a mask is applied to restrict its effects to the edge of the figure's face and leaf hair. This will represent the highlights reflected from above the model.

Figure 3-51
Overlay blend mode set to white paint

The last step is to give the image a little more contrast using the Curve adjustment layer.

Figure 3-52
Completed image—"Emergence," after curve adjustment was applied (© Stephen M. Burns)

Figure 3-53
James Respess

James G. Respess

Pacific Beach, California
jim@greenflashphotography.com
www.greenflashphotography.com

Equipment
Computer: Mac G5, dual 2GHz, with 20GB scratch space and 2GB
    RAM; Sony Artisan Monitor.
Scanners: Microtek 9800XL flatbed, Nikon 4000 ED transparency,
    Epson 3200 flatbed and transparency; VueScan software.
Printers: Epson R800, Epson 9600 Pro.
Favorite Papers: Hahnemuhle Photo Rag and Watercolor, Canvas—
    both matte and glossy.
Any Color Management Systems: Sony Artisan System for monitor;
    ICC profiles for papers, etc.; IT8 profiles for scanners.

About the Artist: Background, Education, Inspirations
My education includes a BA, University of California, Santa Cruz, and
a Ph.D. (Molecular and Cellular Biology), University of Michigan. My
current job is that of an Artist and Master Printer. I own Green Flash
Photography, a business dedicated to the creation of fine art reproductions (giclée). My gallery representation is Off Track Gallery, Encinitas,
CA, and Village Gallery, La Jolla, CA.

Many artists have given me inspiration. I have a strong background
in art and art history. René Magritte stands out as a prominent surreal-
ist that has inspired me.

Creative Process
The most important element in my art is composition. I create photo-
surreal images, often from the ground up, as in the example shown in

Figure 3-58, "Wall of Time," with the aesthetic balance of the imagery always on my mind. The idea for this piece began as a mural replica of a 1943 photograph of a view, looking west toward the Crystal Pier Hotel arch seen at the end of the street in the community of Pacific Beach, California. The hotel as well as the drugstore building are present today. The idea that I wanted to embody was to meld the 1943 war-era world with the present time in a relatively seamless manner such that the folks passing in and out of the 60-year gap appear to be oblivious of or at least unconcerned with their time travel. It is noted that pedestrians on the right side have already passed the war-era signpost and the auto on the left is emerging into the color world of the present, with most of the two-dimensional cinder blocks still imprinted. I photographed the mural (about one-third the apparent size in the composition) with a point-and-shoot digital camera, taking seven shots to avoid the cars parked in front of it. I took an additional 27 photos, standing at the approximate location of the unknown 1943 photographer. I also took several shots of some distant urban landscape shots to add to the background. The mural images were distorted and stitched together to create a giant billboard. I then began to blend in the modern street and sidewalk, adding particularly interesting cars and people. I montage elements (such as the yellow Bronco) by carefully selecting, often by hand using the lasso tool and adjusting the feather at the edge to avoid a pasted-on look. I try to pay attention to detail, taking pictures of the modern scene, for example, at the same time of year and same time of day, to give similar shadows as in the historic scene. The overall artwork is adjusted to ensure that color balance matches throughout the image and sets a mood for the viewer. The piece is finally cropped for compositional balance and maximum impact.

Figure 3-54
Two photographs of the mural to be stitched

Figure 3-55
*Bronco photo on Garnet
Street, Pacific Beach, CA*

Figure 3-56
Background photograph

Figure 3-57
Partially completed image

Figure 3-58
Final image—"Wall of Time" (© James G. Respess)

Figure 3-59
Bobbi Doyle-Maher

Bobbi Doyle-Maher

Seymour, Tennessee
www.rabbittwilight.com

Equipment
Computer: Howard Pentium III 933, Windows XP Pro, 1GB RAM.
Scanner: Nikon Coolscan IV Negative/Film Scanner.
Printer: Epson 2200.
Favorite Papers: Epson Watercolor and Hahnemuhle; custom profile for Epson Watercolor paper.
Cataloging and Archiving: I have a second hard drive, and also back up to CD/DVD. The filing system I use for image files is to name them by year, subject, and date.

About the Artist: Background, Education, Inspirations
I am self-taught. I have worked in traditional mediums since 1974, including watercolor, oil, acrylic, encaustic, printmaking, and photography. I began working digitally in 2001. My job is at the University of Tennessee as a Senior Library Assistant.

The artist that has inspired me the most: I have always been drawn to the work of George Inness. I admire the tonality and light effects in his paintings. Light as a symbolic element is an important part of my work.

Creative Process
In my most recent digital efforts, I am experimenting with taking the digital image beyond the final print. I seal the print with either clear gesso or acrylic soft gel medium and then continue to work further on the print with acrylic, oil, or the monotype process. Exploring these "mixed media" pieces continues to be a great learning experience and

the results are a revelation. I'm including two images; the first is the completed digital print (see Figure 3-77), and the second is that same print done as a monotype (see Figure 3-81).

My usual approach in starting a new digital piece is to browse through my various source photographs. I'm not looking for the perfect image. I tend to select the ones that are inferior in many respects. The challenge is in working with these images to try and create beauty where there seemingly was none. The way that I work digitally is similar to glazing in traditional painting. The layering of image after image gives new color and tonality to the source photo. Details are lost, but can be restored to areas of interest. This digital approach to painting on the computer mimics how an artist using traditional mediums uses lost and found edges, color, and value to lead the eye, but it's all done with pixels!

original photo

door

hills

painting

path

Figure 3-60
Digital photos used to create the final image, titled "Gathering Place"

Figure 3-61

Step One: Opened source photo of the stream in Photoshop CS and made adjustments to levels and hue/saturation. Saved as Figure 3-61 so that original file would remain unmodified.

Figure 3-62

Step Two: Opened Figure 3-61 in Painter 8 and used the color wheel and color palette to mix and select colors to paint over image. Used Oil Pastel with brush size set to 11 and opacity set at 52%. Painted over various parts of the picture to give added color. This part is painted boldly, with no intent to save detail in the original photo. Saved as Figure 3-62.

Figure 3-63

Step Three: Still in Painter 8, used Blender brushes "Just add water," with the brush size 38 and opacity set to 39%. The purpose of this step was to soften some of the oil pastel strokes that were previously painted in Step Two. Saved this step as Figure 3-63.

Figure 3-64

Step Four: Opened Figure 3-61 in Photoshop CS. Opened and brought in as new layer in the Painter file Figure 3-63. The blending mode was normal at 73% opacity. I flattened the layers and saved as Figure 3-64.

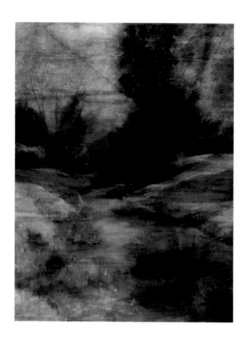

Figure 3-65

Step Five: Opened the close-up photo of the scratched door and inverted this photo by choosing Image/Adjustments/Invert. Then dragged it in as a new layer. Multiply mode was chosen with opacity of 80%. Flattened image, and then used Image/Adjustments/Levels to adjust lights and darks. Saved as Figure 3-65.

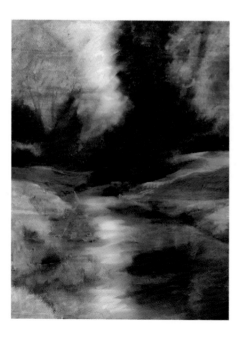

Figure 3-66

Step Six: Brought in Figure 3-64 as new layer. Applied a Layer mask and used brush size 300 to paint out the patches of light that were covered by the new layer. This was done by having the foreground color (on the tool bar) set to black and the background color set to white. (When it is set to black, the brush removes color and reveals the background image, and when set to white you can paint back in colors from the top layered image.) This stage was flattened and saved as Figure 3-66.

Figure 3-67

Step Seven: Duplicated image using Image/Duplicate. Then chose Image/Rotate Canvas/Flip Horizontal. Dragged duplicated image onto Figure 3-66 as new layer. Made larger by grabbing the left corner and using Edit/Transform/Scale while holding down the shift key (to retain proportions), dragged upward to make this layer larger. Using Normal mode set to 73% opacity, I then added a layer mask and proceeded to paint out most of the right side of the picture. The brush for the layer mask was set to 58%. Applied the layer mask, flattened, and saved as Figure 3-67. The purpose of this step was to add trees on the left and then paint out the light areas to regain my light pattern.

Figure 3-68

Step Eight: Opened the photo of the path and brought it as a new layer using multiply mode at 63%. Added layer mask and painted out light areas that I wanted to retain. Applied layer mask, flattened, adjusted levels, and saved as Figure 3-68. Closed image file.

Figure 3-69

Step Nine: Opened Figure 3-61, and applied Buzz Pro, which is a Photoshop plug-in filter set. The filter simplifies basic shapes and diminishes detail. This step brought back some sharpness and hard edges to the painting. Opened Figure 3-68 and brought in as new layer. Used Multiply mode at 71%, flattened, and saved as Figure 3-69. Closed image file.

Figure 3-70

Step Ten: Opened Figure 3-68 and then brought in as new layer in Figure 3-69. Selected Normal mode at 100% opacity and added a layer mask. Painted back in dark tree mass on left and some lights in the water. Applied mask and saved as Figure 3-70. Closed image file.

Figure 3-71

Step Eleven: Opened Figure 3-70 in Painter 8 and set the palette knife for cloning. Painted over the water and sky to get back some harder edges. Saved as Figure 3-71. Closed image file.

Figure 3-72

Step Twelve: In Photoshop CS opened Figure 3-70 and brought in as new layer in Figure 3-71. Selected Normal mode set to 79% opacity and added a layer mask. Painted some parts of background back in, applied layer mask, flattened, and saved as Figure 3-72.

Figure 3-73

Figure 3-74

Step Thirteen: Opened Figure 3-72 in Microsoft Picture It, and applied the filter Paint Long Strokes. Saved as Figure 3-73. In Photoshop opened Figure 3-72 and brought in Figure 3-73 as a new layer in Normal mode at 81% opacity. Saved as Figure 3-74.

Figure 3-75

Step Fourteen: Duplicated image by selecting Image/Duplicate and applied Hyper tiling/cube/procedural from the KPT Effects plug-in filters. Used Normal mode at 41% opacity. Flattened image, adjusted levels, and saved as Figure 3-75.

Figure 3-76

Step Fifteen: Opened hills image, used Edit/Transform to enlarge image. Dragged in as new layer. Selected Multiply mode at 48%. Applied layer mask, painted out lights. Saved as Figure 3-76.

Step Sixteen: Did a test print at this stage. The print was too dark overall.

Figure 3-77

Step Seventeen: Opened Figure 3-76 and then opened the painting image (from the originals) and brought in as a new layer. Selected Normal mode at 59%. Added layer mask and painted out some parts of the layered file to get back to the image underneath. Then used the healing brush to repair some small areas in the water and trees. Saved as final image "stream.final" (Figure 3-77).

Instructions for Mixed Media Monotype
Step One: Opened stream.final (Figure 3-77) and adjusted levels in Photoshop to lighten the print. Printed two copies: one was flipped horizontally to reverse the image, and the second print, used to create the monotype, was printed in its original format only much lighter.

Figure 3-78

Step Two: Image file. Figure 3-78 shows, from left to right: the print that was used for the painting stage, the second print after it had been painted and run through the etching press (note that the painted areas are on the right side of the print), and the Plexiglas plate that was masked out with tape to the exact size of the print.

Figure 3-79

Step Three: Figure 3-79 shows the inkjet print under the Plexiglas plate. The left side and center show the painted areas. To the right you can see the print under the plastic plate. The print is a guide for color placement.

Step Four: Painting on the Plexiglas plate was completed and then the plate was laid on the etching press bed and the inkjet print was placed on top of the plate, face down. After adjusting the roller pressure, the print was rolled through the press and then the paper was lifted off. The print was allowed to dry.

Figure 3-80

Figure 3-80 shows the dry print with pastel applied.
Figure 3-81 is the final mixed media monotype.

Figure 3-81
Final image—"Gathering Place" (© Bobbi Doyle-Maher)

Figure 3-82
Cher Threinen-Pendarvis

Cher Threinen-Pendarvis

San Diego, California
cher@pendarvis-studios.com
www.pendarvis-studios.com

Equipment
Computers: Mac OS X, Mac G5 2GHz, 1GB RAM, 120GB hard drive
and Super Drive; Titanium Laptop with Super Drive; G4 1GHz,
1GB RAM; 80GB hard drive. Monitors: La Cie 22" Electron Blue, 23"
Apple Cinema HD Display, Cintiq interactive pen display. Wacom
Intuos 3 6 × 8 and various Wacom pens and nibs, including the
Wacom 6D Art Pen.
Scanner: Epson flatbed scanner.
Printers: Epson 2200P and Epson 3000.
Favorite Papers: Somerset Bright White, Arches, Hahnemuhle.
Any Color Management Systems: Yes.
Cataloging and Archiving: La Cie Firewire external drives, Super
Drive. I save my images into folders on a Firewire drive and I back
them up to CD or DVD.
Other Art Tools: I also use an artists' easel, oil and acrylic paint,
watercolor, gouache, pastel, pencils, markers, various papers and
other substrates, and my library of conventional sketchbooks that I
use for ideas.

About the Artist: Background, Education, Inspirations

An award-winning artist and author based in San Diego, California, Cher Threinen-Pendarvis has always worked with traditional art-making tools. Also a pioneer in digital art, Cher has created illustrations using the Macintosh computer since 1987. She has been widely recognized for her mastery of Painter, Photoshop, and the Wacom pressure-sensitive tablet, using these electronic tools since they were first released. Exercising her passion for Painter's artist tools, Cher has worked as a consultant and demo-artist for the developers of Painter. Her artwork has been exhibited worldwide and her articles and art have been published in many books and periodicals. Cher holds a BFA with Highest Honors and Distinction in Art specializing in painting and printmaking, and she is a member of the San Diego Museum of Art Artists' Guild and the Digital Art Guild. She has taught Painter workshops around the world, and is principal of the consulting firm Cher Threinen Design. Cher is author of all seven editions of *The Painter Wow! Book*. Her most recent books are *The Photoshop and Painter Tablet Book: Creative Techniques for Digital Painting*, and *The Corel Painter IX Wow! Book*, the latest edition of this highly praised volume of techniques and inspiration.

"My work reflects Pacific Coast roots. I paint real people and places, based on sketches done on location—not to imitate nature, but to express a personal vision. I am passionate about light and color in nature, and how these properties affect form."

As to inspiration, it is difficult to choose just one: John Constable, Jean Gustave Courbet, Eugene Boudin, Edgar Degas, Claude Monet, and Wayne Theibaud. Gallery representation includes the San Diego Museum of Art Artists' Guild and the Digital Art Guild.

Creative Process

After Cher made the sketches in her sketchbook on location, back at her studio, she arranged the drawings so that she could look at them. In Painter, she sketched a loose composition using the Grainy Variable Pencil. Remembering the afternoon light and looking at the sketches helped her to keep the painting loose while working in Painter to rough out the composition. Then she added more colorful strokes, creating movement and activity in the color as she worked. After Cher established the basic color theme using various Artists' Oils brushes, she added details using a small custom Artists' Oils brush (based on the Oily Bristle). To blend areas, she used a low-opacity Wet Oily Palette Knife variant of Artists' Oils, a brush that can mix paint by dragging through existing color. She also used a tiny Palette Knife to move and blend color.

Cher was lost for hours while creating "Quiet Moment at Schwetzingen," busily layering color over color and blending paint using Artists' Oils brushes and blending tools. She spent several creative sessions in her studio while developing the painting.

Figure 3-83

Step One: Create a series of color and value drawings using colored pencils or pastel and graphite pencils. Analyze your subject carefully as you sketch. Back at your studio, assemble your sketches and references near your computer.

Figure 3-84

Step Two: Open a new image in Painter. (Cher's image measured 2000 × 2000 pixels.)

Step Three: Choose a dark gray color in the Colors palette.

Figure 3-85

Step Four: Choose the Coarse Pavement texture from the Papers picker in the Toolbox.

Figure 3-86

Step Five: Add a new layer to your image to hold your sketch. Choose the Grainy Variable Pencil and sketch the basic shapes for your composition onto the new layer.

Figure 3-87

Step Six: When your composition is as you like it, choose the Oily Bristle variant of Artists' Oils in the Brush Selector Bar. In the Layers palette, select the Canvas layer. Using your stylus, begin to brush large areas of color onto your painting. Tip: Turn the visibility of your sketch on and off as needed, using the eye icon in the Layers palette. Keep your subject, lighting, and the atmosphere in mind as you work.

Working from background to foreground, Cher began with the sky, trees, and water, and then she painted the reflections and foreground plants. After laying in overall color with the Oily Bristle, she switched between the Tapered Oils, Dry Brush, and Blender Bristle brushes. She deleted the sketch layer from the image when she had blocked all of the important shapes into the composition. To strengthen the focal point in the composition, she added the large swan later in the painting process. For reference, she used a photo of a swan that she had taken.

Step Seven: For more activity in the brushwork and color, practice varying the size of your brush as you work, using the Size slider in Property Bar.

Figure 3-88

Step Eight: Keep the movement of shapes in the composition and the atmosphere in mind. Remember that objects close to the foreground (such as the foreground grasses in "Quiet Moment at Schwetzingen") are usually more detailed and more vividly colored than the distant trees are.

Step Nine: To blend and finesse areas, use the Oil Palette Knife (Artists' Oils) to pull and blend color. For small details, reduce the size of the knife to about 5 pixels.

Figure 3-89
Completed—"Quiet Moment at Schwetzingen" (© Cher Threinen-Pendarvis)

Figure 3-90
Ciro Marchetti

Ciro Marchetti

Miami Lakes, Florida
cirom@mac.com
www.ciromarchetti.com

Equipment
Computers: Various Macs, OS X; top of my line is currently a G5 Tower, 1GB of RAM.
Scanner: A cheap, small Canon (I don't do much scanning).
Printer: Epson 2200.
Favorite Paper: Epson Premium Luster. I also send out my files for output onto canvas for the larger sized reproductions, using an Epson 9600.
Any Color Management Systems: Basically one of using my own color profiles and settings arrived at after subjective trial and error.
Cataloging and Archiving: I don't have any elaborate catalog or archive of my work. Simply a collection of layered and flattened versions of each piece, along with support files of individual elements of significance from those images that may warrant saving in their own right. I do have an additional library of files that I access. This comprises an eclectic range of images that I've created, such as background skies, cloud formations, animals, birds, insects, flowers, textured surfaces, etc. Many have been created with no specific purpose, and indeed may end up sitting there unused for ages, but most end up playing a role in some future composition, albeit with some modification.

About the Artist: Background, Education, Inspirations
I attended art school in London back in the Jurassic period; since then I've had a full career running my graphic design studio, and in more recent years my personal illustrations. I teach Digital Imagery and Illustration part time at the Fort Lauderdale Art Institute and give

private classes to smaller groups at my studio. I also participate at local art festivals in South Florida. Recent awards include being a finalist of the Macworld digital art competitions in 2000, 2001 (Grand Prize winner), 2002, and 2005. I've also been honored with four GURU awards from the National Association of Photoshop Professionals, and have been featured in a number of publications, including *Digital Graphics* magazine, and *Secrets of Award-Winning Digital Artists* published by Wiley.

I do have a rep that handles the licensing of my work, but I don't have my work placed with any stock agencies, because I'm not particularly proactive in terms of seeking commissions. I now prefer to simply do my own thing, put my work up on my web site, participate in local art festivals . . . and see what happens. My work has been exhibited in a number of galleries as part of a traveling exhibition of digital art, as well as being on a number of virtual galleries.

Creative Process

"The Fool of Dreams" is the lead character from a deck of tarot cards that I've produced titled "The Tarot of Dreams." A modified version of this image is in fact "The Fool," which is the first card of a tarot deck. He symbolizes a somewhat self-assured character, innocently overconfident of the pitfalls the future may have in store, symbolized by his precarious stance which may at any time be unbalanced by the most innocent playful kitten.

When I'm working on personal projects (as opposed to corporate design commissions) I do not use scans, or third-party plug-ins and filters; everything is created within Photoshop. In earlier pieces I simply used a mouse, but mostly with a Wacom tablet and pen.

The various textures, such as the embroidered design of the Fool's costume, are areas initially drawn as an individual shape or pattern in black and white, then placed into a new alpha channel. If the item is one that can be repeated uniformly I may simply define the area as a pattern, and then "fill with pattern." If, however, the overall texture has to be more random or follow a more defined shape, as in the case of, say, the lizard's scales, I produce a small area of scales first, which I then paste repeatedly, giving the various pastes a slight rotation or scale distortion in order to approximately follow the shape of the lizard (which has already been sketched and is prepared as a solid shape that can be seen through the alpha channel as a guide).

Once the overall form is matched by this corresponding alpha channel I continue to mold the shape further by using the Liquify filter, pushing and pulling the textured patterns to follow more accurately the shape of the lizard, trying to form them in such a way as to suggest the contours and folds of skin. Once I'm happy with the result I can load the channel into the appropriate layer and paint through it in any number of ways to suggest the raised surface of the scales. With the use of light and shadow, the volume and folds of the form already created by shape and color can be further defined.

My approach is very informal, I make up treatments as I go along (and all too often forget how exactly I did it . . . duh!!!!), but it's important to emphasize that I don't allow the potential of this digital medium to override or dominate the process. I have a pretty clear idea of what I want; it's just that I get there by knowing what the various tools, color modes, etc. are capable of and applying them intuitively, as opposed to applying precise numbers and percentages, often proposed in various tutorials.

The analogy I use with my students is that you can get by on a vacation in a foreign country using a basic phrase book, but there are only so many phrases you can remember. At some point, to truly communicate you need to apply the basics of the grammar to construct your own sentences, even if they are not perfect; it will still expand your options beyond your hotel and the other places where all the other tourists will be.

Figure 3-91

Iguana illustration step by step.

Figure 3-92

I used a very detailed Victorian illustration as my reference, and sketched in the basic figure, freehand with a Wacom tablet and pen.

Figure 3-93

On a new layer, and using a small hard brush, I follow the outline with a green line, cleaning up curves, etc.

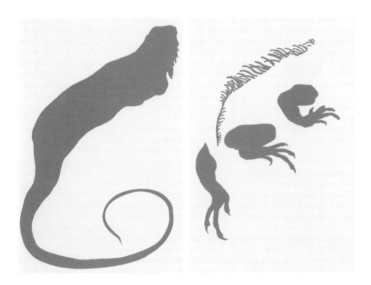

Figure 3-94

These outlines are then filled in to make solid shapes. I keep some of the shapes on separate layers, i.e., the body on one, the legs on another. This makes things more convenient later for adding shadows, etc.

Figure 3-95

Using darker and lighter tones of the base green, I start to suggest muscle shape, and folds of skin, using larger soft-edged brushes.

At this point I would create additional channel layers to prepare my texture of scales.

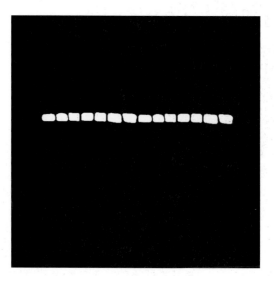

Figure 3-96

This starts with a single row of individual shapes. I try to keep them reasonably straight, but not clinically so. I want to suggest a living natural creature, not a mathematically rendered computer perfection.

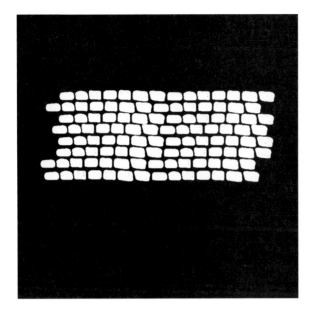

Figure 3-97

I copy and paste the row of scales repeatedly to make a larger area, staggering them like a brick wall.

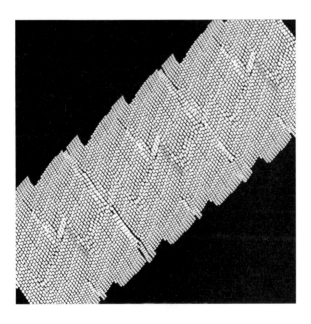

Figure 3-98

The "brick wall" pattern is now scaled down in size, and then once again, by recopying and pasting, a patterned area is produced—enough to cover the body of the lizard image.

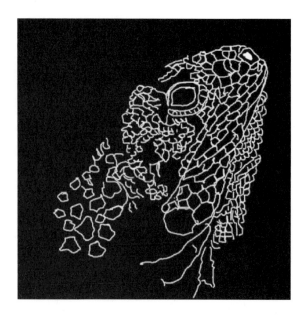

Figure 3-99

There's no shortcut for the lizard's head area; here the scales and pattern are too specific, and have to pretty much be drawn in as a line work, using the original reference material as a guide.

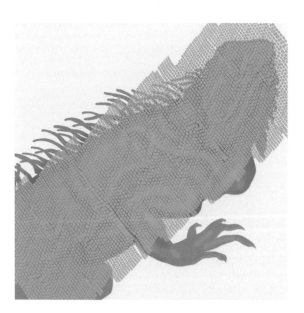

Figure 3-100

I now create a new layer, and "load" the scales channel as a selection and fill with a green color of similar tone to the body shape below. Doing this in a new layer provides many opportunities to try different effects. For example, by changing the "mode" of the scales layer to multiply, darken, or lighten, I start to produce reasonably convincing textures.

Figure 3-101

However, I went one further, and applied a very light bevel and emboss style to the layer. This gives each individual scale a slightly raised surface. I play with the depth and size options to get the effect I feel is natural. I replaced the default color setting with a darker green and multiply for the shadows, a lighter yellow green, and screen for the highlights.

I then go to the layer below and select the lizard's body; with the selection still active, I return back up to the scales layer, invert the selection, and delete. This removes all the scales that extended beyond the lizard's body shape.

Figure 3-102

Now, using the Liquify filter, I start to push and squeeze the scales into shapes that follow the approximate overall volume of the lizard's body, its muscles, and folds of skin. Then using a soft airbrush-shaped brush for dodge and burn, these shapes and folds can be further defined by creating highlights and shadows. I apply an extra pass with the dodge tool in certain areas to suggest a slight sheen to the creature's skin.

Figure 3-103
Detail of "Iguana"

This process is repeated for the different areas, i.e., the legs, which, depending on the overall light source I want to give the image, will require different positions and intensity of light and shadow (that is why I kept them on separate layers from the beginning). But once I'm happy with the various parts, I then merge them into the one layer using a little blur here and there to make the blends of legs to body seamless.

Figure 3-104
Detail of "The Fool"

Figure 3-105

Completed—"The Fool of Dreams" (© Ciro Marchetti)

Figure 3-106
Leslye Bloom

Leslye Bloom

Blacksburg, Virginia
lbloom@vt.edu
www.leslyebloom.com
www.absolutearts.com/portfolios/l/leslye
www.brpas.org/g2/v/Leslye-Bloom

Equipment
Computers: A Mac with four hard drives; also use an ancient G3 laptop and new Epson projector for lectures, photo uploads while traveling.
Scanner: Umax PowerLook 1100.
Printers: Epson 4000; Tektronix by Xerox Phaser 860, Tektronix Phaser 220i, Laserwriter.
Favorite Papers: Phaser 220i needs special paper as it passes through the print head three to four times for each CMY or CMYK wax layer. Other than that, I experiment—since I'll be painting/cutting the papers, I avoid high-end pricey stuff. I've been talking with Dot Krause about printing on aluminum. . . .
Any Color Management Systems: I keep it simple: Screen RGB with autoconversions to CMYK; later in production I control colors by printing small proofs and eyeballing as I work.
Cataloging and Archiving: Photo File Folders by year, then month/day, and place; steps in design by adding a, b, c, etc. to filename; works by title: "3 Irons 2" is the second version (the first was much darker).

About the Artist: Background, Education, Inspirations
Education: BS, MS, Ph.D., Art Education, Penn State; Certified Art Therapist. Retired from teaching (I'm FREEEEEEEEE!) . . . or, you

might say, working under a continuing grant from the Bloom Foundation (that refers to my husband).

Inspiration: There are so many! Right now it's Gustave Caillebotte, an impressionist influenced by photography.

Gallery Representation: I'm represented by local galleries, but I'm looking for others out of town. I want to make, not market.

Creative Process

Figure 3-107
*"3 Irons 2," 10.5'H ×
13.5'W (2005)*

"3 Irons 2" started in an experimental encaustics workshop I taught. A participant, Craig Shaffer, took some wonderful photographs and shared them. Two shots of hand irons dripping wax (left and center, Figure 3-108) sparked my imagination. Craig gave permission to use the images.

Two irons didn't seem to be enough, so I masked one and pasted in a demo encaustic (right, Figure 3-108) I made in the workshop. The fact that this pattern is impossible on a hot iron is a little embedded joke.

Figure 3-108
Source images

I cleaned up the table, added a background (Figure 3-109), and printed it in sections with my Tektronix-Xerox wax printer, then pieced it together. There was a color shift that I liked. Note the blue on the left iron.

Figure 3-109
Print master (© Leslye Bloom)

To quiet the busy background, I added the bluish area of wax by hand. When I burned it in with a heat gun, some of the underlying wax migrated to the surface, making subtle variations (and the gradation to blue-green).

The composition seemed to need another horizontal, so I laid down some red wax on newspaper, tore off a strip, and placed it at the top to pre-visualize. I liked it as it was so I fused the strip to the piece (heat, hold down, and let cool). I broke up the red with manganese blue wax (upper left). When I added the white line it dripped—an unexpected circle that I liked. So I dripped some more at the top and created upwellings (white drop with red center) by spot-heating.

Glossary

Computage: Art created using a computer—I coined the term in 1995 (in the same vein as Collage, Montage, Assemblage. . .).

Encaustic: Pigment bound with wax/damar medium. Heat it to mix and apply, cool it to set or fuse. It can be manipulated while warm. Translucent waxes make even opaque pigments seem to glow.

They are remarkably colorfast. Although encaustics *can* melt (over 200°F), burn, or scratch, they can last centuries or even millennia (e.g., mummies). Archival properties are excellent—the wax forms a barrier to air and pollutants. They can be shown without glazing, cleaned with mild soapy water, reheated and reworked for years, and modeled in three dimensions.

Safety: Good ventilation, a fire extinguisher, and hot pads are a must. Never use open flame. Smoke means overheating, and potentially dangerous pigments have been vaporized. Some heavy metals (e.g., cadmium, manganese) are very toxic.

Tools: Can include hand irons, brass brushes, electric griddles, tjanting tools, and heat guns. Traditionally encaustics are put on gessoed, sanded board (or clayboard) substrates. I like paper so I can easily heat from back or front. Heavy impasto on paper *can* crack. Supplies and equipment can be expensive, but you can use good crayons and an old clothes iron (permanent press or lower heat setting) for first experiments.

Tjanting tool: From Batik, a cone-shaped metal reservoir on a handle for adding liquid wax.

Upwelling: Pigment from lower layers migrates to the top with heating, like a miniature volcano.

Figure 3-110
Luzette Donohue

Luzette Donohue

Arana Hills, Australia
contact@luzette.com
luzette@artnow.com.au
www.luzette.com

Equipment
Computer: Dell Pentium 4 (3GHz), OS = Windows XP Professional, 1GB RAM.
Scanner: Umax Astra 1200S.
Printers: Epson Stylus Photo R800 (home), Epson Stylus Pro 9600 (work).
Favorite Papers: PermaJet Fine Art Inkjet Media range, especially Museum Classic, a 310 gsm, acid-free, mold-made art paper; traditional artist's watercolor papers, e.g., Arches, Saunders Waterford, textured artist's canvas, Hahnemuhle German Etching fine art paper.
Any Color Management Systems: I've always practiced a color-managed workflow but I didn't always achieve consistent color. I read all of the available theory and attended seminars where speakers made recommendations but rarely offered satisfactory explanations. I routinely downloaded the latest generic profiles available from manufacturers and industry gurus, and applied these with a mixture of success and frustration. Then we purchased a GretagMacbeth spectrophotometer and I now produce accurate custom profiles for each media in use. Color management is no longer an issue. I take it for granted that the soft proof I see on screen will be reproduced on paper by the printer. I strongly recommend anyone with a need for consistent color to take advantage of the many services available

that will produce custom profiles for your output device. Despite the initial expense, you will soon save time and money.

Cataloging and Archiving: I catalog my image files using Photodex CompuPic and archive to CD. CompuPic generates previews and thumbnails in offline volumes that I can refer to even after the disc has been removed. It also offers the convenience of searching across volumes using keywords.

About the Artist: Background, Education, Inspirations

When I returned to Australia from living in the UK, no one really understood what I meant when I described myself as a photo illustrator. So I was delighted when the Australian Institute of Professional Photography introduced the Photo Illustrator category. The image I have provided here was part of my winning portfolio when I was awarded the 2004 AIPP Photo Illustrator of the Year. The event served to raise the profile of digital imaging professionals and nurtured the debate concerning manipulation.

My father taught me how to use a camera when I was young and my mother immersed me in good photography. But being a photographer wasn't considered a serious career option so I completed a Bachelor of Education and until recently I've always taught in one capacity or another. I admit to being a perpetual student myself. I always feel the need to know more. When I decided to pursue photography as a career I started with a six-week evening course and ended up studying photography and imaging over six years. A Bachelor of Arts (First Class Honors) enabled me to specialize in teaching digital imaging, in particular, Adobe Photoshop.

That doesn't mean I advocate an academic pathway for anyone who wants to enter the industry. Early in my career I volunteered to assist other photographers, and from them I gained valuable knowledge concerning both best practice and practices best avoided. Even now I attend seminars and meet with my peers at every opportunity. It's vital to keep in touch, up to date, and inspired.

Current job: I am Creative Director for Art NOW, an Australian company producing framed décor art. My role involves creating and acquiring original imagery, and managing our exclusive image collection.

When I first started using Adobe Photoshop to produce montages I relied on experimentation to develop my own style. There was very little documentation available on creative techniques and there wasn't anyone within my network who was producing anything vaguely similar. The imagery I produced was regarded as unique and its content perhaps a little odd. I was fascinated by the results I got from scanning found objects on my flatbed, everything from feathers to whole, decaying birds. I loved the texture, the details, and the fall of the light this approach produced. But at the same time my photographer's conscience argued with me that it was a lazy capture solution. And even when I spent days arranging, masking, and blending layers, I didn't regard the finished piece as being as worthy of admiration as something that had been produced using traditional tools.

Then I came across the wonderful work of Diane Fenster. Diane's success, style, and philosophy helped me justify our form of digital montage as a valid form of art and illustration. There are many people since who have pursued this style, but even when they possess the technical ability, they often lack Diane's talent to convey a concept clearly.

Creative Process

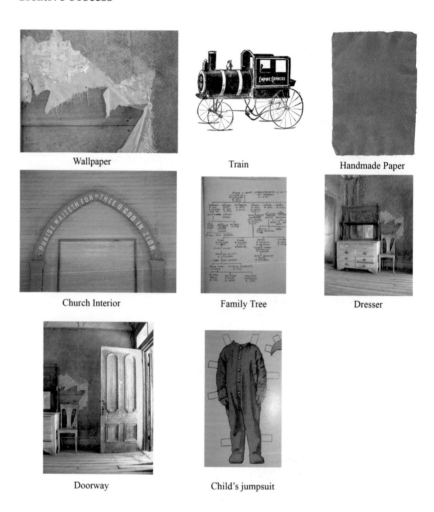

Wallpaper	Train	Handmade Paper
Church Interior	Family Tree	Dresser
Doorway	Child's jumpsuit	

Figure 3-111

"Waiteth for Me" is a reflection on a visit to Bodie, a Californian ghost town in a "state of arrested decay." The remaining buildings and the personal possessions within are so well preserved it is truly haunting. This image captures the feeling that some of the original residents from the 1800s also remain.

When I begin, my intention is always to create a digital image that belies its origins. Characteristic of my work are the textures I use to establish an organic, almost handmade feel. I like to use subtle tones, blends, and strokes that introduce painterly qualities. In the scene "Waiteth for Me," this is further enhanced by the dust, natural light, and peeling paint of three photographs taken on location. They form the foundation to which I've added just a few elements to suggest a narrative. Collecting odd items is an integral part of the process for my collage and I often have to thank my husband for his contributions. The family tree, for instance, that appears in the background was a wonderful discovery inside an antique journal that also contained pressed leaves and handwritten poetry from the 19th century. I have to be very disciplined and stop myself from adding too much. A few thought-provoking additions invite the viewer to linger and construct their own scenario, whereas too many objects or textures overlapping only produces clutter.

Every time I conduct a Photoshop workshop participants are surprised by the simplicity of the techniques I use to combine layers. Inevitably they have already experimented with varying levels of opacity and have only experienced limited success. I rarely reduce the opacity of a layer. The secret instead lies in the blending modes that are available from a myriad of menus. I'm including here a step-by-step description of the process I used to create "Waiteth for Me," so that perhaps you can pull out and use the interesting stages of layer blending.

Figure 3-112
*Prepare background
image—Photomerge*

Select two images in the file browser. Choose Photomerge from the automate menu. In settings check the perspective and keep as layers buttons. Rename the layers in the combined image. Make minor transformations to improve the joins in the wallpaper and floorboards. Add a layer mask and use a soft brush to soften edges where there is a difference in exposure. Link the layers and save the file for future use.

Figure 3-113
*Working canvas: Prepare the
new artwork*

Create a new canvas of the required dimensions and resolution.
Drag the linked layers onto the new canvas, building up the organic
textures. Open the handmade paper file and transfer the paper onto
the working canvas. Transform the paper to fill the canvas. Position the
new layer beneath the photos and name it. Duplicate the handmade
paper layer. Position the duplicate above all other layers. Rename the
duplicate layer texture and turn off its visibility.

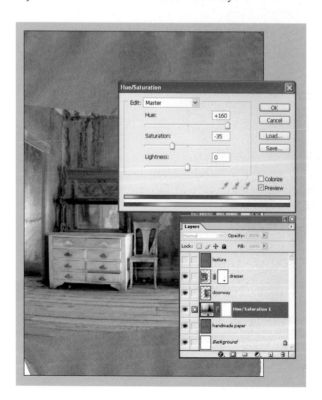

Figure 3-114
*Manipulating color:
Adjust hue*

Return to the handmade paper layer; create a hue and saturation adjustment layer above it. Use the hue and saturation sliders to manipulate the color of the paper background.

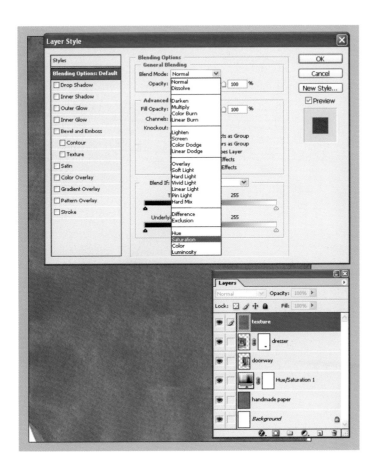

Figure 3-115
Layer blending

Make the texture layer visible. Double-click on the layer in the layers palette to open the layer style dialogue box. Highlight the first blend mode of the dropdown menu and use the arrow keys to scroll down the list, watching the effects of each. Choose saturation.

Figure 3-116
Building texture

Open the wallpaper file and transfer to the working canvas. Use the alternative layer blending mode menu available on the layers palette and choose darken.

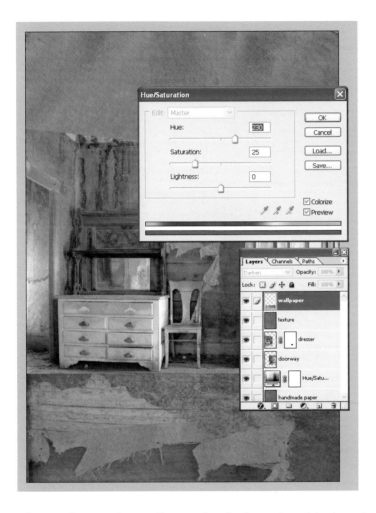

Figure 3-117
Manipulating color: Colorize option

Use hue and saturation again to color the layer, but this time check the colorize box.

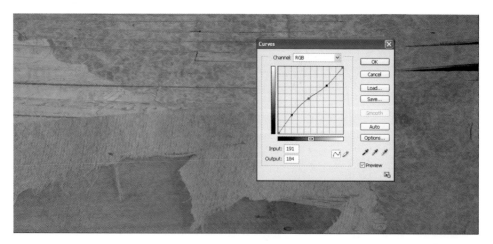

Figure 3-118
Utilizing contrast

Fine-tune the way the layer blends by using curves to control the contrast combining blending techniques. Open the family tree file and transfer to the working canvas. Ensure the new layer is on top of all others. Transform and position the family tree as required from the image adjustments menu; choose invert to produce a negative of the layer, resulting in white text.

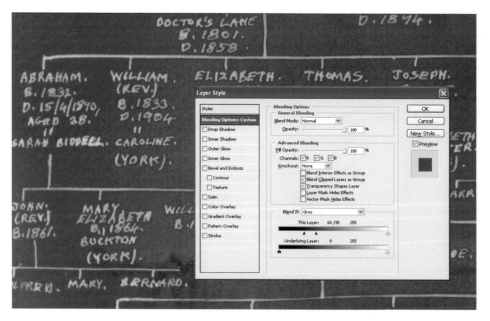

Figure 3-119
Brightness range of blend

Double-click on the family tree layer in the layers palette to open the layer style dialogue box. In the advanced blending area of the layer style dialogue box, use the top slider to set the brightness range of pixels to be blended. Drag the black slider to the right to reduce the visibility of the dark paper. Hold down Alt or Option and split the shadow slider into two and fine-tune the blend for a more subtle effect. Choose soft light from the layer blending mode menu. Use curves to adjust the contrast of the layer.

Masking—Add a layer mask to the family tree layer and use a soft brush to hide or reveal areas as desired. Duplicate the family tree layer; reposition, and swap blending mode to exclusion. Refine mask. Repeat duplication and this time use color burn as the new blending mode. Select one entry of the original family tree layer and edit dates using brush tools. Create a mask for the door layer. Edit both masks attached to the photos to hide unwanted detail. Create a custom brush and use in various modes and opacities to distress the edges of the floor boards.

Adding Elements—Open the child's jumpsuit file. Use the magic wand to select the background. Inverse the selection and drag the jumpsuit onto the working canvas. Transform the new layer. Swap the layer blending mode to luminosity. Use the burn tool set to a low exposure to burn in the shadows as desired. On a new layer use a soft brush of variable opacity to create a shadow for the child. Link the two layers and position. Open and transfer the train file. Transform the new layer and position. Swap the layer blending mode to multiply. Select the text on the train and duplicate. From the edit menu, choose transform; flip horizontal. Replace the reversed text with the duplicate.

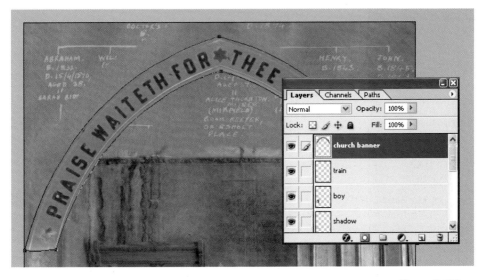

Figure 3-120
Adding elements

Open and invert the church interior file. Create a path to select the banner. Transfer the banner to the working canvas. Swap the banner to soft light and use curves to further soften the appearance of the layer.

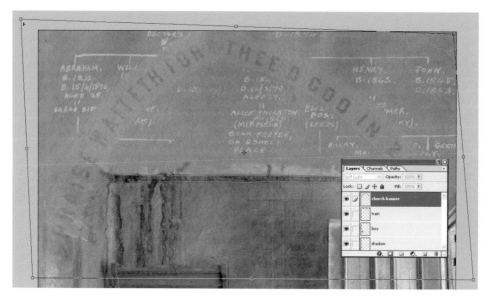

Figure 3-121
Transform

Transform the layer using control to drag individual corners. Select a portion of the boards from the inverted church interior photo and transfer to the working canvas. Swap the layer to soft light mode. Transform and position the new layer.

Minimize Distractions—Select all of the pixels on the church banner layer by holding control and clicking on the layer in the layers palette. Use this selection to delete or mask the boards where they intersect with the banner. Utilize the editing tools to remove unwanted details and burn in distracting highlights.

Print Finishing—Apply an overall curves adjustment layer and enhance color and tone as desired. Pinpoint areas for manipulation on the curve by holding control and clicking on that area of the image. Sharpen appropriately for output.

Figure 3-122

Completed—"Waiteth for Me" (© Luzette Donohue)

Figure 3-123
Ileana Frómeta Grillo

Ileana Frómeta Grillo

Laguna Beach, California
www.ileanaspage.com
Ileana@ileanaspage.com

Equipment

Computer: Apple G5 2.0GHz Dual Processor with ATI Radeon 9600 Pro AGP 64MB (with dual display support), 3.5GB RAM, 160GB hard drive, Pioneer DVR-109 DVD-RW, Mac OS X 10.3.7 Panther, Apple 23″ high-definition cinema display, Maxtor 200GHz external drive.

Scanner: Canon LiDE 30 Scanner (USB), 48-bit color and up to 1200 × 2400 dpi.

Printer: Epson Stylus Photo 2200 (seven colors and UltraChrome inks).

Outside Printers: Dunking Bird Productions (JD Jarvis and Myriam Lozada Jarvis, www.dunkingbirdproductions.com, Hewlett-Packard 2500); for larger prints (over 40″) on canvas I use Duganne Ateliers (Jack and Susan Duganne, www.duganne.com, large-format 12-color Series XII Colorspan).

Favorite Paper: For smaller prints on canvas, Epson Enhanced Matte on the Epson 2200 printer.

Any Color Management Systems: I don't use ICC profiles in the printing of my work. Instead I have created, through trial and error, a color set in Corel Painter that allows me to get bright and consistent printable colors. I also calibrate the monitor frequently (with the Pantone ColorVision Spyder). I use the RGB Adobe 98 option in Photoshop CS for the printing of the final image.

Cataloging and Archiving: I keep a folder for each image in my hard drive. I also keep copies in my backup hard drive and make a DVD of each image for storage purposes. The folder includes the following images: several "in-progress" images, a layered version, a flat version of the final image, an image saved as in Genuine STN format (which will allow me to obtain resized copies when needed), and a folder with the photos used for the background collage.

About the Artist: Background, Education, Inspirations

I have declined several offers from stock agencies in order to remain focused on my overall goal, which is to find an audience in the fine art market. Representation by others has been difficult primarily due to the reluctance of art galleries regarding the digital medium and the lack of an agreeable business model that will keep galleries profitable. Lately, however, I have noticed more openness by galleries that were initially reluctant to accept this medium. I believe this has been due to several factors, such as advantages of the print-on-demand technology, increased use of digital processes by well-known artists, and demand by a public interested in fine images without the exorbitant price tag. On a personal note, the publication of my work in several books and magazines has provided me with a wonderful audience and clientele. Consequently I am able to sell my work without representation, albeit a smaller market than what I would get through gallery sales. I think the most significant changes in this regard have been done through my involvement in the Digital Art Guild in San Diego. Besides becoming a good source for support and exchange of information, the Guild has proactively worked towards gaining exposure in important galleries and exhibition areas. Eventually, groups such as these will be the determining factor in turning the tide around towards a greater acceptance of the medium.

I grew up in a family where art still rules, and was encouraged to pursue a career in the fine arts all along. I, however, took the "scenic route," by first becoming a licensed psychologist in Caracas, Venezuela, and an Art and Play therapist here in the U.S. After working in this field for about 20 years, I finally heeded to the pounding of the Muse, and left an almost finished doctorate degree in Clinical Psychology to become a committed full-time artist, to the delight of my family and husband, who were hoping that one day I would come to my senses. My education in the fine arts began in Caracas, Venezuela, where I was introduced to *plein air* painting, charcoal portraiture, and photography. Once I arrived in the U.S. in 1980, I began my "formal" art education, which included two years of black and white photography at the University of Redlands, California, and three years of fine art studies at the State University in San Bernardino, also in California. At Cal State, I was fortunate to be instructed by a wonderful staff that, in addition to teaching technical skills, emphasized the development of an individual visual language as a lifelong process.

In the mid-eighties, I was offered the opportunity to illustrate a children's book to be published in Venezuela (*La Bicicleta De Nubes*); this led me to do some research into the world of digital graphics. Happy events followed that put me in visual "Nirvana": I bought my first Mac (a II cx with a whopping 20 megs of RAM; I have been a Mac convert since), got my first Wacom tablet (Art Z), and discovered the software Painter (version 1.2), and Photoshop later on (3.0). With the help of knowledgeable friends (and a lot of trial and error) I was able to learn at a fast pace. Having such wonderful equipment and software allowed me to learn intuitively and no doubt made the transition from "traditional" to "digital" a lot easier. As both software and hardware evolved, I was able to create more complex imagery. The rapid development of the wide-format printing and archival inks also helped make the transition into the world of digital fine arts.

My continuing education in Painter is mainly based on books or DVD tutorials that address the software—a few examples: books on Painter by Jeremy Sutton and Cher Pendarvis. Also a Painter workshop by Don Seegmiller, and participation in Internet forums such as the Painter list, Painter world, and www.tutoralley.com (a wonderful forum moderated by the very knowledgeable Jinny Brown). My Photoshop education is based on various Internet forums and DVD coursework by Julieanne Kost. With the sales of my work and the help of a very supportive husband I have been able to realize my dream and become a full-time artist.

Undoubtedly, the use of bright colors and the type of imagery and symbolism that I find attractive is heavily influenced by the sounds and sights of my Caribbean upbringing. I grew up admiring the works of Latin American artists from the Dominican Republic, such as Candido Bidó, and Venezuelan painter Hector Poleo, to name a few. Both artists' work relied heavily on the use of vivid colors and interplay between flat and modeled surfaces. My digital imagery also finds inspiration in the work of Gauguin, the Fauve painters, David Hockney, and surrealistic painters such as Magritte. I have also found inspiration in the works of women artists such as Nivia Gonzales and Pegger Hopper, both artists from the United States.

Creative Process

Sometimes I realize the source of the inspiration only after the work has been completed. I do know that my imagery highly reflects my Caribbean roots, and that the message is viewed from the female perspective. Unless suggested by someone, as in the case of "Snapping Lines," the main image comes to me as a loosely drawn sketch. I also carry my digital camera wherever I go, and store the images taken in CDs for later use; however, at this point, there is nothing specific in mind. I later choose some of the better sketches, scan them into Painter, and use them as the foundation for a finished picture of the main figure. The process of selecting the pictures that will go with this figure is more intuitive. I just look through each one of the pictures taken and put those that "fit" in a folder. Then it is a matter of blending and placing the layers together (in Photoshop) until I achieve the desired composition. The files at this point can get quite large (250 to 600MB) and the most time-consuming part of the project is to combine, blend, and integrate the layers, which can be as many as 22–30.

I work on different projects at the same time, although some sit for a while and are revisited from time to time until I find the right set of images that fit. On the average, once I have a clearer idea of what I want, the work is completed within two to three weeks.

For the image discussed here, I used a couple of "posed" pictures that I had taken with the self-timer and stored in my photo library for later use. Using Corel Painter, and with the photos as a clone source (File > Clone), I traced the outline of the figures using the tracing paper feature (Select All > Delete > Select Tracing Paper button) and the 2B pencil brush. The outline was later transformed until I got a clean outline of each figure that I found satisfying. I also selected different sections of the outline and saved the selection (Select > Save selection). The saved selections will be stored as alpha channel and can be activated when needed. Each outline was later saved in RIFF (Painter) format.

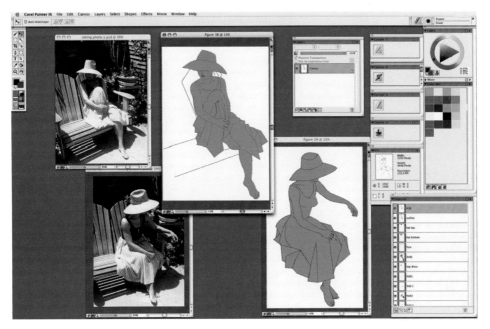

Figure 3-124
Source images and corresponding outlines

Figure 3-124 shows the source images and corresponding outlines with the active masks (in red, list of masks showing in the channel section). Originally the image would only depict one figure, however, I liked the effect of having the two figures side by side and decided to bring them together in one canvas. In order to do this, I selected the black outline of each figure (Select > Auto Select > Image Luminance) and converted it into a layer (click on selection using the layer adjuster tool).

I opened a blank canvas with the dimensions and resolution that I visualized for the final image (30" W × 30" H at 150 dpi) and transferred both figure outlines as separate layers. The layers were scaled and transformed until I found a composition that I liked. Once I transferred the outlines onto the bigger canvas I lost all the channels that I had saved in the original outlines; however, I was able to use the outline layer as a guide for the painting of the image.

The colors were applied on the canvas layer using a custom color palette, several chalk variants, and the "Add Water" brush as a blending medium. I also used the "Pattern Pen" (at a very low opacity) in order to apply a basket weave on the hats.

Figure 3-125
Beginning to paint

Figure 3-125 shows composition first as outline, then painted, and a detail that shows the application of chalk and "Add Water" brush. Once I painted the figures, I discarded the black outline layer and created a new layer with the two figures. Then I began to build a colorful background with a variety of chalk and airbrush applications in different settings and sizes. The "Grainy Water" and "Just Add Water" options in the blending brushes were used to soften and blend the colors. I saved the image in its native RIFF format and saved another version in PSD. (Note: I tend to save multiple copies of the work in progress in both RIFF and PSD.)

Figure 3-126
Painting the background

I opened the PSD version of the image in Adobe Photoshop and transferred in a variety of images that I had taken with my digital camera and which had already been masked and layered. Each photo was scaled and composed until I found an arrangement that I liked. Next I used the blending modes, filters, and hue and saturation levels in Photoshop until I was able to integrate the different elements into a whole image.

Figure 3-127
Transferring layers

The final composition was flattened (after saving a layered version of it). The flattened version was opened in Corel Painter so that I could work on the final touches (such as smoothing layer edges or painting highlights). Along with a flattened and a layered version, I keep a saved version in Genuine Fractals (STN format), which, in this case, came in handy, since it allowed me to enlarge the image to its final 42″ × 40″ print size.

Figure 3-128
Final image—"In the Garden" (© Ileana Frómeta Grillo)

Figure 3-129
Fay Sirkis

Fay Sirkis

Brooklyn, New York
fay@faysartstudio.com
www.faysartstudio.com

Equipment

Computers: Power Mac G4, OS 10.3.8 Panther, with two CPUs (speed, 1GHz; memory, 1GB); PowerBook G4 15″ (Mac laptop), 10.3.8 Panther, with two CPUs (speed, 1GHz; memory, 1GB).

Scanner: Epson Expression 1640XL.

Tablets: Two Wacom Intuos 3 6 × 8 tablets, one Wacom Intuos 2 6 × 8 tablet, and one Wacom Intuos 2 9 × 12 tablet (I need many tablets, for teaching and travel).

Printer: Epson 9600.

Favorite Papers: All my watercolor portraits are printed on beautiful acid-free textured fine art paper. Each print has a special matte coating, designed for high-quality fine art reproductions. I print on the Epson 9600, directly out of Photoshop. The inks used are guaranteed to last 100 years, under normal lighting conditions. I like to use Epson Somerset Velvet, for my outdoor scenic paintings. For my portrait work I like to use the Hahnemuhle papers. They have some beautiful textured fine art papers. My favorite is Torchon; it has a lot of texture and it brings out a lot of the detail in my work. William Turner is another watercolor paper from Hahnemuhle; it has a very smooth texture and looks really beautiful in pastel colored paintings. I like to print my simulated oil paintings, which usually are my lower key images, on canvas. I use the Satin Canvas from LexJet; it's a quick-dry fabric, and prints out beautifully.

About the Artist: Background, Education, Inspirations

Fay Sirkis is an internationally recognized portrait artist, photographer, and instructor. She is a New York-based contemporary digital artist, with a background in traditional fine art. In the 1990s Fay moved into the graphic design industry. She attended the Pratt School of Professional Studies in New York City, where she became certified in Graphic and Web Design. She also attended Rockhurst College CE in New York City, for her certification in printing and pre-press. She worked as a freelance graphic artist as well as a graphic design instructor. She designed book covers and the total design of the books for a children's book publishing company.

Fay is a beta tester for Corel Painter, and was instrumental in the launching of Painter IX. Her work is featured in Corel's Painter Masters Art Gallery, as well as their numerous ad campaigns. Her commissioned portraits and paintings are held in private collections internationally, and also exhibited in museums and art galleries. She is best known for her simplistic way of teaching, making the learning curve in the digital world easier to master.

"I knew that I wanted to paint from the time that I was very young. My parents enrolled me in art classes at the Y. While my friends studied music, I studied art. For me, art was my music! I could see the colors sing on my canvas!"As a child I would find myself staring at Norman Rockwell's paintings, whenever I had the chance. I would always wonder, 'Are they paintings, or photographs?' Rockwell's paintings always told a story, and the detail of his work could hold my attention for a very long time. Norman Rockwell remains my favorite contemporary artist. I am a still a student of his works today. I can look at his paintings many different times, and each time I see something else.

"Until the late 1930's, Rockwell painted from life . . . then he went for photography in a big way. Photography enabled him to paint action, and so much more that he could not do without the camera; it expanded his options enormously. Rockwell had his assistant photograph the models, in the pose he wanted to paint them in. Sometimes he would include backgrounds in the photograph, that he would want in his paintings as well. Rockwell would project the photograph onto a large sheet of canvas, and literally trace the photograph, producing a sketch. When the image was all sketched out, he would proceed to paint it.

"That is how Rockwell captured reality onto the canvas. I do the same thing today, by capturing my image (my portrait model) with a digital camera, and then I bring it into Photoshop, where I retouch and enhance my portrait, and then I bring it into Painter, where I clone the image (much like projecting) and then add a new layer above the canvas, and then I proceed to paint and blend my painting. I named my favorite brush 'The Rockwell.' It is a very small digital airbrush, from the Airbrush category in Painter, which I paint all my details with, the same details that I have grown to love in the paintings of Norman Rockwell.

"Today you don't have to be a Norman Rockwell to create beautiful paintings. We are living in the new digital era, where so much technology is available for us to help with the creative process. My primary focus is to capture the character and vitality of my subjects. Fine portrait painting is more than a likeness, it is the story of an individual and the person's great uniqueness."

Creative Process

The painting "Ashlie" is based on the original photograph captured by the late Don Blair. Don was the recipient of virtually every award and honor in professional photography. He was best known for his technical mastery of lighting and posing. You can imagine my excitement when Don asked me to paint his images.

Figure 3-130
Original photo by Don Blair

This painting is one of my favorite portraits. It is the first digital portrait where I achieved the look I was trying to mimic from my traditional painting days. In the original photo, Don captured Ashlie with a low-key background. Its impact is beautiful. Because Ashlie is a young teen, I wanted to paint her in high to medium key, with a dramatic background. I started to use the palette knife background effect first, on Ashlie's portrait. Since then, you will find that effect on many of my paintings.

I tend to outline a lot of my edges. I like to keep my paintings very sharp. By exaggerating the contrast between light and dark colors, you accomplish the look of your subjects popping off the canvas. It takes on almost a 3D effect. To outline my edges I use two brushes, one giving me a softer edge, and the other a sharper edge. For a softer edge, I select the Airbrush category from the brush selector, and then I select the Digital Airbrush variant, from the list on the right. I paint with a brush size as small as 1.7 to outline. When I need a very sharp edge, I use the 2B pencil, from the pencil category, sometimes going as small as 1.0 in size. In the painting "Ashlie" I used these brushes to paint the seams on the girl's jacket, as well as the hood string. The sharper the detail, the more the painting takes on dimension.

Figure 3-131
Detail of painting

The Painting Process—First, I bring the original image into Adobe Photoshop, and do all my retouching, taking care of unwanted color casts, bags under the eyes, and any skin imperfections. I use Curves, Levels, and Hue and Saturation to obtain the perfect skin tones for the portrait painting. Once the image is ready for painting, I bring it into Painter and make a clone copy, a regular clone, not a quick clone. I don't trace the image, nor do I paint with the clone brushes. Many artists do work this way and achieve beautiful results. My approach is different.

I rename the clone copy and proceed to paint. I start by adding a layer on top of my canvas layer (which is really my reference photo) I don't trace the photo, but paint directly on top of it (on a separate layer), adding more color and detail; the photo acts as a good foundation for your painting. Eventually you won't see any pixels from the photo, once you merge the new layer with the canvas layer.

The key to this technique is to check "Pick up underlying color" in the layers pallet. By checking this box, you will be merging colors from the photo with the colors that you will be applying to your new layer, once you start to blend them.

Equally important as to what colors and brushes you use, is how you apply and blend your colors. My choice, and in my opinion, the only choice is to paint with a stylus pen, using the Wacom 3 Intuos tablet.

Because my final image is printed on fine art watercolor paper, I don't add a paper texture from Painter to my image. All the textures on my paintings are either from the final paper output or a natural painting result from various combinations of brushes that I use together in Painter.

Figure 3-132
Completed digital painting—"Ashlie" (© Fay Sirkis)

Figure 3-133
Jeremy Sutton

Jeremy Sutton

Jeremy Sutton Studios
San Francisco, California
Jeremy@paintercreativity.com
www.paintercreativity.com (Painter resources)
www.jeremysutton.com (art galleries)

Equipment

Computers: G5 Duo, Mac OS X (Panther), 1GB RAM, 80GB hard drive, 1.5GHz, 21″ Apple Cinema display; G4 PowerBook, Mac OS X (Panther), 1GB RAM, 60GB hard drive, 1GHz, 15″ display.

Scanner: Epson Perfection.

Printers: Epson 2200, Epson 9600.

Favorite Papers: Crane's Museo for 2200, Epson Fine Art and Hahnemuhle Etching for 9600, plus PremierArt Water Resistant Canvas for Epson for 9600.

Any Color Management Systems: None as yet. Currently evaluating systems.

Cataloging and Archiving: Methodical file naming (subject—version number—note.file type) within project folders, periodically backed up in duplicate onto DVD, one set of which is kept in studio and the other of which is sent to the UK for secondary backup.

About the Artist: Background, Education, Inspirations

My educational background includes attendance at the Vrije Akademie, The Hague, The Netherlands, 1985–1988, where I studied lithography and life drawing. I earned a Bachelor of Arts degree (later converted to Masters of Arts Oxon) in Physics at Pembroke College, Oxford University, 1979–1982. While at Oxford I studied etching, sculpture, and life drawing at the Ruskin School of Drawing and Fine Art. I earned

A-Levels in Physics, Chemistry, and Math at Latymer School, London, 1972–1979.

I work full time in the field of fine art as a portrait artist and author, and I split my time between making commissioned portraits and fine art, using a combination of media (digital and traditional), and writing books and articles, producing instructional DVDs, teaching seminars and workshops, and speaking to professional photographers and artists at regional, national, and international conferences and conventions. My commissioned portraits include collages similar to the one I describe in this chapter. You can see examples on my art web site at www.jeremysutton.com.

Inspiration: My mother, Margaret, is probably the single artist who has been the most major influence on me being an artist today. I grew up surrounded by Mother's art at home. She exposed me to the wonderful art galleries and museums of London and elsewhere. She has often been a useful sounding board and artistic mentor in my adult life. My mother would talk to me about drawing, encouraging me to explore and experiment.

Other influences include my sister, Debbi, also an artist, though with different media and approach (she creates installation and conceptual art); she has also been a great sounding board for ideas and a source of constructive critique for my art. When I lived in The Netherlands my greatest artistic influences were two artists who were both my mentors and friends, Martin Helm and Let Bijkersma.

While living in The Netherlands I was exposed to the beautiful art in Dutch museums such as the Kroller Muller, the Van Gogh, and the Stadelijk; in Denmark, there was the Louisiana, and, in Paris, the Picasso and Rodin museums. In these museums I grew to appreciate the qualities of different artists whose work, or aspects of their work, resonated with my own approach and vision.

Artistic qualities that struck a chord for me included the colors and bold brush strokes of the Fauvists, such as André Derain, Wassily Kandinsky, Maurice de Vlaminck, and Henri Mattise. I like the thick, loose expressionistic brush strokes and application of paint of Post-Impressionists, such as Vincent van Gogh, and of Bay Area Figurative Movement painters, such as David Park. I like the playfulness of Pablo Picasso and Andy Warhol. I like the sensitivity of Renoir's paintings, the quality of light in the Impressionists' work, and the passionate sensuality of Auguste Rodin's sculptures.

Creative Process

The art I chose to discuss here, "Dad," is a collage portrayal I created of my father, Maurice Sutton, who passed away in 1988, just after I had moved to live in the U.S.A. The principles and techniques used in this case study can be applied to any collage project. In dissecting and analyzing the steps that went into making this collage, I share my intuitive approach to combining imagery. I have not sanitized the serendipitous nature of the way the collage unfolded. It didn't go exactly as planned, and it didn't end up looking how I initially envisioned it. The steps didn't follow the most logical or efficient path. Real-life creativity is not a perfectly running, pre-programmed script—it is a series of mini-adventures and unscripted happy accidents. The description I share with you here of how I created the collage portrayal "Dad," is based on the chapter on collage in my new book, *Painter IX Creativity: Digital Artist's Handbook.*

Trusting in the Process: Creating this collage was a scary yet exciting proposition. I felt a sense of responsibility to my Dad's memory, to create something worthy of him. I also felt a sense of responsibility to my feelings. Would I express myself in a way that would convey how deeply I love him and miss him?

In starting off there is only a blank canvas. I could not predict what would emerge, or how successful it would be, or how beautiful, or how powerful. I had only the trust in the process. I had to acknowledge and then let go of my fears. I had to jump in and take the risk. It felt like stepping off a high diving board, trusting that I would survive the fall. . . .

Research and Collect Imagery: Having selected my subject, the next step was image research and image collection. By "image" I mean all kinds of images, not just photographs. An image can be anything visual that conveys, or relates to, my subject. It can be a sample of their writing, an object or place you identify with them or that was/is meaningful to them, and so on. I created folders outside and inside my computer, for collecting potential source material. I created a main Project Folder in my computer, and within that folder created a 'Source Images' folder into which I collected all my potential source images, and a Working Images folder into which I saved all my working images. In this case study I ended up with a Source Images folder containing 29 documents (taking up a total of 485MB), and a Working Images folder containing 46 saved versions (taking up a total of 1.41GB), each sequentially numbered.

Some of my source images that were particularly significant were the following:

a) Picture of when my Dad was a little boy (two and half years old) with his two older sisters (taken in London, 1930).
b) Wedding picture of my Mum and Dad (London, U.K., 1954).
c) Picture of Grandma and Grandpa Sutton (London, 1963).
d) Author description from the back of my Dad's book, *Cancer Explained* (published in 1966).
e) Mum and Dad hiking (Lake District, U.K., 1973).
f) Sketch I did of my Dad at a conference (Oxford, U.K., 1983).
g) The last pictures taken of my whole family together, one outside my parents' home and one at Heathrow Airport, as I was leaving to come and live in America (April, 1988).
h) Pictures of me, my Mum, and my Dad in Big Sur, California (October, 1988).
i) Picture of outer space from the *Times Atlas of the World* that Mum and Dad gave me after visiting me in California (Dad loved astronomy and space).

j) A letter my Dad sent me on November 18th, just a month before he died.

I used Photoshop's Adjustment Layers (Levels, Hue/Saturation) to optimize my source imagery. I saved flattened versions of the files for opening in Painter. I could get a quick overview of my source images using Photoshop Bridge (CS2) or Browser (CS).

Figure 3-134
Using Photoshop's browsing function to view source images

To give myself the maximum flexibility and choice of imagery I sometimes digitally capture the same image using both my digital SLR (single lens reflex) camera with a soft-focus lens and with my flatbed scanner. You may notice in the browser view shown here that I have several pairs of the same image, but one (the one taken on the SLR with the soft-focus lens) looks slightly fuzzier than the other. I will not necessarily want to use the most precise or detailed image in my collage. Sometimes a more diffuse, abstract image works better.

My Key Foundation Image or Images: It's easy to put a jumble of overlapping and juxtaposed images together on a page. However, it's a whole other challenge to create a powerful, evocative composition that grabs the viewer's attention and tells my story in a compelling way. Just like a painting, my collage composition needs a focus of attention, a simple key image, or group of images that ground the piece and form a foundation, or framework, that I can build up on. The key foundation image, or images, may also act as a background to start the collage with, rather like an underpainting, or I may select another background image and combine that with my foundation images. Frequently the main foundation image jumps out. It speaks loudly. In this case I envisaged from the start a central main portrait of my Dad being the root image of the collage. I found one head shot photo of Dad smiling, hair blowing in the wind, with the sea in the background, that I thought would work perfectly as a foundation image. Since Dad loved astronomy, I pictured using the stars in the background behind the main portrait.

As I did further image research I came across the letter dad had written to me the month before he died. I loved the way he'd signed off at the end with a joyful "love & kisses from all of us, Dad xxxxxxx." As soon as I saw that I knew I wanted to have that portion of his letter clearly visible in the collage.

Customized Palette Layout: Before diving into action in Painter, I took the time to create a "collage shortcuts" custom palette (those commands and brushes you are likely to use repeatedly while creating a collage) and then set up and saved a custom palette layout called "Collage" specifically suited to working on collages.

Besides the Collage Shortcuts custom palette I also had open on my Painter desktop the Toolbox, Property Bar, Brush Selector Bar, Colors palette, Brush Controls Size palette, Layers palette, and Papers palette. I minimize what I have visible to just those palettes that are essential. The more I clutter my workspace the harder it is to work efficiently. When I had everything laid out to my satisfaction, I chose Window > Palette Arrangement > Save Layout.

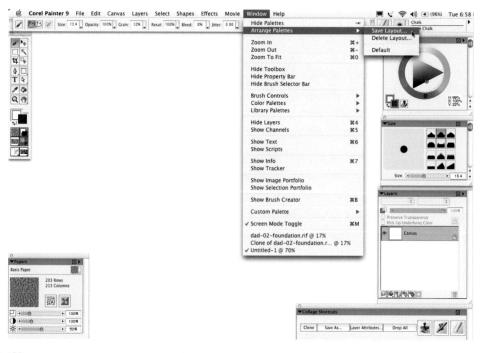

Figure 3-135
Saving a custom palette layout

Canvas Size: The foundation canvas is the canvas from which I started building up the collage. The foundation canvas sets the scale, proportion, and size of my artwork, at least for the duration of the creative process. I first established the proportions of the canvas (ratio of height to width) and then, second, the overall size of the canvas (the physical dimensions and pixel resolution of my artwork).

In this case the proportions were determined by the scale of the central portrait versus the overall size of the canvas: in other words, how much of the canvas would be taken up with the central portrait. I opened the scan of the central portrait, my main foundation image, in Painter. I chose Cmd/Ctrl-M (Window > Screen Mode Toggle). I chose Canvas > Canvas Size and added 200 pixels all the way around.

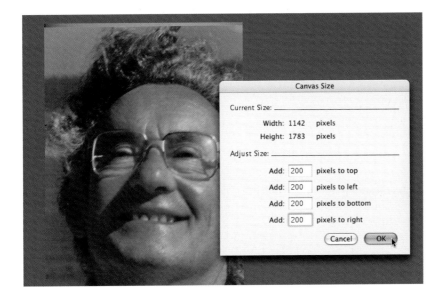

Figure 3-136
Establishing canvas proportions

After adjusting the proportions I saved this version of the file. Throughout this collage project my layered working files were saved in RIFF file format with sequential version numbering, and intermittently backed up in Photoshop file format (always back up layered files in Photoshop format before closing Painter, since large RIFF files occasionally become corrupt). Although there is some overlap between Painter Composite Methods and Photoshop Layer Blending Modes, there are Composite Methods in Painter that are only preserved in RIFF format and will not be preserved in Photoshop file format.

Saving My Reproportioned Image: The next step is to look ahead at the final print size you envisage making. I envisaged a print approximately 20 inches by 30 inches and resized (Canvas > Resize with Constrain File Size unchecked) the file to that size with a pixel resolution of 150 ppi.

Figure 3-137
*Resizing foundation canvas
to suit final envisaged print
dimensions*

I then saved, and renamed (as dad-02-foundation.rif), the resized file. This is my foundation canvas.

Having generated my foundation canvas, my next stage was to generate a series of variations that I could use as clone sources to bring imagery into my collage. The key point with any clone source for this project is that it would have exactly the same dimensions as my working file (that is, the same dimensions as my foundation canvas). I use my foundation image to create a series of clone copies (using the Clone button in my Collage Shortcuts custom palette), which will automatically be of exactly the same size and proportions, and use these clone copies as "base canvases" for my clone source variations.

Preparing a Background Canvas from the Stars Image: I clicked on the Clone button in my "Collage Shortcuts" custom palette. This created a clone copy of the foundation image into which I would be pasting the stars background. I chose Cmd/Ctrl-M (Window > Screen Mode Toggle), which mounted my clone copy in screen mode. I opened the stars source image in Painter. I chose Cmd/Ctrl-A (Select > All). I chose Cmd/Ctrl-C (Edit > Copy). I chose Cmd/Ctrl-W (File > Close) and closed the stars image without saving changes. With the clone copy of the foundation canvas being the active image in Painter, I chose Cmd/Ctrl-V (Edit > Paste). This pasted the stars image as a layer above the background canvas. With the stars layer active (highlighted) in the Layers palette, I chose Effects > Orientation > Free Transform. Holding the Shift key down, I dragged one of the corner Free Transform control handles and resized the layer to cover the whole canvas. In the Layers palette I lowered the layer opacity slider so I could see the portrait underneath.

Figure 3-138
Lowering the opacity of the resized Free Transform star layer

I used the ability to see through the stars layer to position it so it would work compositionally with the portrait. I increased the layer opacity to 100%. I chose Drop from the layer pop-up menu. I drop the layer primarily to keep the file compact and to prevent accidentally moving the layer. Note that you can equally well keep the layer and just click on the padlock icon in the Layers palette while the layer is selected in order to lock it in position. The advantage of keeping the layer is if you wish to vary its scale or position in the future.

Figure 3-139
Dropping the resized star layer

I saved the flattened file, renaming it with the filename dad-03-starbckgnd.rif. It is important in collage to name every file clearly so you know exactly what it is. This is especially true of those files you may use as clone sources, since you'll be searching for the right file to assign as clone source purely by filename in the File > Clone Source menu. For this reason I do not recommend using Iterative Save in collage (it automatically creates filenames that do not include descriptive notes, just sequential numbers added at the end of the filename).

Capturing a Paper Texture from the "Dad" Letter: I selected the foundation canvas (it is listed at the bottom of the Window menu) and made that the active image in Painter. I followed the exact same procedure for the letter image as I did for the stars, first making a clone copy of the foundation image, then pasting in, resizing, and repositioning the letter layer until I was satisfied, finally saving that resulting file as dad-04-letterbkgnd.rif.

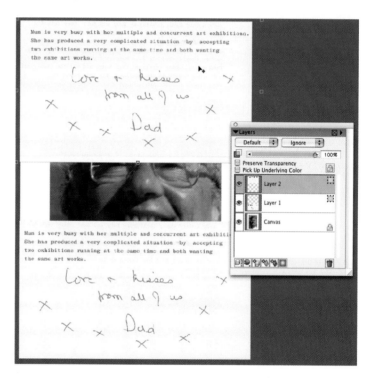

Figure 3-140
Creating the letter background image

My vision with the writing from Dad's letter was to introduce that into my collage as a paper texture rather than just clone in with the Soft Cloner. To do this I needed to capture the letter as a paper texture. Capturing a paper texture the same size as my foundation canvas is the best way for me to control exactly where the writing appears in the image and what scale it is. Thus my goal was to take the letter background image I had just created, change it into a high-contrast black and white image, and then save that as a paper texture. The first step of this was to select the background canvas in the Layers palette. I then chose Cmd/Ctrl-A (Select > All). I then pressed the Backspace/Delete key. This cleared the background image, which I didn't want to be part of the texture. I then clicked on the Drop All button in my Collage Shortcuts custom palette. This flattened the image. I then chose Effects > Tonal Control > Adjust Colors. I then reduced the Saturation slider in the Adjust Color window to minimum (−139%). This desaturated the image.

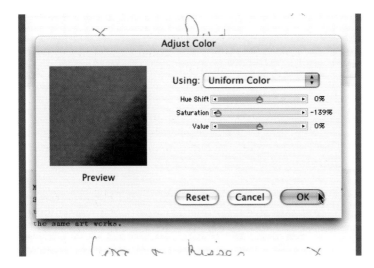

Figure 3-141
*Desaturating the image
using the Adjust Color effect*

I clicked OK. I then chose Cmd/Ctrl-E (Effects > Tonal Control > Equalize). I then brought the black and the white points close together in the Equalize window histogram. This created extreme contrast in the image so the writing was black and everything else was white.

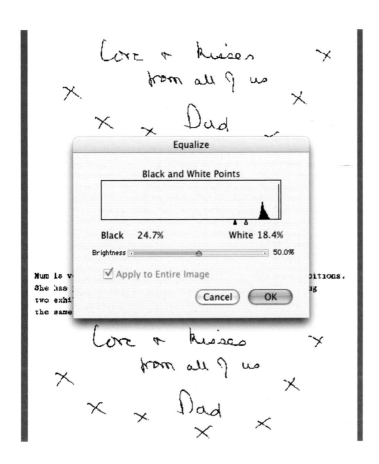

Figure 3-142
*Increasing contrast using the
Equalize effect*

Saving Large Papers into a Custom Paper Library: Before capturing this relatively large image (3179 × 4500 pixels) as a paper texture I knew ahead of time it would be a memory hog and I wouldn't want such a large paper texture sitting in my default paper library. Therefore I chose Open Library from the Papers pop-up menu and opened a custom library, "JeremyExtraPapers," I had created specially for my large custom papers. I recommend you do the same. The detailed technique for creating my own Paper Library, involving use of the Paper Mover, is described in my book *Painter IX Creativity: Digital Artist's Handbook*. After opening and using this custom paper library, I would then open the default "Paper Textures" library so that was the one open next time I worked with Painter. That way I could avoid the large custom papers affecting the efficiency of Painter when working on other projects. I then chose Cmd/Ctrl-A (Select > All). I then chose Capture Paper in the Papers palette pop-up menu.

Figure 3-143
Capture Paper in the Papers palette pop-up menu

I named the paper, adjusted the Crossfade slider to zero, and clicked OK. The paper was now saved in my custom papers library for use anytime in the future.

Capturing Photocopies as Paper Texture: One great aspect of capturing material as paper textures in Painter is that it frees you up from having to have perfect color reproductions of your images. The source images of my Dad and me, and of my family at Heathrow Airport as I was about to leave for America, were both poor-quality black and white photocopies dating back almost fifteen years! However, I knew that they would make a great paper texture. In fact, the poor quality was almost an asset, since each picture was already a high-contrast black and white image. I did add a little Equalize to increase the contrast even further.

With these photocopies, I just chose Cmd/Ctrl-A (Select > All) and then chose the Capture Paper command from the Papers palette pop-up menu, and captured these images as a paper textures in my custom papers library.

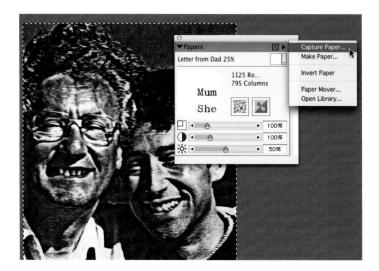

Figure 3-144
Choosing Capture Paper for the photocopy of Dad and me

Figure 3-145
Choosing Capture Paper for the photocopy of my family saying goodbye to me at Heathrow Airport

Pasting Childhood Photo into Image for Use as a Clone Source: I chose to use the softer, fuzzier version of the photograph of my Dad and his sisters, the one I recorded with my SLR rather than the scanner. I increased the contrast a little and then copied and pasted the image into my base canvas (clone of the foundation image). I positioned the newly pasted image layer in the bottom left corner of the canvas.

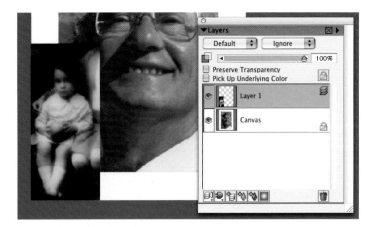

Figure 3-146
Photo pasted and positioned on the base canvas

Making a Paper Texture from the Sketch: I copied and pasted the sketch onto another base canvas (a clone copy of the foundation image in which I had cleared the canvas to white). After positioning the sketch I dropped the pasted image layer. I increased the contrast with the Equalize command and then captured the entire canvas as a paper texture.

Figure 3-147
Naming the sketch paper texture

Using Paint Bucket to Fill Foundation Canvas Border with Blue: I wanted to fill the white border around the central portrait image in my foundation canvas with blue instead of white. I wanted to avoid any accidental harsh boundaries when cloning. I chose the Paint Bucket tool in the Toolbox. In the Colors palette I picked the color I wanted to fill the border with. I clicked once in the white border region. I noticed that some of the blue had "leaked" into the photograph. In other words, the default Painter Bucket Tolerance setting of 32 (in the Property Bar) was too high.

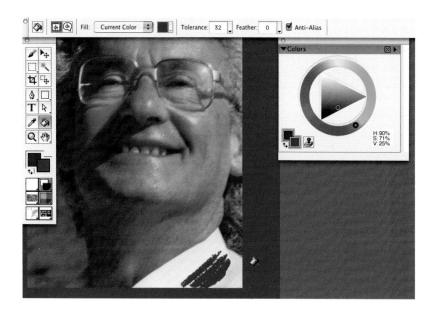

Figure 3-148
*After filling the border
with default Paint Bucket
properties*

I lowered the Paint Bucket Tolerance setting to 9. It worked perfectly.

Figure 3-149
*Paint Bucket Fill with Toler-
ance lowered to 9*

Using my Save As button, I then saved the foundation image with an appropriately descriptive name. I chose File > Clone Source and set the blue-bordered foundation image to be clone source.

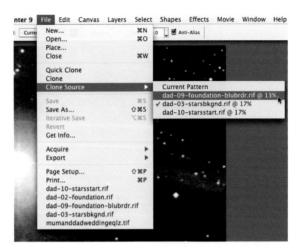

Figure 3-150
Setting the blue-bordered foundation image to be clone source

Free-Hand Painting from Observation and Using Clone Reference: With a clone copy of the stars background image being my active working image, and the foundation image with a blue border being my clone source, I started the process of painting the main central portrait onto the stars. I chose the Artists > Sargent Brush. I was about to use Tracing Paper and clone color when I stopped myself. I picked up the photo of my Dad that I had scanned for the central portrait and decided to start painting it just from observation of the photo that I had sitting beside my computer, rather than using Tracing Paper. I specifically wanted to create an expressionistic portrait with loose, free, gestural brushwork. I knew that relying on the Tracing Paper would stilt the expressive quality of my brush strokes. Thus I started the portrait.

Figure 3-151
Painting the portrait free-hand against the stars background

At a certain point in my painting process I turned on Tracing Paper (Cmd/Ctrl-T) to compare my free-hand brush strokes with the underlying photo. I had painted the portrait larger and displaced down to the lower right side of the canvas. Rather than try to distort my painting to match the scale and location of the underlying photo in the clone source, I decided to do the opposite and resize and reposition my underlying photo to more closely match the brush strokes I had already placed on the working image. This is an example of what I referred to earlier as "flowing with the unexpected twists and turns of my creative process." Don't be too attached to your plans! I made the clone source the active image in Painter. I chose Cmd/Ctrl-A (Select > All). I chose Select > Float. This made the whole source image a layer. I chose Effects > Orientation > Free Transform. This made the layer a reference layer, which I could resize with minimum loss of quality. I held the Shift key down while dragging one of the corner Free Transform control handles away from the center. This enlarged the layer image. I adjusted the layer size until it matched my painted version of the portrait. I then dragged the layer (with the Layer Adjuster tool, which had been automatically selected when I created a layer) into a position that matched the painted version. To do this I had to do some trial-and-error moving, returning to the working image and turning on and off Tracing Paper to align the features like the eyes.

Figure 3-152
Aligning the eyes of the underlying photo with the painted portrait using Tracing Paper to view both simultaneously

Once I had rescaled and repositioned the clone source, I then started using a combination of clone color with my own color on the portrait. I chose the Jeremy Faves 2.0 > JS—Luscious Squiggle brush.

Figure 3-153
Applying the Luscious Squiggle brush using clone color

I continued the painting process with a modification of the Cloners > Oil Brush Cloner, one in which I changed the Brush Controls Impasto "Draw to" setting from "Color and Depth" to "Color."

Figure 3-154
Painting with a modified Oil Brush Cloner

I continued painting until I reached a stage where I felt there was a sufficient likeness combined with sufficient roughness of brushstrokes. I didn't want the portrait to look photographic or over-realistic.

Figure 3-155
The painted portrait

I added the "Mum and Dad at Big Sur" image using Difference Composite Method and a mask.

Figure 3-156
Detail

I added the "Dad Hiking" image as layer using Gel Composite Method and a layer mask. I selected the "Dad and me" paper texture in the Papers palette paper selector and I chose the Chalk > Large Chalk brush, increased its size, and reduced the grain slider (Property Bar). I applied the paper texture in the upper left side of the working image on the background image.

I began adding in images like "Grandparents" image as layer, using Luminosity Composite Method. I added "Mum and Dad" hiking with the Shadow Map composite mode. I Added "Family Goodbye Outside House" image using Default Composite Method. I added "Mum and Dad Wedding" image as layer using GelCover Composite Method.

After saving a RIFF version with all my layers intact, I flattened the image. Using the Large Chalk, I then applied the "Sketch" and "Letter" paper textures in the flattened image.

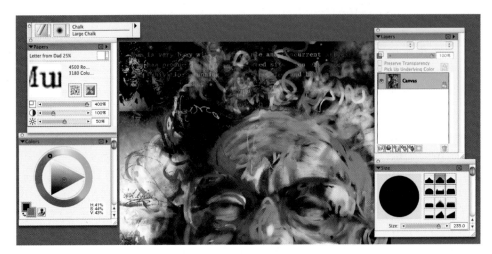

Figure 3-157
Applying the "Letter" paper texture

In lieu of a signature I decided to add a personal note. I chose the Pencils > 2B Pencil, with Grainy Soft Buildup to Cover and Grainy Soft Cover. I de-emphasized the writing with use of the Soft Cloner.

One element remained, the write-up on Dad that was on the back of his book. I wanted this in the collage. My final steps were to blend away a couple of harsh straight edges that I found distracting. I chose the Blenders > Round Blender Brush 30 and applied this gently to the back of the couch behind my Grandparents (bottom left) and also where the edge of the original portrait photo was showing on the upper right.

Figure 3-158

Completed—"Dad" (© Jeremy Sutton)

Figure 3-159
Paul Elson

Paul Elson

North Bergen, New Jersey
paulge@att.net
www.elson.cc

Equipment
Computer: Mac G5 dual 2GHz, 8GB RAM, OS 10.3.9.
Scanner: Epson Perfection 4990 PRO; digital files also created with a
Canon EOS 1Ds Mark II camera (16.7-megapixel sensor).
Printers: Epson Pro 10600 (UltraChrome ink), Epson Stylus Photo
1280.
Favorite Papers: PremierArt Water Resistant Canvas for Epson, Epson
Premium Luster Paper, Epson Textured Fine Art Paper, Epson Smooth
Fine Art.
Any Color Management Systems: Via Photoshop CS2 and profiles
via GretagMacbeth, iPhoto hardware, and GretagMacbeth Eye-One
Match 3.0 software; image manipulation with Photoshop CS2 and
Painter 8.
Cataloging and Archiving: External Firewire drives and DVDs.

About the Artist: Background, Education, Inspirations
Education: Antioch College, BA in Philosophy; then a different kind of
education—14 months in flight training to become a U.S. Navy pilot.
I'm working full time creating/selling my images; I still get commercial
assignments from previous clients, but I no longer solicit this work. My
inspirations are Ernst Haas and Camille Pissarro.

Creative Process

My preference has always been to live, vacation, and work at the seaside. "The House on the Dune" was created with several images, but the dominant one was photographed on a trip I took along the ragged edge of Maine up into Canada. I shot the image with a Nikon F5, Fuji Provia film (100 speed), and a 28 mm PC lens with a polarizing filter. It happened to be a beautiful day as I crossed the border, and although I do not remember the name of the nearest town, I know the slide from which the image began was taken on that first day in Canada. Much is different from the final image, but I remember quite distinctly the stillness and haunting quality of the scene. The gentlest of zephyrs soughing through the sand grass, the arrhythmic crash of waves a counterpoint, the occasional wheeling and caw of a seagull—somehow all seemed to lend an air of foreboding to the dilapidated house crumbling about itself. Perhaps it was the severed boat, or the lobster cages rotting in a jumble of chicken wire and moss-covered, weathered wood. But most, it was the little girl's bike, rusted, bent, abandoned in the tall grass far from the house.

Figure 3-160
Original photo—Beginning

I remember thinking, "who abandons such a beautiful property at the edge of the sea, what child abandons her bike, perhaps her most cherished possession; what tragedy presaged such neglect?" Very quickly, in my mind's eye, the unremitting sunlight of that cloudless day rose several hundred degrees Kelvin as it passed through a gray and threatening sky. Very quickly the serenity I first observed, turned into a mask over a sad, untold tale.

I remembered these thoughts when I returned home and began the image transition by duplicating the scanned image. Working on the duplicate in Photoshop, I selected the sand grass surrounding the house with the Magic Wand and the Lasso, and went to Image/Adjustments/Replace Color to begin the transition to the image I felt, as much as saw, that day. Ultimately, I could never get the yellow color exactly as

I wished in certain areas, so I exported the file to Painter and adjusted in the color in the areas where needed. I also drew in several of the longer stems of the foreground sand grass.

Figure 3-161
Sky area used previously in
"Metro Gas"

The sky is a portion of a sky I created in a previous image, "Metro Gas." "Metro Gas" started as a slide of a closed and deteriorating gas station outside a dying town in the high desert of Nevada. The coming of the Interstate left this once-main approach to the town on the wrong side of the traffic flow, and the "House on the Dune" reminded me again of someone's dreams gone awry. (You'll probably think I'm hopelessly neurotic, despondent, or depressed—actually, I consider myself a most sanguine fellow. And I have no idea why these lugubrious inclinations emerge every so often—and fortunately, I do not have the time, the patience, or the income for the long-term therapy that might explain it all.)

Figure 3-162
Birds on a wire

You'll notice the telephone pole with its solitary wire and silhouetted birds is not in the original slide. I thought a leaning pole and a line of crow-like birds could suggest abandonment, symbols of a melancholy and ominous site.

There is a small lake in a park where I live in northern New Jersey. In late fall and winter, the pigeons that normally hop the paths take to gathering on the electric wires that surround the lake. One gray and misty day, I noticed several of them huddled in the dank wind, swaying the wire. I went home to get a camera—as it turned out, an all-automatic point-and-shoot film camera loaded with 400-speed print film. I knew if I aimed the camera from a low angle and cropped everything but the wire and part of one pole against the sky, the birds would silhouette, and I would have an easy time selecting out the elements I wanted to eliminate.

I scanned the 35 mm negative into Photoshop, removed the sky, and duplicated several of the birds in various groupings on the wire. I added and rearranged them until I thought I had the correct composition, and hit Command T to get the Transform tool. I elongated the birds so they looked more like crows than pigeons, and tilted the upright pole toward the catenary curve of the wire. I then made a Levels adjustment layer and dragged the Shadow input slider on the left toward the middle so there was no detail in the birds.

At this point, the image was a composite of several photographs/slides. As I've long admired the Impressionist painters, I like to experiment with the image by creating several new layers and combining

Painter, Photoshop filters, blending modes, and an application I use occasionally, Studio Artist, in an attempt to shift the image from its realistic look of a photo. I try to do as little as possible to achieve the painting-like effect, and I find it's easy to go just a little too far, and the image starts to go south really quickly. That's why it's a good investment to have a fast CPU and lots of RAM so you can pile on the History States, Snapshots, and multiple layers as you're wending your way through all the pixel pushing. Turning on or off a layer or dropping back through the History States/Snapshots is a most enlightening method of figuring out where the image slid over to The Dark Side.

I have anything but a set method with each image at this painting stage. As with any endeavor that is considered art, it should have an emotional element that feels right. It's not necessarily about correct perspective or the rule of thirds—or maybe it is. And that's one of the joys of art: as an artist you can define art as what you do. And one of the less joyful parts: to be a successful artist, someone has to agree with you.

Figure 3-163
Complete—"The House on the Dune" (© Paul Elson)

Figure 3-164
Bill Hall

Bill Hall

Cedar Hill, Texas
bill@billhall.com
www.billhall.com

Equipment
Computer: Macintosh G5, OS 10.4, 1GB RAM; ACOM Data removable hard drive, 80GB.
Scanner: Hewlett-Packard ScanJet 8200.
Tablet: 9" × 12" Wacom tablet, Intuos 3.
Printers: Epson Stylus 1520 Color Printer, Hewlett-Packard LaserJet 5100 Black and White Printer.
Favorite Papers: For internal proofs I prefer Epson Glossy Photo paper. Most often my fine art is reproduced outside my office as giclée prints.
Cataloging and Archiving: I back everything up to external hard drive, then burn to DVD after the project is completed.

About the Artist: Background, Education, Inspirations
My current job is full-time artist/illustrator. I operate an illustration and design studio with my wife of 35 years, Anita. We have been in business together for 25 years. Illustration clients come from local and national advertising agencies. Advertising design, web site, and audio/visual clients come from local businesses and nonprofit agencies. My education includes:

1964: Student of artist Chapman Kelly, Dallas Museum of Art.
1967: American Motors Art Scholarship recipient.
1970: BA, University of Texas, Arlington.
1972: Northwood Experimental Art Scholarship recipient.
1983: Illustrators Workshop, Tarrytown, NY.

I was greatly influenced by the work of Bart Forbes because his work elevated illustration into the realm of fine art. My fine art is represented by art4love.com and Art Exchange online fine art galleries, by Evviva Gallery in Beverly Hills, CA, and by Visual Expressions Gallery in Cedar Hill, TX. My illustration work is represented by ispot.com and images.com for second rights sales.

Creative Process

The painting of a horse race, "Finish," was inspired by my own original photographs taken at the event. I use photo reference with practically every painting, but am careful not to paint directly from images I didn't shoot myself. In this case, I opted to go with the positions pretty much as is and changed the faces, numbers, and silk colors to avoid trademark or licensing issues.

Figure 3-165
Original photo

Figure 3-166
Sketch

To begin the painting, I opened my photo reference on a second monitor, where I also organize my application tools, then opened a blank document in Painter IX. After making sure that "Preserve Transparency" was unchecked in the layers palette, I created a new layer and named it "Pencil." At this stage I modified the "Pencil" tool using the options under "Brush Controls" to get the feel of a real pencil sketch.

Figure 3-167
Filling in blocks of colors

Using my photo as reference, I did a freehand sketch on the pencil layer. This was easy using my Wacom tablet and stylus, because it so closely emulates the act of drawing on paper, with the added benefit of being able to "undo." Even though tracing an image is easy to accomplish in digital art, I'm much happier with the looser, more natural feel of a freehand pencil drawing. After completing the pencil drawing, I cleaned it up using the eraser tool, leaving only the main contours. Then I selected the canvas below the pencil layer, and used the Lasso tool in Painter to define areas that I wanted to fill with flat color.

Figure 3-168
Completed color blocking

The resulting blocks of color were imprecise and loose, and served as an undercoat for the painting. Since I was working below the pencil layer, I continued to use it for reference throughout the painting process. Figure 3-169 shows a close-up of the painting before the modeling process.

Figure 3-169
Close-up

Figure 3-170
Adding lights and darks

Having completed the color blocking, I created a new layer above the canvas and below the pencil, and named it "modeling." On this layer of the canvas I applied the lights and darks that defined the forms.

Figure 3-171
Palette knife work

My favorite Painter tool for defining the form is the palette knife. Having spent many years of my life actually working on canvas, this tool is comfortable and gives me the painterly look I desire. I can even use an unloaded Painter palette knife to work the pencil into the paint so that some disappears and some doesn't. Figures 3-172 and 3-173 show more palette knife work on the modeling layer defining the form.

Figure 3-172
Progress on modeling phase of painting

Figure 3-173
Detail on modeling phase of painting

I consider myself an artist, and prefer not to be categorized as illustrator or fine artist. I treat work assignments from clients with the same aesthetic approach that I pour into work done to satisfy my own creative drives. The only difference is the client gets to pick the subject matter when I am painting commercially.

Figure 3-174
Completed painting—"Finish" (© Bill Hall)

Figure 3-175
Steven Friedman

Steven Friedman

Parker, Colorado
www.digitalartmasterworks.com
sfriedman@digitalartmasterworks.com

Equipment
Computer: PC Windows XP with 512MB RAM, Wacom 4 × 5 tablet.
Scanner: Acer.
Printers: Epson 3000, Canon 9100, Hewlett-Packard CP 1700, ColorSpan 5000 (outsourced).
Favorite Paper: Intellicoat.
Any Color Management Systems: None.
Cataloging and Archiving: ACDsee.

About the Artist: Background, Education, Inspirations
My education includes an Associate in Photography. I'm self-taught in digital techniques, pioneering the techniques found in my work. My current job is as a physical therapist in the Denver Metro area. I am a digital artist on nights and weekends.

I consider myself a hybrid artist—one-half in photographic arts and the other in traditional painting. Although I never really learned to paint until recently, the digital element really frees me to concentrate on artistic interpretation rather than technique. I've always been captivated by the works of John Singer Sargent, Mary Cassatt, Winslow Homer, and Charles Russell. My artistic goal is to totally capture the look and feel and style of traditional artistic mediums so that even artists who work in those mediums are fooled by my work. I am presently working on my second audiovisual instructional tutorial set that will focus on specific techniques for creating different natural medium looks.

Figure 3-176

Creative Process
Since my background is photography, I was really anxious to try out my new digital art techniques on some scenes that wouldn't sit still long enough for me to paint them. Rodeos naturally fell into this category. I shot the original picture shown in Figure 3-176 with a Pentax SLR 35 mm camera and then had the image scanned onto a CD.

Figure 3-177

Masking the Image and Changing the Background—To do this I first captured a small swatch of the foreground to use as a fill pattern and then masked the surrounding areas and filled it with that swatch.

Figure 3-178
Version 1

Figure 3-179
Version 2

Figure 3-180
Version 3

Applying Artistic Effects—Using the now defunct Microsoft PhotoDraw II, I applied a number of the Artistic Filters using my own custom brush templates to create several renditions of the masked image, each version emphasizing different levels of details and abstraction.

Blending the Images—I then opened these images in Painter and using the straight cloner brush, painted in parts from versions 2 and 3 onto version 1, until I had a good mix of detail and abstract. I also increased the saturation to give it more vibrant pure colors.

Enhancing the Image—Then I went to work on the piece in Painter using the oil brushes, palette knives, and gooey brushes using a clone of itself as the color source (Figure 3-181). Today I would have used the new Artists Oil Brushes in Corel Painter, but they weren't around at the time I did this piece. I really wanted to get a richly colored and highly textured oil paint look made up of colorful, richly textured brush strokes.

Figure 3-181

At the stage shown in Figure 3-182, the clown and bull rider were working beautifully, but the background still looked vacant.

Figure 3-182

Adding 3D Scrumbling Marks—I decided to experiment with a technique of adding scanned acrylic brush marks into the image to give it a 3D texture and brushed-on look. My template for this was similar to Figure 3-183. I selected parts of the brush marks using the color mask. The first thing I did was to add the impasto 3D effect using the Surface Control > Add Surface Texture > Image luminescence and then copied and pasted in pieces onto the bull rider image.

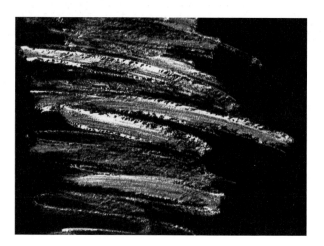

Figure 3-183

Finally, I also added a slight impasto 3D effect to the base image before combining all the layers. I had the final piece printed 36″ × 44″ onto coated canvas using a Roland Printer and coated it with Sign-Painters one-shot acrylic coating that is made for giclée prints. People often come up to touch the piece at art shows to see if the paint actually is three-dimensional.

Figure 3-184
Completed painting (© Steven Friedman)

Figure 3-185
Audrey Bernstein

Audrey S. Bernstein

Dobbs Ferry, New York
audreysb@yahoo.com

Equipment
Computer: Mac G4 with 512MB RAM.
Scanners: Imacon, Epson 1680.
Printer: Epson 10000 (pigment based).
Favorite Paper: Roland canvas.
Any Color Management Systems: Color Bite Image Print.
Cataloging and Archiving: I catalog my work on CDs and zip disks.

About the Artist: Background, Education, Inspirations
My work has been published in three recent publications: *Visions of Angels*, by Nelson Bloncourt and Karen Engelmann; *Photomontage, A Step-by-Step Guide to Building Pictures*, by Stephen Golding; and *Exploring Color Photography*, by Robert Hirsch. I have been very active in numerous shows in the New York City area. In 2001, I had a one-person show at Saint Peter's Church in New York City, as well as a show at the 92nd Street Y in New York City. In 2001, I had a show at the Hopper House Art Center in Nyack, NY, and I was included in a show at the Alternative Museum in New York City in 1999.

My educational background includes an MFA (1982) from the Visual Studies Workshop, Rochester, NY, and a BFA (1979) from Cornell University, Ithaca, NY. Since 1997, I have been an Associate Professor of Photography at Long Island University. I juggle full-time teaching, a career as an artist, and three daughters.

Christian Boltanski is the artist that I most admire. He is one of the most compelling producers of post-Holocaust artwork in the last decade. Using very simple materials, Boltanski is able to address issues such as death, loss, and memory in an evocative and unique way. I admire his ability to tackle the tragedy of life and the horror of war in an intimate, almost personal way.

Creative Process

"So Much to My Sorrow" is composed of a portrait photograph and an old letter digitally scanned with an Epson 1680 flatbed scanner. Using Photoshop 7, I collaged the images into a different background. The digital image was enlarged using Image Print and printed on Roland canvas using an Epson 10000 pigment printer. The large canvas was stretched traditionally as an oil painting. The digital collage was painted with oil paints to create more shadow and depth.

I have always been fascinated by the creative possibilities afforded by combining hand-worked media (such as painting, drawing, and collage) and digital/photographic tools. My interest lies in blurring the distinctions among the processes I use, specifically between photography and painting. I want my work to embody both the uniqueness of a handmade object, along with the reproducibility of a photograph or print.

The collages are layered with paint, double exposed, or I use Photoshop to create a multitude of layers. Over time, by covering, erasing, and revealing layers, it becomes hard to tell if one sees a photograph or a painting. The final painting has become worked and kneaded into a texture that creates an illusory reality. This process of rewriting and reworking a photograph mimics the experience of memory. Over time, our experiences erase and recreate our memories. These issues of memory, of compelling realities, and of erasure have always been a central theme in my artwork.

The original image was from an old SX-70 I took of my friend. The image was blurry and impressionist. I liked the feel of it, so I scanned it in on an Epson flatbed 1680 scanner.

Figure 3-186
Original SX-70 photo

Figure 3-187
Another layer added

The portrait needed a background, so I found an image in an old magazine. It was scanned in and added to the portrait using Photoshop CS (Figure 3-187). I erased the area behind the portrait so it could show through.

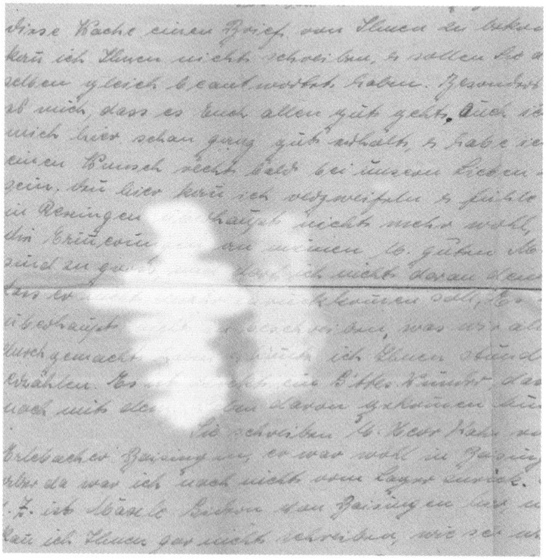

Figure 3-188
Old letter text added

I added text from an old letter. Again, I scanned in the letter and simply layered it in using Photoshop CS (Figure 3-188).

Figure 3-189 is the final painting. I printed the image on a large piece of canvas using an Epson 10000 printer. This image was enlarged using an interpolation program called Image Print. After printing, I painted over the whole image using oil paints.

Figure 3-189
Completed—"So Much to My Sorrow" (30″ × 30″) (© Audrey S. Bernstein)

Figure 3-190
Artful interpretation of Rick Lieder

Rick Lieder

Berkley, Michigan
rick@dreampool.com
CollectingDreams.com

Equipment
Computer: PowerMac G4 Dual 500, OS 10.3.9, 1.28GB RAM, two monitors.
Scanners: Flatbed: Epson Perfection 2450, Microtek 9800XL, 35 mm Film Scanner: Polaroid Sprint Scan 4000.
Printer: Epson 2200.
Favorite Paper: Epson Enhanced Matte.
Any Color Management Systems: Spyder2 Monitor Calibration.
Cataloging and Archiving: Archive everything on CDs and now DVDs.

About the Artist: Background, Education, Inspirations
Education: University of Michigan.
Current Job: I have operated an art/illustration studio, Dreampool Studio, for 20 years.
A few influences: Bosch, Brueghel, Tiepolo, Rembrandt, Goya, Daumier, Whistler, Degas, Sargent, Picasso, Schiele, de Chirico, Burchfield, Ernst, Gorky, Bacon, and Fischl.

Figure 3-191
Antique watch

Creative Process

Time is both a construct and a medium. As the clock ticks off its minutes, we move bodily through change, growth, decay as if through water, an invisible river flowing all around us. When my grandfather died, I was given several of his old watches, one of which struck me as very handsome, with its intricate Art Nouveau center and archaic, arresting typeface.

Some years ago, I came into possession of an old photo album filled with small portraits of children, probably made before 1920. One image stood out for me, despite the extensive fading of the image: a boy, his hair mussed and tie askew, looking intently into the camera. I generally use only my own photographs in my work, but this portrait was very powerful and I wanted to share it somehow.

I decided to combine the watch with the boy's portrait and create an image with a sense of the passing of time. Perhaps the boy in the photo recalled to me the boy my grandfather had been, so many years ago.

The watch measured less than an inch and was quite tarnished. My final image size would not be very large, 2800 pixels tall (9.3" × 5.3" at 300 ppi). I often photograph a small object with my digital camera (a Canon 300D) and a macro lens to get an image into my computer, but in this case I decided to scan the watch on my Epson 2450 flatbed scanner, even though this would give me a file with less resolution than I needed. I knew that the scanner light would reflect off the metal watch, and introduce some interesting reflections in that carved Art Nouveau center. I removed the watch case before scanning, even though it was interesting in its own right, and decided to crop the watch background to include only the numbers.

I sharpened the scanned watch image slightly and resized it in Photoshop CS to a height of 2800 pixels. The watch background was a little soft because of this resizing, but I decided the scanner lighting effects offset this. I used an adjustment curve layer to increase the contrast of the watch face, and another curve layer to darken the numbers with a mask. I added a Hue/Saturation layer to greatly increase the saturation, which added quite a bit of color noise. I like the visual feel of texture in many of my images, and the saturated noise worked well.

Next I scanned the boy's photograph at 1200 ppi, sharpened it, and cleaned up a few of the most obvious blemishes. I left most of the flaws and scratches in the watch and portrait since I found them visually interesting, and they added to the sense of age and time's decay. I moved the portrait to the watch document, resized it to its final dimensions, and sharpened it slightly again. I used a mask to remove the boy's background and set the blending mode to Luminosity, which allowed the portrait to take on the mottled color of the watch background. I duplicated the lower right quadrant of the image and masked off everything but the numbers 4, 5, and 6, to float them over the portrait. There was too much masking on the portrait layer already, and this separated the numbers from any adjustments I would make later.

I then used several curve and hue/saturation adjustment layers to lighten or darken the portrait and watch, increase or decrease the contrast, and alter the color in subtle ways. I never hesitate to add a layer to make a change to an image, even a very small change, and always archive the final layered image in case I want to change the image in the future, which happens often. When the image was completed, it spoke to me of both a lost and a vibrant youth, an innocent determination to resist the grip of time, even as the minutes ticked away. My grandfather was 95 when he died, but a part of him will live forever in this image.

Figure 3-192
*Circa 1920 vintage photo of
a boy*

Figure 3-193
Completed—"Moments Big as Years" (© Rick Lieder)

Figure 3-194
Pep Ventosa

Pep Ventosa

San Francisco, California
info@pepventosa.com
www.pepventosa.com

Equipment

Computer: Dell Dimension 8200, 1.50GB of RAM; Dell P1130 19" Trinitron color monitor, two 80GB internal hard drives, two 200GB external hard drives, one 20GB portable hard drive.

Scanner: I don't use a scanner. I work entirely with digital photographs.

Printers: Epson Stylus Pro 7600, with UltraChrome pigment inks, Epson Stylus Photo 1280.

Favorite Papers: Epson Premium Semimatte Photo Paper, Epson Enhanced Matte Paper.

Any Color Management Systems: ColorVision Spyder2 PRO color calibration system. For printing I use the custom RGB ICC Profiles from Epson.

Cataloging and Archiving: It's a challenge. The nature of my work involves a constant influx of thousands of new images as well as the creation of huge new final artwork files. Incoming images are cataloged by date, place, and subject matter. Final artwork, my digital negatives, are archived by year and title. I use a combination of hard drives, DVDs, and CDs for storage and backups.

Cameras: Nikon D70, Nikon Coolpix 995.

About the Artist: Background, Education, Inspirations

I attended Escola d'Arts i Oficis Artístics de l'Alt Penedès in Barcelona, Spain, but my work with photography, digital compositions, and printing is primarily self-taught. I also have a degree in Tourism Economy from the Tourism School of Sant Pol de Mar in Spain.

I work full time in my artwork. (I juggle countries, Spain and my home in San Francisco.) In my native Spain, I am represented by Palma Dotze Galeria d'Art. Additionally, the Winn Devon Art Group publishes fine art reproductions of some of my work. I'm inspired by bits and pieces of many different people, places, and things. At the moment, I am entranced with photographer Stephen Shore's "Uncommon Places." I love his eye for the ordinary. He frames daily things we don't stop to look at because of their banality. As he says, "I'm interested in the process of how to be consciously casual."

Creative Process

The piece "Kearny Street" was selected by Guggenheim Museum curator and New York University Art Professor Robert Rosenblum for a summer 2005 show of artists in a Chelsea gallery. I was attracted to this street scene because of the contrast between the old brick buildings that border San Francisco's Chinatown and the new iron and glass skyscrapers of downtown—the overlapping boundaries between old and new, the past and the present.

As with most of my work, I shot "Kearny Street" in fragments—about 30 or 40 separate digital photographs, each capturing a different part of the scene. Then I reconstruct it like a puzzle in Photoshop. On a blank document, I open each photograph as a new layer, building "Kearny Street" piece by piece. The work flow results in a very large digital negative, with intense resolution: a backwards digital wide-format camera. But when I piece the puzzle together, I'm not interested in stitching a seamless photograph of the entire scene. I'm interested in creating a brand new image I've never seen before, one that's real in all of its parts, but not in the whole. It's the mystery of what emerges that intrigues me.

In piecing together "Kearny Street," I looked for natural symmetries in the overlapping lines of the individual photographs and some balance in the colors, textures, and way images mix together. I moved and combined different layers to find some natural order and shape for the final image. One by one, I edited each of the 30 or 40 layers of separate photographs until I felt something interesting there. That's the most creative part of the process for me, spending hours editing and experimenting to slowly uncover the hidden soul of a reconstructed work. I look for some kind of rhythm and harmony in how the pieces relate to the emerging whole. An example in "Kearny Street" is the skyscraper sky, where the blue sky puzzle pieces were accentuated to give the same overlapping feel of the buildings.

Technically speaking, I work mainly with levels, layers masking, and blending modes in Photoshop. Sometimes I combine duplicated layers or selected parts. When I'm finished with the entire piece, I flatten the image, crop it, and make final little adjustments. The miracle of digital allows me to make endless experiments. It's often hard to decide when to stop. When is the final work ready? What else could "Kearny Street" have become? I enjoy the mystery of this process. You just never know what's going to happen.

Figure 3-195
Completed—"Kearny Street" (© Pep Ventosa)

II

Step-by-Step Painting

4

Painting in Photoshop with Your Photos

The concept of painting digitally is a strange one to most people. Using the mouse to paint is like drawing with a bar of soap in some ways. Digital tablets and styli seem to be more natural implements to use with digital art tools. They offer the wonderful ability to experience the impact of touch and the strength of a stroke. Their pressure sensitivity allows for a powerful laydown of color or a thin, wispy veil of color. This alone recommends them. If you do not have a tablet and stylus, however, don't despair. All the following techniques can be performed with a traditional mouse.

When asked about why he photographed, the famous photographer Henri Cartier-Bresson said simply "That it was quicker than drawing." In his modesty he was suggesting the incredible immediacy of photography. His work was both intuitive and disciplined. His photography was not casual. Composition was paramount and, of course, his renowned "decisive moment." All of this is to say that, as a photographer, you have responded to an impulse to originally make your photograph. That impulse was recorded on film or digital media.

I often feel the need to dig into the image still further. In my wet darkroom days, that meant learning and using a vast array of alternative processes. Some of those techniques allowed me to further manipulate the captured image into the one I saw in my mind's eye. The extraordinary range of possibilities in the digital art arena is truly amazing. In this chapter I'll share with you some of my favorite techniques of digital painting in Photoshop. Photoshop alone can offer a far greater range of artistic potential than most users realize.

Take a look at your contact sheets, trays of slides, or file browser. The time has come to select an image to which you would like to give a painterly rendition. Some images will speak to you more than others. Follow your intuition and select from your heart. Of course, that is not to ignore the basic principles of design, composition, color, line, etc.

It is often necessary to "clean up" a photo to ready it for the painting. Perhaps there was debris on the street, power lines over a bucolic rural landscape, or an unnecessary element in the photo that distracts from the central impact. Look for these problem areas and correct them in Photoshop before starting to "paint." Preparation of the photograph will often include the use of the rubber stamp, healing brush, patch tool, layer adjustments, and more. These are vital preliminaries that need to be executed with skill before starting the painting. Compare it, if you will, with the traditional preparation that a painter does with his canvas in advance of painting. The canvas needs to be sealed, gessoed, and made ready to receive paint. These time-consuming traditional painting steps assure that the painting has a greater chance of archival survival.

We do not see things as they are, we see things as we are.
—*The Talmud*

Once you have eliminated the distracting elements and feel comfortable with the contrast and saturation of your image, it is time to decide how you will execute the digital painting. Most Photoshop users don't get further than running a single filter on the image. Using a watercolor filter on the image does not make it a watercolor painting. Oh that art were indeed that easy! Art is often seen best in its subtlety. Just think how van Gogh's paintings would have looked if his brush strokes were always uniform in size and directionality. You want something that is unique to you and your sensibilities. Passing your image through a filter, lock, stock, and barrel, will yield an image that lacks your touch and imagination. The rendering, or mark making, should truly be your own. How can we achieve this kind of individuality in Photoshop, using the tools it has to offer? Let's take a look.

How to Use Photoshop Filters and the History Brush to Create a Digital Painting

Filters are the first place that many photographers go to for an artistic rendition of their photograph. Photoshop offers many, many options for your artistic interpretation. One of my favorite methods involves the history brush. What a wonderful tool!

Figure 4-1
Original photograph of a Roman café table

This photograph was a grab shot, as I walked the streets of Rome recently. I liked the neutral tones and the simple arrangement of café chairs and table. The bouquet of daisies was an added plus.

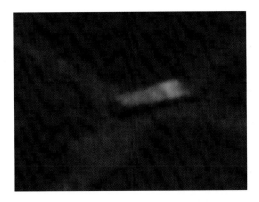

Figure 4-2
Cigarette butt that needs to be removed before we begin

Correct any flaws that exist in the original photo

To make Figure 4-1 ready for painting, I first needed to become the street sweeper or maid for the establishment. There was a piece of debris under the table and a stray cigarette butt nearby, both of which were captured in this image shot with a Nikon D100 camera.

A simple minute or two with the rubber stamp tool cleaned up the sidewalk for our ensuing painting. Look around for any other distracting elements. Does the image need to be cropped? Does the color need any alteration? Use a critical eye when analyzing the image at this stage of the process. The success of the end product may well be dependent on this crucial first step.

This technique relies on the ability of Photoshop to make a history state that can be revisited as necessary to complete the painting. In order to show the effect of the filter on the image, I've included a close-up view of the daisies on the table with each step. Let's begin.

Figure 4-3
Filter—Artistic—Cross Hatch

Apply the Artistic—Cross Hatch Filter
Make a copy of this History State, by clicking on the camera located at the bottom of the History Palette
Name the History state
The Artistic Filter, Cross Hatch, was applied to the image using a stroke length of 14, a sharpness of 7, and strength of 1. I then took a snapshot of the image with that filter applied. Use the little camera at the bottom of the history palette. The "snap" of this current history state will appear under the snap of the original image in the history palette, as it looked when the file was opened. Take the time now to name that history state, Cross Hatch. Simply double-click on the name and retype its title. As we add more history states this naming convention will become more important as we search for the intended filter effect. Now return to the original image, walking backward in your history palette.

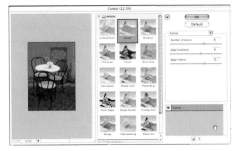

Figure 4-4
Filter—Artistic—Cut Out

Apply the Artistic—Cut Out Filter
Make a copy of this History State, by clicking on the camera located
at the bottom of the History Palette
Name the History state
The next step is to repeat the process, but using the Artistic Filter—
Cut Out, with the number of levels set at 6, the edge simplicity set at
6, and the edge fidelity set at 2. Although I give the particular settings
that I used on the image, please experiment with the sliders to create
the effect that you want for your image. Make a snapshot of this history
state and again return to the original image, as it was opened.

Figure 4-5
Filter—Artistic—Dry Brush

Apply the Artistic—Dry Brush Filter
Make a copy of this History State, by clicking on the camera located at the bottom of the History Palette
Name the History state

The next filter that was applied was the Artistic Filter known as Dry Brush. I set the Brush Size at 2, the Brush Detail at 8, and the Texture at 1. A snapshot was made of this filter effect and we again returned to the original image in our history palette.

As you can see by now, we are accumulating various filter effects with our snapshots of each particular effect. Please take the time to name each effect to make things easier later. We will eventually be using these history states to paint from and it will be important to discern which one was dry brush or watercolor.

Figure 4-6
Filter—Artistic—Rough Pastels

Apply the Artistic—Rough Pastels Filter
Make a copy of this History State, by clicking on the camera located at the bottom of the History Palette
Name the History state

The next filter employed was the Artistic Filter—Rough Pastels. This is a good one for showing brush strokes and texture. The settings used were Stroke Length 11, Stroke Detail 7, Texture—Sandstone, Scaling 100%, Relief 20, and Light from the Top. There is a variety of textures that you can use. They include canvas, brick, sandstone, and burlap. Rough pastels allow a color to be carried through another color mass with a stroke effect. That can be very nice for a painterly feel. Pastel artists often use a sanded colored board to draw on. The sand actually saws off the soft chalk, capturing the particles of chalk, giving a gritty kind of look. This filter can mimic that look well. Again take a snapshot in the history palette, rename that history state, and then return to the original image.

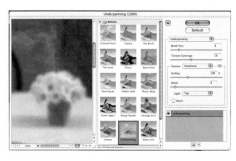

Apply the Artistic—Underpainting Filter
Make a copy of this History State, by clicking on the camera located at the bottom of the History Palette
Name the History state
The next filter, Artistic—Under-painting, is a great one to loosely map out the colors that will be used. Underpainting is a technique used by painters to block in where the major color masses will be in the painting. It is used for composition placement and establishing color tonal areas. This technique has been used for centuries and was the basis of the finished painting that followed. It is virtually the foundation that the completed work is built on, especially oil painting. You will notice a blurry kind of effect in this digital version of underpainting. This is not a filter that will render crisp details, but instead, loose color masses. The settings on this filter were set to Brush Size 6, Texture Coverage 16, Texture—Sandstone, Scaling 100%, Relief 4, and the Light from the Top. Take a snapshot and name it, again returning to the original image.

Figure 4-7
Filter—Artistic—Underpainting

Art is an extension of language—an expression of sensations too subtle for words.
—ROBERT HENRI,
The Art Spirit (1923)

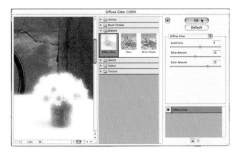

Figure 4-8
Filter—Distort—Diffuse Glow

Apply the Distort—Diffuse Glow Filter
Make a copy of this History State, by clicking on the camera located at the bottom of the History Palette
Name the History state
The next filter comes from a different category, that of Distort, and its name is Diffuse Glow. This filter gives a halo effect and blurs the image. I often use this filter to help simulate an infrared effect. The settings used were Graininess 6, Glow Amount 10, and Clear Amount 15. It offers a soft, rather romantic effect that can also be used for dreamy portraits. Again, take a snapshot, name this new history state, and return to the original image.

Figure 4-9
Filter—Sketch—Graphic Pen

Apply the Sketch—Graphic Pen Filter
Make a copy of this History State, by clicking on the camera located at the bottom of the History Palette
Name the History state
The next filter can be found under the filter category called Sketch.—Graphic Pen yields a nice sketch effect created by a directional mark. The settings were set to Stroke Length 15, Light/Dark Balance 50, and the Stroke Direction coming from the right side diagonally. By itself, this filter can make a nice illustration from a photograph for perhaps a newsletter, magazine illustration, or annual report. But we will use its mark making effect in our digital painting. Take a snapshot, rename the layer, and return again to your original image.

Figure 4-10
Filter—Texture—Grain—Stippled

Apply the Texture—Grain—Stippled Filter
Make a copy of this History State, by clicking on the camera located at the bottom of the History Palette
Name the History state

Another sketchy-like filter is the one under Texture, called Grain—Stippled. You will notice that under Grain, there are a lot of various options for making marks. We chose stippled. This would be the effect an illustrator would achieve with a very fine pen point, creating an illustration from thousands of dots of ink. The settings were set at Intensity of 40, Contrast of 50, and the Grain Type to Stippled. Again, take a snapshot of the effect and name it properly and return to your original for one last filter.

Figure 4-11
Filter—Stylize—Find Edges

Apply the Stylize—Find Edges Filter
Make a copy of this History State, by clicking on the camera located at the bottom of the History Palette
Name the History state

This filter, located under Filter—Stylize, is called Find Edges. It looks for differences in contrast along edges. There are no sliders to adjust. The effect is automatic, but you can fade it as much as you would like. To fade any filter simply go to Edit, Fade (whatever the name of the filter was). Again, and finally, take a snapshot, name the layer, and return to the original layer. We are now ready to "paint" from our history state wells.

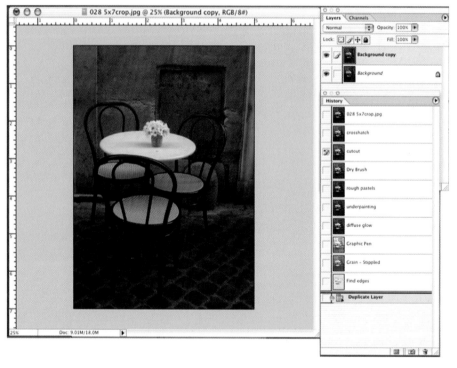

Figure 4-12
The stack of previous History States, made from the use of filters

Art is the stored honey of the human soul, gathered on wings of misery and travail.

—THEODORE DREISER,
  Life, Art and America
  (1917)

We will be using the history states that we created from each filter we applied. To the left of the snapshot of that remembered history state is a "well." When we want to apply some Rough Pastels to our image, we will dip our History Brush into the well beside the snapshot of Rough Pastels.

I recommend that you set your opacity on the history brush to a low amount (5–20%); this can give a more subtle effect and can be increased by simply brushing over an area again and again.

Figure 4-13
The digital painting starts to evolve, using the History Brush to apply strokes, derived from various filter effects

Using the History Brush, dip into the "well" of the history state you want to use
Use a low opacity for subtlety
Grab that History Brush and, with a low opacity setting, brush light applications from the history palette. Place the History Brush in the well to the left of that snapshot, and brush away.

Figure 4-14
Light, transparent applications of various filters are applied with the History Brush

I wanted to place an irregular edge on this piece and chose an eraser technique. It is so easy.

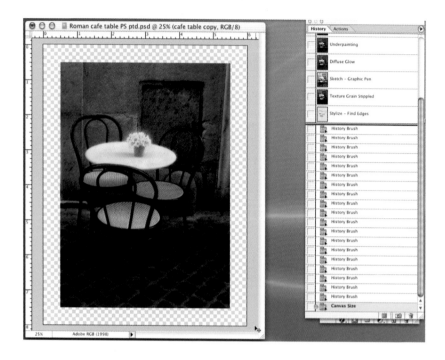

Figure 4-15
Canvas was added around the completed image

Add an inch all the way around the image by going to Image—Canvas Size and adding the extra space

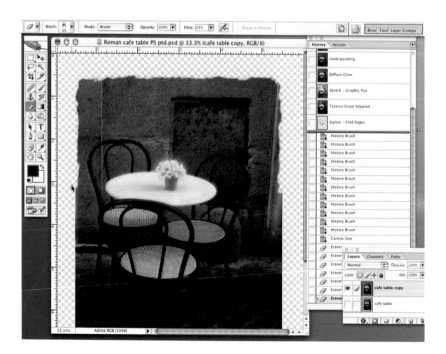

Figure 4-16
An eraser was used on the edges with an irregular brush shape

Erase around the edge with an irregular, textural brush

There are a lot of crazy brushes. We traditionally use a hard-edge brush or a soft-edge brush, but there is much more available. There are brushes that resemble bristle brushes, that give an irregular, scratchy kind of effect, and are wonderful for scratching away at the edges of an image. The effect is distressed and more interesting. Try some of these irregular brushes for painterly edges using the eraser.

I paint as I feel like painting; to hell with all the studies. An artist has to be a spontaneist.
—EDOUARD MANET
in *The World of Manet*,
by Pierre Schneider
(1966)

Figure 4-17
Finished artwork with irregular edges; "Roman Cafe Table"

Using the Art History Brush to Create a Digital Painting

The Art History Tool is generally underutilized by most Photoshop users. It is a little quirky, but lots of fun. As always, select a photograph on which you would like to apply a painterly effect.

Correction of Flaws

Figure 4-18
*Original photo that was
captured digitally*

If there is any correction that needs to be done to the image prior to working, please do that first. In my example I increased the contrast a bit in Curves before starting.

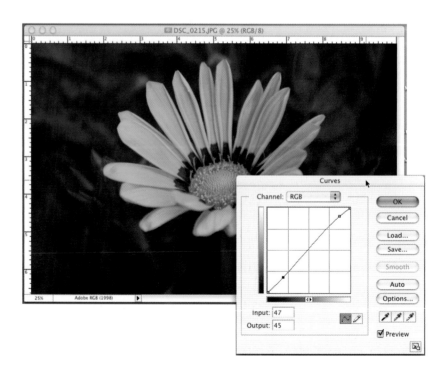

Figure 4-19
*A little boost in contrast was
made in Curves*

Contrast was increased in Curves

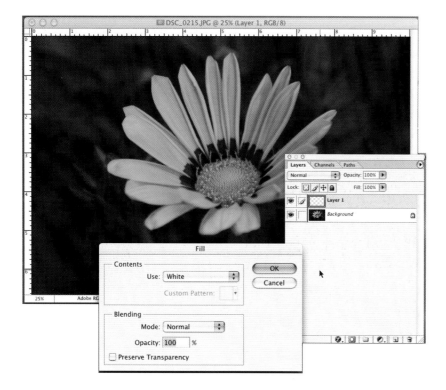

Figure 4-20
A new layer was added on top and filled with white

Add a new layer and fill it with white

Using the Art History Brush requires adding another layer above the photograph and filling it with white. Think of this layer as your sheet of watercolor paper, where you will deposit the paint.

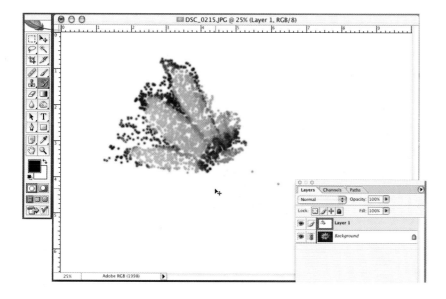

Figure 4-21
Art History Brush using the Dab method

Select the Art History Brush and the Dab method to "paint" the image

Select the Art History Brush. It is nested with the History Brush and can be easily identified by its distinctive curly-cue top on the brush icon. The modifiers for this tool are, of course, in the upper menu bar. There are lots of different brush strokes. (See Figure 4-29.)

I selected one of my favorites, the Dab method. Start brushing on your white layer and see what effect you can achieve. I used a brush size of 32 for this example. The bigger the brush you use, the less detailed your image will be. Conversely, the tinier the brush you use, the more detail you will achieve. The choice is yours.

Painting is like making an after dinner speech. If you want to be remembered—say one thing and then stop. Have the ability to see largely.

—CHARLES HAWTHORNE,
Hawthorne on Painting
(1938)

Figure 4-22
White layer opacity lowered

Lower the opacity—It is like using tracing paper!

It sure would be nice to see where you are painting, in relationship to the photograph. No problem. Just lower the opacity of the white layer to see through to the photograph beneath.

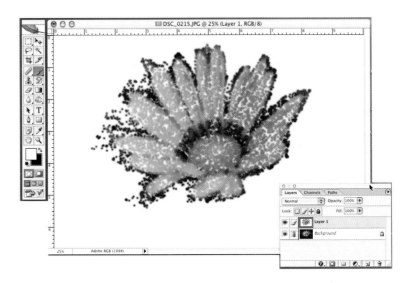

Figure 4-23
Flower made from Dab stroke with the Art History Brush

Continue brushing the dabs of color on the white layer

Continual brushing using the Dab method yielded the image shown in Figure 4-23. I decided not to brush the green area outside the flower. Only a small bit of green was used to establish the outside edges of the flower.

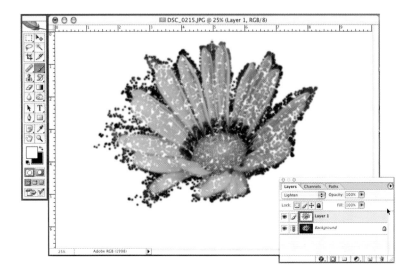

Figure 4-24
Blending Mode set to Lighten

Set the Blending Mode to Lighten

In the Blending Mode—Lighten, the white area of the upper painted layer will be ignored, but the colored areas will interact with the photograph beneath it, yielding a bit more detail. Figure 4-24 shows the Lighten mode utilized for the current blending mode. Experiment with various blending modes.

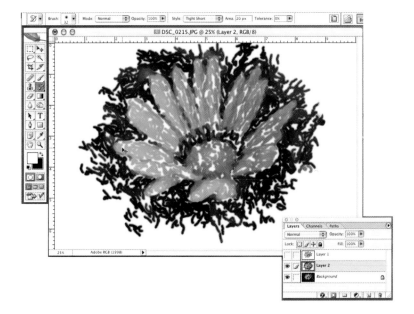

Figure 4-25
Tight Short Stroke used with the Art History Brush

Art History Brush—Tight Short Stroke was explored for effect

Just to satisfy my curiosity, I also tried the Tight Short Stroke with the Art History Brush. I still preferred the Dab method on this flower, but it was worth the try.

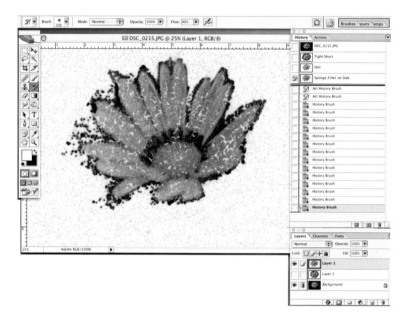

Figure 4-26
Filter—Artistic—Sponge was used on the Dab version

Apply the Artistic—Sponge Filter

I seem never to be satisfied with a result and I am always asking "what if" questions. In response to that urge on this piece I ran the Filter—Artistic—Sponge on the dab layer. I liked the variegated gray spotting in the background. If you do not, it would be easy to remove with the History Brush set to a previous white layer. I think the sponge effect added some texture that was interesting.

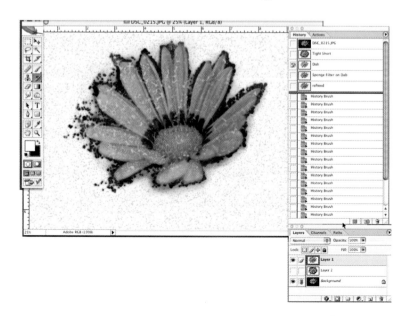

Figure 4-27
History Brush was used to produce a light shadowed area under the flower

A soft shadow was added by using the History Brush

The History Brush was used in the original photo well and set at a low opacity to achieve a soft shadow under the "painted" flower.

A great work of art is like a great shock.
—ALEXEJ VON JAWLENSKY, *Das Kunstwerk II* (1948)

Figure 4-28
Completed flower using the Art History Brush method of brushwork

This interpretation is a little reminiscent of the pointillism era in painting. That movement, led by Georges Seurat, featured the application of paint in a dabbing style. The eye blended the various colors together. A similar effect can be achieved in Painter. We will explore that later in Chapter 5.

Dab   Loose Curl Long   Loose Curl

Loose Long   Loose Medium   Tight Curl Long

Tight Curl   Tight Long   Tight Medium

Tight Short

Figure 4-29
Types of Art History Brush strokes

Try the various brush offerings in the Art History Brush repertoire. Remember that you can vary the amount of detail by changing the size of the brush. For purposes of illustration here, the brush size was 70 on all the examples in Figure 4-29. And, of course, there is no reason that you can't combine various brush strokes all in the same piece, by simply changing the stroke selected.

Figure 4-30
Art History Brush painting of sunflowers

Using the Pattern Stamp to Create a Digital Painting

Pattern Stamp for a painting? You must be kidding. No. This may seem like a crazy way to make a painting, but it works. Bear with me on this one. The first order of business is, as usual, to get your photograph ready to make a painting.

Figure 4-31
Original digitally captured image and the "doctored" version

Photo was lightened, using Curves, and the color saturation was increased

The photograph I used was taken on a gloomy day that was heavily overcast with a light rain. It certainly wasn't very promising. In Photoshop the image was "doctored" by working in Curves and increasing the color saturation.

Choose Pattern Stamp Tool—go to Edit—Define Pattern—identify current open photo and click OK

The next step seems bizarre, but try it. Choose the Pattern Stamp Tool that is bundled with the Rubber Stamp Tool. Go to Edit and then to Define Pattern. A dialogue box will appear. In the window the current open image will appear along with its name. Click OK. You will notice that the photograph now appears as an option in the pattern options available in the top menu bar. That indicates that when the Pattern Stamp Tool is selected the and desired pattern is selected, you will be pulling the color information from the original photograph.

You should rely on sensation rather than thought.
—KIMON NICOLAIDES,
  The Natural Way to Draw (1941)

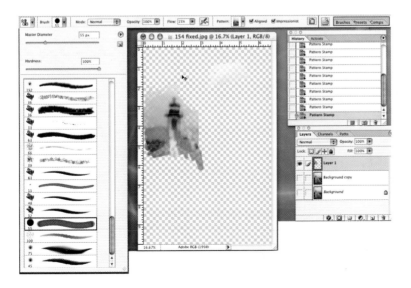

Figure 4-32
Using the Pattern Stamp with a blurry brush

Create a new Transparent Layer (it has the checkerboard pattern effect to indicate transparency)
Paint with the Pattern Stamp Tool, using a loose, sloppy brush
If we now selected a regular brush from the options available to us in the brush palette, we would simply be making a clone of the original image. We want more than that. We want a painterly effect, like the look achieved with a real brush loaded with wet paint. So we need to experiment a little. As you can see in Figure 4-32, I selected a brush that gave me wet edges. I also checked the box for Aligned and Impressionist, on the modifiers for the Pattern Stamp tool.

Create a new transparent layer and begin to "paint" with the Pattern Stamp Brush, using the original photograph as your selected pattern. You will get a blurry, stroke-like effect.

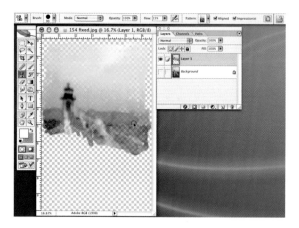
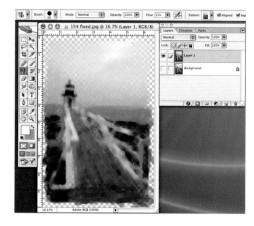

Figure 4-33
Continuing to paint with the Pattern Stamp Brush

Continue painting, building up color
Continue to build up your brush strokes. You will see that it will build up in the color effect after repeated applications. I like the messy edges, but that is your artistic choice.

Figure 4-34
Boosting the Saturation and changing the Hue balance

Saturation was increased again and a shift was made to Hue
After looking at the painting layer, I decided it still needed an additional boost in Saturation and a shift in the Hue balance.

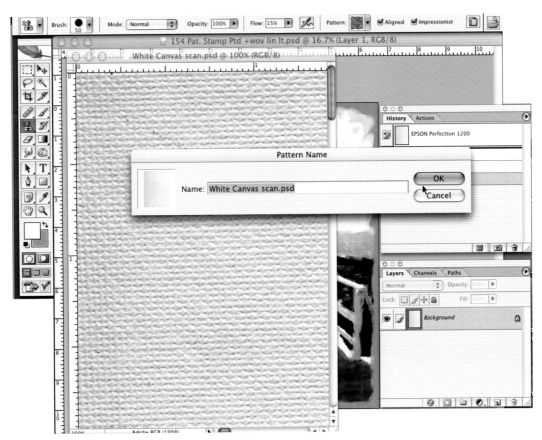

Figure 4-35
A scanned piece of white canvas board used as a pattern

Scan a piece of white canvas board
Create another pattern, using the Canvas Board
Now for another marvelous trick using the pattern stamp. Using the flatbed scanner, I scanned a piece of white canvas-covered board. You know, the kind of board sold to amateur oil painters, who don't want to stretch canvas over stretcher strips. It is a cheap and easy way to secure a "ground" to paint on. They are usually pre-gessoed, so the artist can jump right into the painting. You are going to be able to use this scanned piece of board over and over, every time you want a canvas texture to appear on your paintings. Hint: Once you learn this great technique you can imagine scanning burlap and other textured surfaces to use in a similar fashion. I proceeded to use the canvas to create a new pattern to draw from, just as we did with the lighthouse. That will stay in my pattern stamp brush options, every time I open Photoshop.

Figure 4-36
Blending Mode set to Multiply

It needs a certain purity of spirit to be an artist of any sort.
—D.H. LAWRENCE,
    "Making Pictures," in
    Assorted Articles (1928)

Create a new transparent layer
Paint with the newly created canvas pattern stamp
Set the Blending Mode to Multiply
Create a new transparent layer, inserting it between the original photo and the "painted" layer. Using the pattern stamp, paint the new layer with the canvas variation, now available. Set the "painted" layer Blending Mode to Multiply. Voilà! The painting now takes on the texture of canvas.

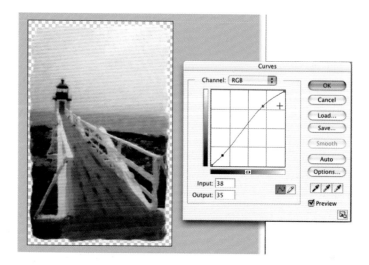

Figure 4-37
Contrast increased in Curves

Contrast was increased in Curves
The image was still too drab, so I increased the contrast with a Curves adjustment.

Figure 4-38
Completed piece made with the Pattern Stamp technique

Using the Art History Brush and Emboss Filter to Create a Textured Digital Painting

I am always amazed at how much detail exists in a photograph that is over- or underexposed with a digital camera. The bouquet of mixed flowers in Figure 4-39 was dimly lit by window light. One of my favorite Blending Mode techniques is to duplicate the layer and set the Blending Mode to Screen to lighten a photo that is too dark. I'm going to assume that you will have some photographs that are not perfectly exposed. The legendary master, Ansel Adams, burned and dodged with his wonderful negatives. Chances are that we will need to do a "little work" with our digital negatives. Here is a great technique for improving that photograph before we begin to paint.

Figure 4-39
Original digital photograph—poor lighting

You can never do too much drawing.
—Tintoretto,
in *Tintoretto*, by Evelyn March Phillipps (1911)

Copy the layer and set the Blending Mode to Screen
This brightens the image. It virtually looks like you turned the flash on, rendering more detail in the shadows. It can, however, blow out your highlights at the same time.

Figure 4-40
Blending Modes and masking used to correct exposure

Add a Layer Mask to create the proper lighting

The left side of the photograph was now too light. Using the Screen Blending Mode technique for lightening a dark photograph is a great trick. But it works globally, across the entire photograph. In most instances you only need a portion of the image to be rendered lighter in tone. This calls for masking. Using a mask will hold the desired highlights in place but open up the areas that are too dark. I always tell my students that "Masking is your friend." A mask allows you to really burn and dodge with a great deal of control. This technique has much more control than using the burn and dodge tools that are available to you in the Photoshop tool window.

Figure 4-41
Photo corrected and cropped—ready to begin painting

Crop Photo for composition

The photograph has been cropped and the exposure manipulated to give an image that can be used in a painting.

Figure 4-42
Saturation was beefed up for more color

Increase color saturation, using Hue/Saturation Adjustment Layer

Rich, saturated color is desirable in some paintings. For this example we increased the saturation through an adjustment.

Figure 4-43
Colored ground layer is introduced

Create a new layer and fill it with a color. Brown was used on this example

The old master's style of oil painting was frequently made on a colored ground. The canvas or board would be sealed with various chemical agents such as rabbit skin glue, white lead, etc., and then covered with a pigmented layer. This allowed the artist to paint in the highlights and shadows and work towards a middle tone, using the colored ground as that middle tone. Today, most artists choose to gesso their canvas to seal it. If they are working in the style of the old masters, they may then apply a layer of color. This layer is usually made from some paint and a painting medium. I often use a brown or gray color for my pigmented layer, which is applied on top of the dry gesso. In order to replicate that effect digitally, I created a new layer and filled it with a brown tone. I reduced the opacity of that layer, in order to see through to the photograph beneath.

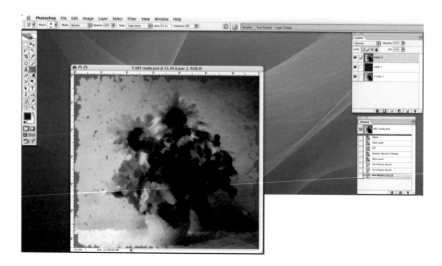

Figure 4-44
Art History Brush is used for initial laydown of color

Select the Art History Brush (Tight Short brush strokes) and "paint" in image

To create a simple underpainting, roughing in the color tone masses, I painted with the Art History Brush using the Tight Short brush option. This maps out the basic colors and forms. It is rough, but a good technique. This is a good place to step back and analyze the composition. Are there any changes that become apparent now? If not, proceed.

Figure 4-45
More detailed brushwork

Lower the brush size to achieve more detail

More details are needed now. I lowered the size of the brush to bring in some details. The smaller the brush is, the more details are shown. The larger the brush is, the looser the paint effect will be.

Figure 4-46
Using a chalk-like brush

Fine art is that in which the hand, the head, and the heart go together.
—John Ruskin, lecture: "The Two Paths," in *Art and Life* (1886)

Choose a rough, textured brush from brush options available

You are not limited to the commonly used brushes, even when you are in the Art History Brush category. So become daring. Go for a brush that mimics texture. I chose a chalk-like brush, found in the lower part of the brush palette. I love these brushes! They are great. Using this brush now introduces a wonderful texture to the brush strokes.

Figure 4-47

Examine closely, inch-by-inch, for corrections now

It's time to stop and look at the painting. The painted layer sits above the brown-colored ground layer, which, in turn, sits above the original photograph. This is the time to slowly examine the painting in a detailed and thorough way. I usually zoom in to the painting and carefully go over each part of the painting, section by section, for additions, deletions, and corrections. Your painterly effort is almost complete at this point.

Figure 4-48
Added duplicate layer set to Overlay Mode

Duplicate the layer and set the Blending Mode to Overlay

The next step is to duplicate the painted layer, by simply dragging that layer to the new layer icon. Now set the Blending Mode on this new layer to Overlay Mode. It will look really strange, with colors that border on neon, glow-in-the dark, bizarre shades. Relax, we are only partially there.

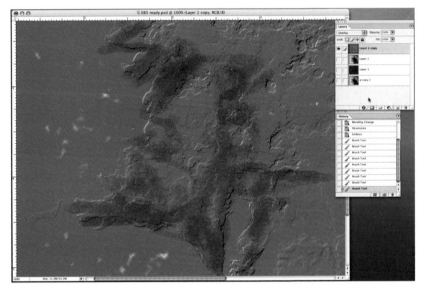

Figure 4-49
Duplicate layer is desaturated and the Emboss Filter is used

Desaturate this duplicate layer and use the Filter—Emboss

Use Image—Adjustments—Desaturate to remove the color from the duplicate layer. To achieve the texture of an application of opaque paint, like oil paint, the next step is to use Filter—Stylize—Emboss. The effect will be determined by how you move the sliders. They predict the thickness of the paint effect. To isolate the effect, you may wish to turn off the visibility of the other layers to concentrate on the fine-tuning of the effect.

The hand is the tool of the tools.
—ARISTOTLE,
   in *Aristotle's Theory of Poetry and Fine Art*, by S.H. Butcher (1951)

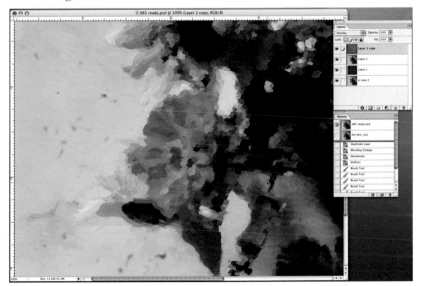

Figure 4-50
Close-up of the embossed effect

With all the layers turned on, zoom in to check out the embossed effect on your painting

Figure 4-51
Chalk effect adds texture

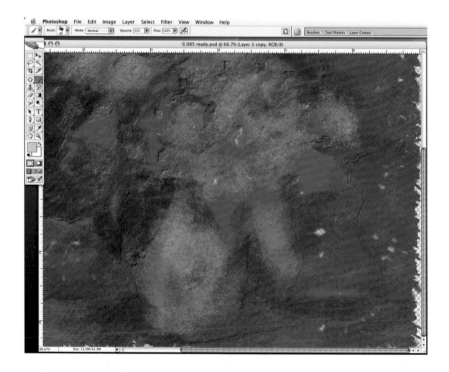

Figure 4-52
Varied gray tones for Textural Effect

Brush light gray for a lightened effect
To increase the textural effect, I used the earlier chalk brush to brush light gray on the desaturated layer in areas where I wanted a little lightening and a textural feel.

Figure 4-53
Details added with History Brush

The next step was to add a new layer and, using a small History Brush, add a little bit more detail

Art lies hidden in nature—he who can wrest it from her possesses art.
—ALBRECHT DÜRER,
The Writings of Albrecht Dürer, trans. by
W.M. Conway (1958)

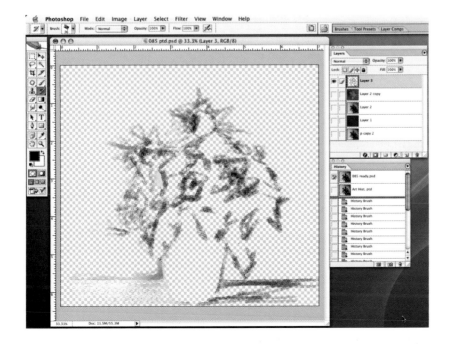

Figure 4-54
Actual detail

Figure 4-54 isolates the actual detail that was added in this new layer

Figure 4-55
Details Layer and Emboss Layer

Art is not a pastime, but a priesthood.
—Jean Cocteau,
 The New York Times
 (September 8, 1957)

Figure 4-55 places those details in context, with the lower emboss filter allowed to show through

Figure 4-56
Close-up

Figure 4-57
Close-up

Close-up examination of brush stroke effects
These close-ups reveal the paint stroke effect and the application of
an embossed thickness and texture to exaggerate the brush strokes.
It is wise to go over the entire painting, section by section, looking at
minute detail. This close examination will show you areas that might
need more work.

Figure 4-58
*Completed painting with
brown canvas edge*

Brown Edge Effect
This version allows the brown canvas ground to be seen along the
edges and peeking through the paint strokes, in areas that were not
covered by color. You may decide that this is the final version.

Figure 4-59—*"Mixed Bouquet"*
Completed painting with white painted edge

White Edge Effect—Paint with white using the textural chalk-like brush

If you want a white edge that still looks painterly, try painting with that chalk brush again with the normal brush tool selected and the color white. Figure 4-59 shows this white chalk edge effect.

Photo Illustration Using the Find Edges Filter

Figure 4-60
Original photo shot in Venice

Use a photo with good edge contrast

The next example is an interesting way to make a photo illustration. Select a photo with some edge detail. I used a photo that I took while on a gondola ride in Venice (Figure 4-60).

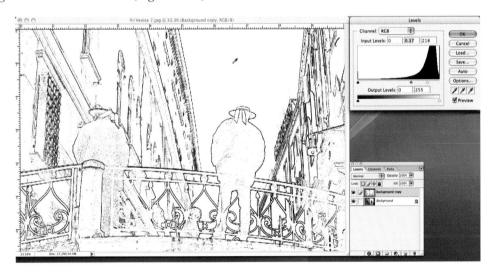

Figure 4-61
Stylize—Find Edges Filter

Copy the layer
Apply Filter—Stylize—Find Edges
Use Adjust—Levels to remove small unwanted particles
Copy the layer by simply dragging the layer to the new layer icon at the bottom of the layer palette. On that new layer use Filter—Stylize—Find Edges. I really like the effect that this filter gives, but often there are mid-tone areas that look like the windshield of your car when it has been sprayed with dirty water by a passing car. These areas just give a messy gray texture. To remove them and crisp up the contrast, go to Adjust—Levels and pull the sliders in until you like the effect. This clears out the unwanted gray areas. I also desaturated that layer, creating only a black line—no color.

Figure 4-62

Use the History Brush, at low opacity, to brush back some of the original photo's color image
Now we can color back into this area using the History Brush. Set the opacity low and gradually stroke the color from your original back into the illustration. Leave some areas empty of color to enhance this interesting effect. This would be a great technique for illustrations in newsletters, annual reports, and magazines, but don't rule out the use of this style when making images that are more fine art oriented.

Figure 4-63
Close-up

Figure 4-64
Bridal illustration

Follow steps in previous image
Duplicate the Find Edges Layer
Set the Blending Mode to Multiply
Add a Layer Mask, as needed

Figures 4-63 and 4-64 illustrate how this technique might be used for wedding photography. To intensify the dark edge effect, the Find Edges Layer was duplicated and placed above the History Brush Layer. The Blending Mode was set to Multiply. A layer mask was applied to the face area to remove any remaining residual gray areas, which may appear as acne or freckles in the finished piece. A digital facial!

Hand-Color a Black and White Photo

Figure 4-65

Create a new layer and hand-color with the Blending Mode set to Color
Simply select colors and brush them on in the new layer
Duplicate the colored layer twice
Apply the Artistic—Rough Pastels Filter to one new layer
Apply the Artistic—Watercolor Filter to the other new layer
Use a layer mask on both filter layers, to allow some of the filters to show, concealing some areas
You can use transparency, by lowering the opacity of the black that you brush onto the masks

While we are on the subject of bridal art, let's look at Figure 4-65. The bride was photographed by a pond of lotus blossoms with black and white infrared film. Those negatives were scanned and then hand-colored in Photoshop. Hand-coloring is easily achieved on a new layer, with the Blending Mode set to Color. The hand-colored image was duplicated twice. The Rough Pastels Filter was used on one new layer. The Watercolor Filter was used on the other new layer. A layer mask was used on the Watercolor layer (which was on the top of the layer stack), to see through to portions of the rough pastels layer. Masking allows you to use more than one layer effect on the same image.

Figure 4-66
Infrared black and white film scanned

An old-fashioned hand-colored look can be achieved with a black and white image. Our example is from infrared film that was scanned (Figure 4-66).

Beauty is the expression, in matter, of reason, which is divine.
—Plotinus,
   Enneades (c. A.D. 70)

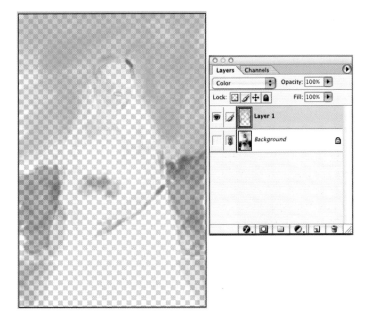

Figure 4-67
Color Layer with Blending Mode set to Color

Add a new layer. Choose the Color Blending Mode
Select colors and paint to your heart's delight. Use a light opacity. If you make a mistake you can erase the color layer, sparing the original image from any harm.

Figure 4-68

Combine the Colored Layer with the Black and White Layer
The combination is reminiscent of the vintage postcards from the 1930s to 1950s. Of course, you can alter your own personal palette as much as you like.

Figure 4-69
Commercial assignment for a bridal magazine, done in the manner described in the text

Chapter 9, "Filters," has even more painting techniques available to you in Photoshop. Be sure to investigate those techniques.

Edge Effects for FREE!

Imagine painterly edges in Photoshop that you can create without buying a program. There are many edge effects software programs available today. They range from wildly funky edges to painterly edges to faux photographic edges. The prices range broadly also. They are quick and generally easy to apply to your images but they can be expensive. Let's explore a few free ways to make interesting edge effects.

Scanner Edge Effects

Your scanner can be a wonderful assistant in this first type of edge effects. There is no limit to the variety of edges you can create with this method.

Materials
White artist's paper (experiment with rough cold press watercolor
    paper and smooth hot press paper).
Black ink.
Artist's brush (I like a wide Japanese brush).
Scanner.

Figure 4-70
Ink-coated paper

Brush ink on good quality, thick, artist's paper. Leave rough edges
With a ruler and a pencil I map out the proportion of a 35 mm negative, with a very light pencil mark. This is a rough guideline to assist me in making a black rectangle. I brush the ink on the paper using the guidelines as a template. I intentionally make the edges rough, showing the brush strokes. Let this dry. If the black area has sections that are not dense with black, it may require a second coat of ink.

Scan this black rectangle. Save it and give it a name that will indicate the nature of this template (Rough Edges on Watercolor paper, thin wispy brushy strokes, etc.). Develop a whole library of different brush edges that you can use on your work.

Now how do you use these edges? Open a photo or digital painting on which you would like an edge effect. Open the scanned edge effect.

Figure 4-71
Bring the ink/paper scan on top of the photo

Copy the edge effect template onto the layer above the photo

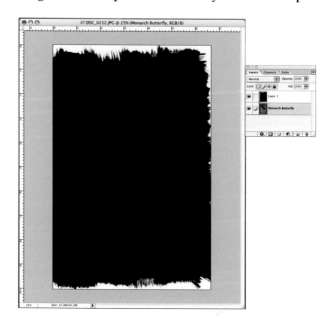

Figure 4-72

Combine ink-coated paper scan and photograph
Set your Blending Mode to Screen
This produces the desired edge effect. In my example, the scale of the
edge template needed to be adjusted to fit the photo beneath.

Figure 4-73

Choose Edit—Free Transform and pull the bounding box edges to
make the edge effect "fit" the photo
I stretched mine to fit the proportions of the underlying photograph.

Instead of trying to
reproduce exactly what
I have before my eyes, I
use color more arbitrarily,
in order to express myself
more forcibly.
—VINCENT VAN GOGH,
letter to his brother, Theo,
in *The Letters of van Gogh
to His Brother, 1886–1890*
(1929)

Figure 4-74
White edges

Set the Blending Mode to Screen

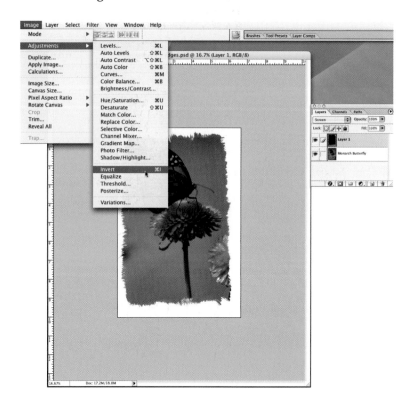

Figure 4-75
White edges being inverted

Image—Adjustments—Invert

How would you like to double the usefulness of your edge effect? Try this trick. On the edge effect layer go to Image—Adjustments—Invert. What was white will turn black, and vice versa.

Figure 4-76

Change your Blending Mode to Multiply

Your outside edge is now black!

Two for one! One edge effect template will allow you to make two different edge effects.

Figure 4-77
White edges and black edges

Do you want to try for three? Once you understand what can be accomplished with the use of blending modes, all sorts of possibilities open up. Let's duplicate the edge effect template layer. Simply drag that layer to the new layer icon at the bottom of the layer palette.

Figure 4-78
Duplicate the Edge Layer

Duplicate the Edge Layer
Set Blending Mode to Screen
Image—Adjustments—Invert
Free Transform to change the size of the bottom Edge Layer, just slightly

Change the Blending Mode on the new layer to Screen. Invert the black and white areas on the new layer, by again going to Image—Adjustments—Invert. The next step will give us a bit of a three-dimensional effect, similar to a drop shadow. Using the Free Transform command, simply pull the edges of this layer a little bigger than the layer above it.

Figure 4-79
Shadowed edge

Voilà! Three edge effects from one edge template. The possibilities are endless. Experiment. Try different kinds of brushes on a variety of paper textures. Each template will be unique to you, as each brush stroke will be different. It's fun, practical, and economical.

Figure 4-80
Completed edge effects

Film/photo edges

Let's use that scanner again and scan in a Polaroid transfer image. The edges on this type of process are unique. They give a telltale reminder to the viewer of how the image was made. The Polaroid gel that oozes out along the edges during this process leaves a trace of color that is identifiable as a Polaroid transfer. We can mimic that effect through scanning and transforming.

Polaroid transfer edges

Figure 4-81

Figure 4-81 shows two separate Polaroid transfers. Each has a unique border that is a result of this process. Notice also the softness of the image and a texture that resembles grain.

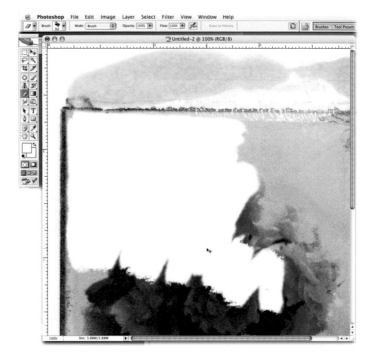

Figure 4-82
Erasing Polaroid transfer

Use a Rough Brush to erase the actual Polaroid transfer image
We want only the outside edge of the scanned transfer. With the eraser
set to a rough brush (number 60), the inside of the transfer is erased.

Figure 4-83
*Empty Polaroid transfer
edges*

Only the edges remain. Transfers that are hollow can be kept in a
library of edge effects to use on later projects.

Figure 4-84
Photo and Polaroid edge are joined

Join the Polaroid edge and the photograph. You will probably need to use Free Transform to get the proportions just right. If I am trying to truly mimic a Polaroid transfer, the photograph is too sharp.

Figure 4-85
Gaussian Blur and filter Noise

Apply Filter—Blur—Gaussian Blur
Apply Filter—Noise
To continue along with the concept of creating a faux Polaroid transfer, I then ran two filters on the photograph layer. I first used a light application of Filter—Blur—Gaussian Blur, followed by Filter—Noise. The filter applications move the image closer to looking like a real Polaroid transfer.

Film Edge Effects

Good composition is like
a suspension bridge—each
line adds strength and
takes none away.
—ROBERT HENRI,
The Art Spirit (1923)

Occasionally you will see a photo that has, as its frame, the edge of a
piece of film. This seems to be a popular edge in recent years. We can
mimic this effect also.

Figure 4-86

Lay a strip of film on your flatbed scanner and scan it. Save that file.
Take a portion of that filmstrip and copy it into its own document. For
this example (Figure 4-87) I've shown you the scan on the right, and
on the left I have inverted the image. Either way will work. Your own
taste will determine which version you like best.

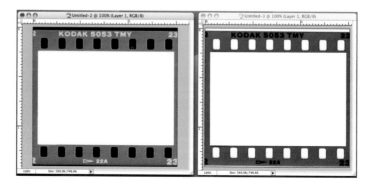

Figure 4-87
Film edges

Figure 4-88

In Figure 4-88, I've inserted a photograph under the layer of the film edging. Again, either one would work. It's a matter of taste.

Figure 4-89

You can take this a step further and select the film edging (I used the Magic Wand tool) and darken it. Darkening is done easily with either an adjustment in Curves or levels. I also cropped the film edge down a little. This gives a contemporary feel to the edge effect.

There is absolutely no limit to the number of edge effects that you can personally make, creating a library of edges that you can use well into the future. The bonus is that they are all unique to only your work.

I would encourage you to explore the painting possibilities within Photoshop. Try combining some of the techniques shown in this chapter using Filters, the Pattern Stamp, Art History Brush, and History Brush. Try some of the more irregular brushes. In Chapter 12 you can discover how to make your own unique brushes.

5 *Painting in Painter*

Artists often have a variety of art supplies in their studio spaces. My studio contains oil painting supplies, watercolors, gouache, pastels, charcoals, colored pencils, inks, encaustic paints, oil sticks, dry pigments, and more. There are brushes galore. They each have special uses. My expensive sable brushes are only for my watercolors. There are natural bristle and plastic bristle brushes for oil painting. My large map case holds drawers full of different papers in various textures and colors. Although many artists specialize in a particular medium, such as watercolors, they often have dabbled at using other mediums over the years.

Wouldn't it be wonderful to have all those tools, and more, at your fingertips? Wouldn't it be wonderful to never spend time washing and

If one hasn't a horse, one is one's own horse.
—VINCENT VAN GOGH, letter to his brother, Theo, in *The Complete Letters of Vincent van Gogh*, ed. by V. Willem van Gogh (1958)

cleaning up your brushes and gear? It is possible to use these tools in their digital version with the software called Painter. Painter began as a great little black and white program, called Sketcher, that came in a cigar box-type packaging. In time it grew into a paint can and was marketed as Painter. It has had several owners over the years, but has been owned by Corel for several years. Although many digital artists use the variety of art mediums available in Painter, without using photographs, we will not address those applications. Our task, in this book, will center on how photographers can use the digital art materials available in Painter. Be prepared to be amazed with the realistic effects those art materials will lend to your work. Another pleasant side effect of using these digital art materials is the lack of fumes and odors associated with some art materials. You will not be digging pigment out of your fingernails or wiping paint off your hands and clothes. Hooray!

Painter uses several traditional file formats, including PSD, TIFF, JPEG, etc. What may surprise you will be the native format of Painter called RIFF. You won't see that format in any other program. It is particular to Painter. If you are going to use your file in another program, such as Photoshop, just be sure to save it in a file format accepted by the other program. This native painter format of RIFF allows you to keep a watercolor "wet" over a prolonged period of time. In real life, if you are painting and your long lost college roommate calls from three thousand miles away, necessitating an extended phone call, your painting will have dried out on your return. If you had been painting digitally and saved the file in the RIFF format, you could return to the "wet" paper two weeks later. Also with digital watercolors in Painter, you can instantly "dry" your painting to apply another medium, such as pastels, on top of your painting. This is an artist's dream come true.

I prefer drawing to talking. Drawing is faster, and allows less room for lies.
—Le Corbusier, *Time* magazine (May 5, 1961)

As a photographer, you will want to prepare your photograph before bringing it into Painter. I usually do any cropping, image adjustments (such as rubber stamping to remove objectionable areas), and contrast, tonal, or color adjustments, etc. in Photoshop. After all, Photoshop is the photo manipulation program: let's use it for what it does best. In fact, the primary question that I ask repeatedly is "What program will be best for the task at hand?" I often go back and forth between Photoshop and Painter, according to the job I need to do. It is just common sense. The look of the Painter interface has improved in recent versions. In the past, the tools consumed so much of the screen real estate that there was barely room to work. It has a much more practical and streamlined look now. But, of course, you will still not want all of the windows and palettes open at once. If you are comfortable with the Photoshop layout, then the Painter interface will be similar in design and will reinforce your instinctual impulse, as you reach for a tool.

Painter is a wonderful asset to photographers who desire to make their work more painterly. It is good for portraits, photo illustrations, still lifes, landscapes, and much more. We will explore a few of those applications in this chapter. If you need to brush up on your Painter skills or you are a novice at Painter, please refer to Chapter 13, concerning essential skills.

Simple Cloning Techniques

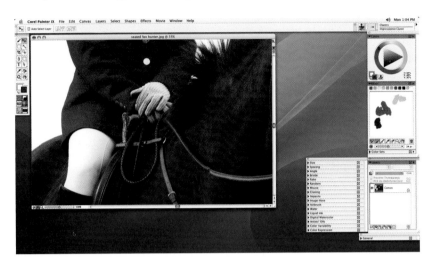

Figure 5-1
Original photograph

File—Open (choose the photo you want to use)
File—Clone
Now, on to working with photographs in Painter. Go to File—Open (just like you do in Photoshop), and select the file you want to open. You now have your photograph in Painter. The first step is to clone your photograph. This preserves the original. We are never working on the original. Simply go to File—Clone. A clone of the original image will appear with the name Clone of . . . (whatever the name of the original image was).

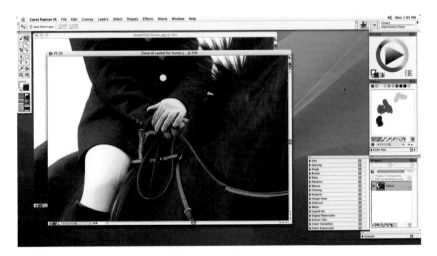

Figure 5-2
Clone created

The artist expresses only what he has within himself, not what he sees with his eyes.
—ALEXEJ VON JAWLENSKY, *Das Kunstwerk II* (1948)

Select—All
Delete
The next step seems counterintuitive. Choose Select—All and hit the delete key. You have just eliminated the clone, right? Wrong! The upper right-hand corner of the image has a button for tracing paper. You can toggle the tracing paper on and off, revealing and concealing your original image.

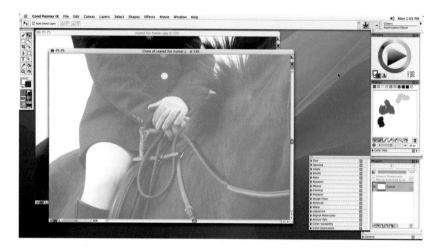

Figure 5-3

Select the cloning tool
Select the cloning icon (looks like a rubber stamp) in the Color Picker

Select the cloning tool. Hint: it looks like a rubber stamp. There are tons of different types of brushes and different art media that can be used in cloning. My personal favorites include the Impressionist Cloner, Chalk Cloner, and Watercolor Cloner. The vibrant Color Picker needs to be disabled to pull from the colors of the original cloned image. Just toggle the "rubber stamp" icon, located next to the foreground and background blocks, in the lower left-hand corner of the Colors palette. If the Color Picker Palette is enabled, it will pull from the current color selected. When the cloning color method is activated, the color wheel will appear grayed down. Simply click on or off the "stamp" icon to activate or deactivate the Clone color option or the Color Picker option.

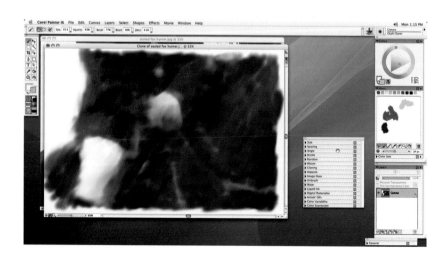

Figure 5-4
Begin to brush Chalk Cloner onto Clone image

Choose Chalk Cloner from the various Cloner variants
Begin to brush the Chalk Cloner onto the "blank" cloner

For this example I chose the Chalk Cloner. I used a large brush (size 63) and roughed in the cloned colors. This provides an underpainting, indicating the shapes and approximate colors. The larger your brush, the rougher the image, and less accurate the colors. The large brush pulls from a large selected area on the original image and averages out the approximate color from all the pixels selected. A smaller brush will give you more detail and more accurate color. Our image is very rough, painterly, and smudgy now.

Calamity is a time of great opportunity.
—CHINESE PROVERB

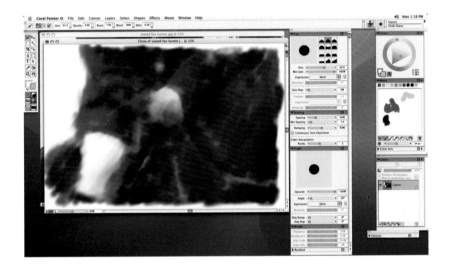

Figure 5-5
Try to vary the brushes that you use

In Painter it is possible to design a brush to your specifications. You can see in Figure 5-5 some of the selected characteristics of the brush used here. You can choose the size and type of bristles and how the brush will interact with the paper selected. Go crazy on this and try a variety of different types.

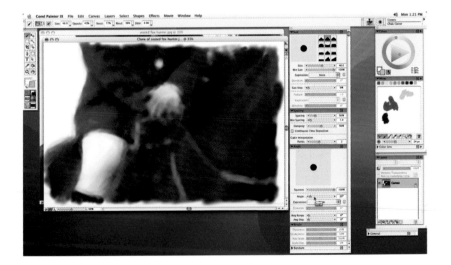

Figure 5-6
Detail added

Use a smaller brush for more detail

Next, I wanted to firm up the painting a bit and selected a smaller brush
(size 40). Working with the smaller brush brought in more detail. The
strokes were made in the direction of the object (e.g., fold of sleeve,
leather reins). Make your brush stroke on the painting as your hand
would do if it were following the contour of the object that you are
painting.

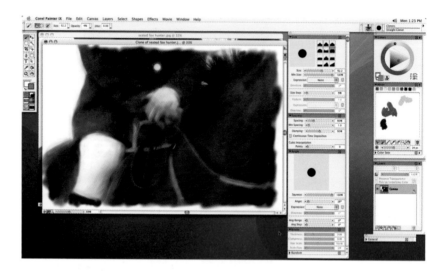

Figure 5-7
*Straight Cloner used for
more detail*

Use Straight Cloner at a very low opacity (4% or less)

At this point in the process, I usually like to bring back some of the
detail from the original image. I chose the Straight Cloner. This brought
the exact photo up. That, however, was way too much. We would have
been merely restoring the image to its photographic beginnings. We
wanted just a hint of the details. The opacity was set very low (4% or
less) and strokes were added, as if adding a light transparent veil over
the original, only in the areas where more detail was desired.

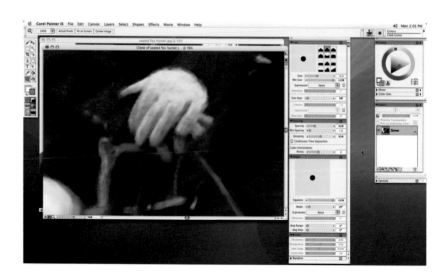

Figure 5-8
*Loose painterly strokes
reapplied*

Chalk Cloner reapplied to areas that are too photographic
If you bring back too much detailed photographic information, just go back to the Chalk Cloner and again stroke on those loose colors. Try doing that at a very low opacity. This is helpful if a diffusion effect is needed over any area that is too sharp.

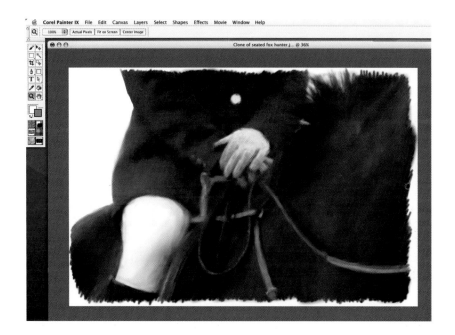

Figure 5-9
Assess the painting

   It was time to stop, step back, and assess the progress to this point. What did the painting need? In this example I felt that I wanted to brighten and exaggerate the colors, especially those in the woolen riding jacket of the fox hunter.

Michelangelo's energy terrified me; I felt a sentiment I could not express; on seeing the beauties of Raphael I was moved to tears and the pencil fell from my hand.
—JEAN-HONORÉ
   FRAGONARD,
   personal notes on a
   visit to Italy in 1752,
   in *Letters of the Artists*,
   by Richard Friedenthal
   (1963)

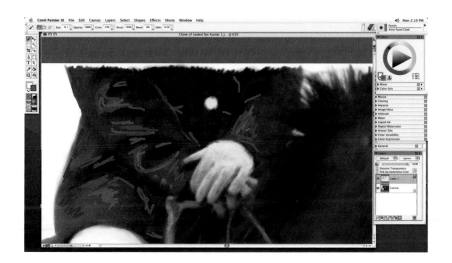

Figure 5-10
Color painted on using Artist Pastel Chalks

Create a new layer
Use Artist Pastel Chalk to paint in brighter colors on the new layer

I created a new layer on the Layer palette and chose the Artist Pastel Chalk as my Brush. I selected brighter colors that I wanted to blend into the underlying painting. By keeping these rough strokes on a separate layer, they are more easily corrected or erased without marring the painting. Needless to say, but I will say it any way, save your image frequently. Computers can and do crash, the phone can ring, and the cat can jump up on the keyboard as you chat in another room. You can return to a deleted or damaged file. It is just common sense to frequently save your images. It is your digital insurance policy.

Figure 5-11
Strokes are blended into the painting

Drop the new layer with bright paint strokes
Use a Blenders brush to blend the paint strokes into the painting

The next step was to "drop" that layer into the painting. A Blenders brush was used to blend those colors into the existing painting. Be sure to take your time, and vary the size of your brush, as needed.

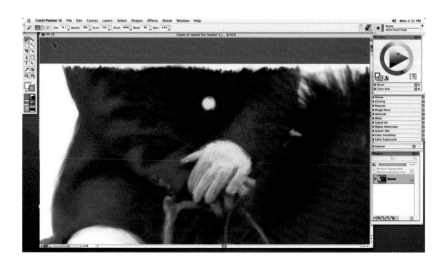

Figure 5-12
More chalk added

Apply more Artist Pastel Chalk

The result is more color vibrancy in that woolen jacket. The riding gloves, riding pants, and horse needed a little help. Again, the Artist Pastel Chalk is the brush that applied the additional color.

Figure 5-13
Grainy Blender used

Grainy Blender used to blend the color into the painting

A Grainy Blender was used to blend the Artist Pastel Chalk colors into the existing painting.

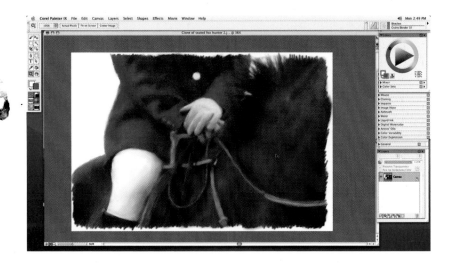

Figure 5-14
Assess the painting again

The end of the process was near. This was an excellent time to step back and assess the image so far. What did it need? Did the edges need help? Did it need more detail somewhere, or, perhaps, less detail somewhere? Did I need to add more color or, conversely, tone down any existing color? You need to be your own harshest critic, and try to have an objective eye for needy areas.

A painter paints a picture with the same feeling as that with which a criminal commits a crime.
—EDGAR DEGAS,
The Notebooks of Edgar Degas, trans. by T. Reff (1976)

Figure 5-15—*"Waiting"*
Print is pulled for proofing

Print and assess the proof

After the corrections were made, a proof was pulled. The image was printed and again evaluated for color, quality of brush strokes, etc. The final image was printed on a heavy inkjet watercolor paper.

Figure 5-16
Sepia rendition from the same image

The completed painting was made primarily with Digital Chalk and Artist's Pastel Chalk. That same source image was used for the sepia-toned sketch seen in Figure 5-16. This version was made in Photoshop with filters and masks. (See Chapter 9 for details on using filters.)

Painted portraits are challenging work. You don't want the image to be photographic in nature. You really want a painting. Figure 5-17 illustrates a digital painting I made of a friend. Every portion of this large work has been painted. Most of the work was done in Painter. Many various brushes were used, including cloning ones, pastels, and gouache paint. Although I can make a passable piece in an hour or two, this painting took the better part of a weekend to achieve the look that I wanted. Digital painting is not done in an instant. Time is needed for the discernment and study that are necessary throughout the art-making process. Give yourself the gift of time and patience to see yourself through to a satisfying conclusion and pleasing piece of art.

The wonderful responsiveness of the chalks and pastels make them some of my favorite tools. The colors are true to your selection, and the ability to have the paper surface interact with the pastels is a wonderful textural element. The digital painting of a statue in a small village in Provence, France (Figure 5-18) was made with these techniques. Another painting made this way is the vase and stairs shown in Figure 5-19. It also began as a slide taken in France.

If I didn't start painting, I would have raised chickens.
—Anna M. Moses, *Grandma Moses, My Life's History* (1947)

Figure 5-17
Painted portrait—"Scott"

Figure 5-18—*"Les Bastides de Jordan, France"*

Figure 5-19—*"Les Baux, France"*

Impressionist Cloner

Figure 5-20
Photo that was corrected in advance in Photoshop

Another favorite cloning tool is the Impressionist Cloner. The shape of this brush leaves a mark that is similar to a grain of rice. You can make the size of that mark vary by enlarging or shrinking the brush size. For this exercise I thought it would be fun to use a photo that has the feel of a painting from the era of impressionism. The photograph was taken at a Civil War reenactment. There were lots of people, trucks, food tents, etc. in the original photograph. The distracting elements were removed in Photoshop.

An artist should paint as if in the presence of God.
—MICHELANGELO,
in *Michelangelo's Theory of Art*, by Robert C. Clements (1961)

Figure 5-21

File—Clone
Select Clone and Delete

The image was cloned (File—Clone). The clone was selected and deleted. The "tracing paper" was turned on, for our visual orientation.

Figure 5-22
Chalk Cloner applied for an underpainting

Cloner—Chalk

Before I begin with the Impressionist Cloner, I like to rough in the painting with large, loose areas of color. A different cloning technique was used for this. I chose the Chalk Brush with the Tapered Large Chalk variant (brush size 66.6). The cloning option needs to be selected on the Colors palette. Chalk gives an initial laydown of color. It also allows the texture of the selected paper to show through. The Basic Paper was selected for this image. This initial coloring with chalk avoided lots of bare spots that would have appeared if I had begun right away with the Impressionist Cloner. The Impressionist Cloner, used alone, will yield bare spots, unless there is extensive repeated use over an area. We avoided that problem by supplying a solid laydown of color with the Chalk Cloner, before moving on to the Impressionist Cloner.

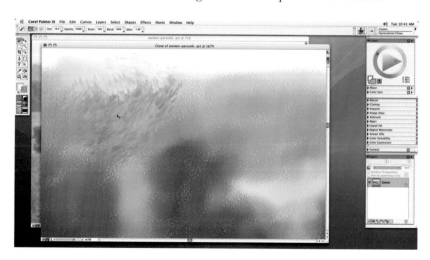

Figure 5-23
Impressionist Cloner applied

Use Impressionist Cloner Brush

Once the entire painting had a good underpainting of color it was time to use the Impressionist Cloner. A brush size of 19 was used over the entire painting. In Figure 5-23, you can see the texture of the previous step with chalk and paper and the beginnings of the Impressionist Cloner in the upper left-hand corner.

Painting must be impulsive to be worthwhile; an aesthetic excitement.
—CHARLES HAWTHORNE, *Hawthorne on Painting* (1938)

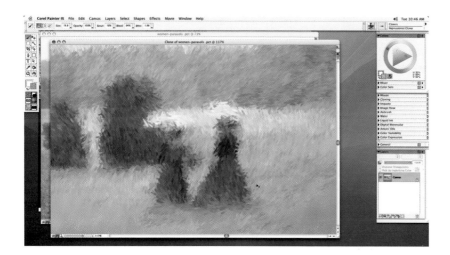

Figure 5-24
Large, chunky, Impressionist effect

The entire painting got an application of the Impressionist Cloner. Any areas of blank paper, which would have peeked out, were covered by the first layer of chalk underpainting. At this point the painting was loose, with large marks from the cloner.

Figure 5-25
Smaller brush used for more detail

More detail was definitely needed on the women and their dresses and parasols. The size of the Impressionist Cloner brush was lowered to 4.8. Compare the woman on the left in Figure 5-25 with the figure on the right. The woman on the left had been stroked with a small brush size, which yielded more detail.

Figure 5-26
Smaller brush used throughout in selected areas

The smaller brush size was used on both women and in occasional spots throughout the painting.

Straight Cloner used in a very low opacity to restore some detail
For some finishing touches the Straight Cloner was used with a 2% opacity to bring back a little of the grasses in the foreground and more definition to the parasols. It's not a Monet, but it gives a bit of the flavor of that era.

Other paintings made with this Impressionist Cloner technique are shown in Figures 5-28, 5-29, and 5-30. The sky in Figure 5-30 was purposely made to resemble the sky in Vincent van Gogh's *Starry Night*. The original slide was shot with a medium-format slide film in a sunflower field at dawn, near van Gogh's residence in the south of France. The sky treatment was a bit of homage to the way van Gogh applied those marvelous marks of color on his canvas. The foreground of the sunflowers relied a bit more on the Chalk and Straight Cloner brushes.

Why talk when one can paint?
—MILTON AVERY,
   in *Milton Avery,* by
   Barbara Haskell (1982)

Every time I paint, I throw myself into the water in order to learn how to swim.
—EDOUARD MANET,
   in *The World of Manet,*
   by Pierre Schneider
   (1966)

Figure 5-27—*"Parasols"*
Tiny touches of Straight Cloner applied

Figure 5-28—*"Lavender Field, France"*

Figure 5-29—*"Arles Lane, France"*

Figure 5-30—*"van Gogh's Sunflower Field, St. Remy, France"*

Pastel Cloning

Figure 5-31
Original Roman sculpture photo

File—Clone
The next example of cloning relies on the custom brush function that is so powerful in Painter. This technique delivers an effect like a chalk drawing on a rough, colored, charcoal paper surface. Open your photograph as usual in Painter and Clone the image.

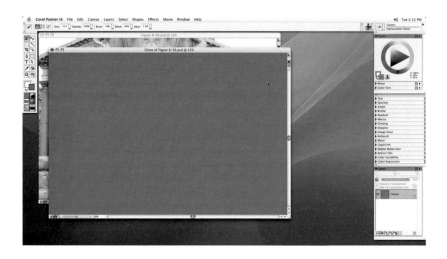

Figure 5-32

Delete the cloned image
Pick a color
Effects—Fill—Current Color at 100% opacity
The cloned image was selected and deleted. A color from the Color Picker was selected for our charcoal paper. Try looking at your original photo and make a color decision that complements the image. Opposites on the color wheel are frequently good possible choices. Go to Effects—Fill—Current Color at 100% opacity. This will create the colored charcoal paper.

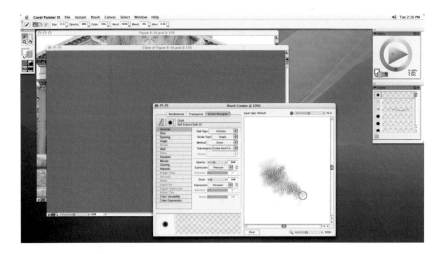

Figure 5-33
Use Brush Creator

Window—Show Brush Creator
Choose modifiers

The next step in this process was to create a special brush. Go to Window—Show Brush Creator. This brings up a fairly large menu. There are lots of ways that you could modify a brush and preplan how it will react with the surface on which it draws. I picked the Chalk Brush with the Dull Grainy Chalk variant. The modifiers that I selected were:

Dab Type: Circular
Stroke Type: Singular
Method: Cover
Subcategory: Grainy Hard Cover
Opacity: 30%
Grain: 10%

You will find that the possibilities for variations are virtually endless. Experiment!

Figure 5-34

Dull Grainy Chalk used at 30% opacity

The "tracing paper" icon was turned on, and an application of the Dull Grainy Chalk variant was used. Since the opacity was set to 30%, it was possible to build up color with many strokes or allow some areas to be more thinly painted. The paper type selected for this image was the Italian Watercolor Paper—a good selection since the photo is of a fountain in Rome.

Painting begins with outlining of key areas.

I think I'm beginning to learn something about it.
—Pierre-Auguste Renoir,
his last words about painting, at age 78, in *Renoir, An Intimate Record*, by Ambroise Vollard (1930)

Figure 5-35

Use the tracing paper feature to paint over the outlines of the photo
Turn tracing paper off, once the outlines are established

I generally use the tracing paper feature to map out the contours of the photograph (see Figure 5-35) and then turn the tracing paper off. I like to really see the effect the strokes are having on the painting. If the photograph is still visible, it can distract me and I'm less able to see the quality of the marks that I am making. I occasionally turn the tracing paper on and off to check with the information available in the original image.

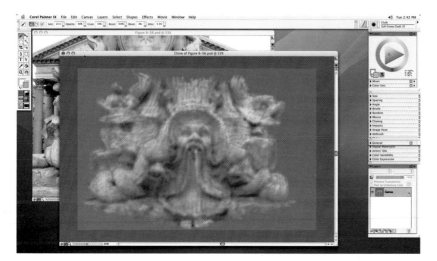

Figure 5-36
Assess your work

Most of the painting is done without the tracing paper turned on. This is the honest version of what you are creating. After the application of chalk was completed it was a good time to, again, step back and analyze the painting. What were its strengths? What were its shortcomings? What did it need?

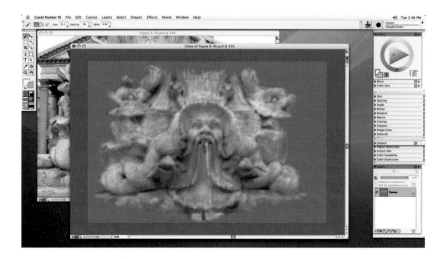

Figure 5-37
Straight Cloner used for detail

Use the Straight Cloner for areas needing more detail (2% opacity)
A little more detail was needed on the smaller aspects of the photo. The Straight Cloner was used sparingly at only 2% opacity to bring a little more clarity to the final touches on this piece.

The final painting retains a chalk drawing feel and enough detail to carry the image successfully.

Other images made with this technique are shown in Figures 5-39, 5-40, and 5-41.

Painting is the grandchild of nature. It is related to God.
—REMBRANDT,
   in *Rembrandt Drawings*,
   by Paul Nemo, trans. by
   David Macrae (1975)

Figure 5-38
Final version

Figure 5-39—*"Roman Piper"*

Figure 5-40—*"Florentine Lion"*

Figure 5-41

Oil Paint Cloning

One of the wonderful techniques available to you in Painter is the ability to apply paint that has a thickness, like oil paints. A thick application of paint is often called impasto. In the next example I used a photograph that I had taken in Venice (Figure 5-42). The nature of the image led me to believe that it might be a good image to work from, using the Wet Oil Cloner. The brick work, which was showing the passage of time, would work well with a thick brush stroke of paint.

Figure 5-42
*Original photo, taken in
Venice*

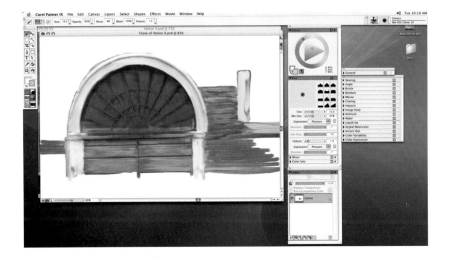

Figure 5-43
Wet Oil Cloner selected

Create a clone (File—Clone)
Select and delete the clone
Select Cloner brush—Wet Oil Cloner
The image was cloned, selected, and deleted, as we have done in previous examples. The Cloner brush was selected and the Wet Oil Cloner variant was the type of brush used. A size 10 brush was applied for preliminary brushwork. That size was great for dragging in horizontal strokes over the brick area. You will notice that a previous laydown of color will smear into the next stroke, if overlapped. That is just the way real oil paints interact when painting. The cloner is pulling the color information from the underlying photograph. The larger the brush, the more color samples that are selected and averaged for the color application. A smaller brush will always yield more detail and accurate color sampling, as per the photograph.

Figure 5-44
Use tracing paper to establish outlines

Use the tracing paper feature to establish key areas
Turn tracing paper off to see the "real" painting and the marks that you are making
It is occasionally helpful to use the tracing paper feature to see where you are on the original image, as you paint. I like to rough out the outlines of areas, using the tracing paper, and then turn the tracing paper off. With the tracing paper turned off, I can see more clearly the type of brush stroke I am making and how it interacts with previous strokes (directionality of the pull of the brush, and the amount of color blending that is occurring as the paint smears). I can concentrate more on my mark making without the distraction of the underlying photograph.

Figure 5-45
Straight Cloner applied lightly for detail

Assess the painting
Use Straight Cloner at 2% opacity for details in selected areas
Select Oil Brush—Glazing Brush variant—lay down a light glaze
After covering the canvas with paint strokes using the Wet Oil Cloner, it was time to step back and assess the painted image. I used the Straight Cloner at 2% opacity to bring a little of the window-box foliage into view, instead of green smears. The next step was to leave the Cloning brush, and go to the Oil—Glazing Brush, also set at a low opacity. I picked a rich dark brown and glazed over the shadowed areas on the left, intensifying the shadows and depth.

Figure 5-46
Glazing brush used

Use Glazing Brush to deepen shadows, lighten highlights, and add detail

The Glazing Brush was used with various shades of aqua, green, pink, and yellow to add some color interest in the window boxes. More flowers were added, using this brush. The photograph was taken in January and the geraniums were just hanging on to life. The Cloning brush was akin to adding fertilizer into the dirt. The growing conditions improved immediately. Feel free to use your creative license.

The completed painting has the look of an oil painting. There are smears, loose blending of colors, and the appearance of a thick, impasto, paint application. There are several oil options to use, and many different brushes. Experiment with thick paint. Be selective with the photograph that you choose. Not all images will look good rendered in oil paints. Some images are better suited to a delicate watercolor rendition than to a thicker, more opaque application of paint. Choose the medium to match the feel of the photograph. This image was printed on inkjet canvas.

Figure 5-47—*"Venetian Canal"*
Completed painting

More Oil Painting

Use Oil Paint Cloner on the clone

I'm going to show a few more variations on the Oil Paint Cloner, since the look of an oil painting is often an effect that many photographers desire. In Figure 5-48 the Oil Paint Cloner was used for the first painterly effect.

Figure 5-48
Oil Paint Cloner used

Figure 5-49
Oil Paint—Glazing Round brush used

**Light application of color gazing was added with the Oil Paint—
Glazing Round brush**

The next brush that was used was the Oil Paint—Glazing Round variation. Colors were selected from the Color Wheel and stroked lightly into
the hair area. The opacity was set low to give a feel of transparency.

Figure 5-50
*Highlights and shadows
intensified*

**Highlights and shadows were intensified with the glazing brush
Blender brush—Oil Blender was used on the floor area**

That same glazing variation was used on the ballet skirt to add highlights and shadows. An oil blender (from the Blender brushes) was
used on the wooden floor.

The finished piece (Figure 5-51) takes a snapshot of a teenager's
ballet recital and turns it into a little painting, worthy of framing and
displaying.

Figure 5-51
Completed painting

Figure 5-52
Original photo and oil painting rendition

Our next oil variation is the Bristle Oil Cloner. Think of this as a brush made of coarser hairs, similar to a boar's bristle brush, made from the thick, strong, and stubby hair on the back of a pig. In real oil painting a variety of brushes are available. Some are softer for more delicate blending and some are coarser for a more textured mark. In Figure 5-52 we compare the original photograph, on the left, to the Bristle Oil Cloner painted version on the right.

Figure 5-53
Underpainting, using Fuzzy Cloner

File—Clone
Select and delete the clone
Select Cloner brush—Fuzzy Cloner variant to create an underpainting of color
One of the techniques I use for a quick underpainting is to paint the clone with the Fuzzy Cloner. It is an amusing cloner that makes pompom type marks with variations of the color that were sampled in the cloning area. It works quickly and gives a rough underpainting of color. In my work, this underpainting is almost always covered later by other brushwork. Figures 5-53 and 5-54 show a close-up view and an overall look at the Fuzzy Cloner used on the whole painting.

One wants the spirit, the aroma, don't you know? If you paint a young girl, youth should scent the room; if a thinker, thoughts should be in the air; an aroma of personality . . . and, with all that, it should be a picture, a pattern, an arrangement, a harmony, such as only a painter could conceive.
—JAMES ABBOTT MCNEILL WHISTLER,
The Gentle Art of Making Enemies (1890)

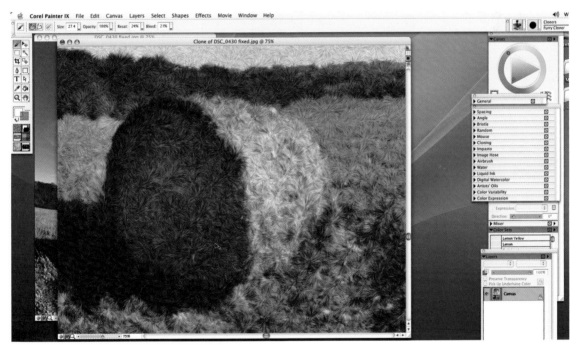

Figure 5-54
Completed Fuzzy Cloner painting

Cloner brush—Bristle Oil Cloner used throughout the painting
Oil painting brush—Glazing Round used for accent color glazing
The Bristle Oil Cloner was used for the majority of the actual painting. That brush most closely resembled the type of brush mark that I wanted in the painting. Figure 5-55 shows a close-up of the brushwork and the addition of extra colors, using the Oil Paint variant, Glazing Round.

Figure 5-55
Bristle Oil Cloner

Figure 5-56 shows the completed painting. Many additional colors were added with that oil glazing brush. More color was added in the autumn trees to the rear of the image and in the haystack.

Figure 5-56—*"Hayroll"*
Completed Bristle Oil Cloner painting

Combining a Variety of Mediums into One Painting

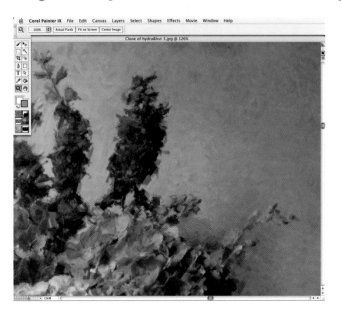

Figure 5-57
Oil Cloner, Bristle Oil Cloner, and Van Gogh Cloner

File—Clone
Select and delete the clone
Cloning made with three cloners: Oil Cloner, Bristle Oil Cloner, and Van Gogh Cloner
The next oil painting (shown in Figure 5-58) was made with the Oil Cloner, the Bristle Oil Cloner, and the Van Gogh Cloner. Figure 5-57 shows a close-up of the loose brushwork that was applied using all three cloners.

Figure 5-58
Light glaze applied to wall

Figure 5-59
Glazing effect intensified

A glaze was brushed onto a separate layer to add color effect in specific areas

After finishing most of the painting (Figure 5-58) I wanted to warm the background wall a little with a glaze of a soft apricot color. That was applied on a separate layer and combined using the default blending mode (Figure 5-59). The effect would be like putting a gel over your lighting source in studio photography, but limiting the effect to certain areas.

The flowers used in the digital oil paintings shown in Figures 5-60 and 5-61 were photographed the day after the wedding of my daughter, Emily. The flowers had been used in the wedding and the lace under the vase was the lace handkerchief that she carried with her bouquet that day. I wanted to make a painting using some photographs of those items, as a special gift for the newlyweds. As I worked on the photography that day, a beautiful blue and black butterfly kept coming into my picture frame as I made photos. In Figure 5-60, I decided to welcome the butterfly into the composition. I decided not to question the serendipity of his presence. That painting actually used all of the following brushes: Watercolor Cloner, Bristle Oil Cloner, Fine Gouache Cloner, Van Gogh Cloner, and Watercolor Run Cloner. I switched vases for Figure 5-61. This painting has a slightly different feel and more closely resembles an old Dutch still life painting.

You will paint well when you are able to forget that you are painting at all.
—KIMON NICOLAIDES,
The Natural Way to Draw (1941)

Figure 5-60
Completed painting

Feel like you are touching the model while you draw and paint and forget you are drawing or painting.
—KIMON NICOLAIDES,
The Natural Way to Draw (1941)

Figure 5-62 shows the detail of brushwork used in the painting. Notice the addition, again, of an apricot-colored glaze on the back wall. This was made with that wonderful oil Glazing Round brush.

Figure 5-61—*"Wedding Bouquet"*
Completed bridal bouquet still life

Figure 5-62
Detail of painting

Adding Texture to Your Painting

Figure 5-63
Original photograph

The next still life has a Spanish flavor and incorporates the ability of Painter to render a surface texture. For this photograph I selected items that I had brought home from a trip to Spain (a fan and a hand-tooled metal box from Toledo). The bouquet was made with red peonies. The background was actually the fabric of a jacket, not wallpaper. Go to the fabric store and buy inexpensive remnants for interesting background colors, textures, and patterns. I probably took over sixty versions of this still life, moving items and lighting until I found the one that was most pleasing to me, in terms of lighting, color, and composition.

Figure 5-64
*Cloned with Chalk Cloner
and Van Gogh Cloner*

File—Clone
Select and delete clone
Clone Brush—Van Gogh Cloner and Chalk Cloner
The entire painting was cloned with the Chalk Cloner and the Van Gogh Cloner. Notice the evidence of the Van Gogh Cloner in the fabric background. The Van Gogh Cloner gives wonderful strokes of color. I next used the oil cloner to give a thick, impasto brush stroke throughout the painting. That version was saved.

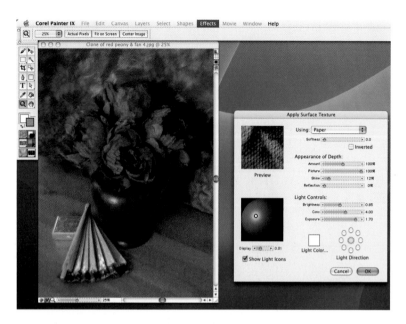

Figure 5-65
Apply Surface Texture

Duplicate the layer
Effects—Apply Surface Texture—Coarse Cotton Canvas
Adjust the light source
Here comes the fancy footwork, folks. I reopened that saved file and duplicated the layer. I then selected a paper texture (Coarse Cotton Canvas). Under Effects I chose Apply Surface Texture. That dialogue box and the settings used are shown in Figure 5-65. Try moving the light source around. A slight adjustment has a profound effect on the texture.

Figure 5-66
Canvas texture applied

Figure 5-66 shows the canvas textural effect on the painting. It seemed a little too strong for my tastes. Here is where that duplicated layer comes in handy. The layer that had the textural effect applied was named "canvas" and was at the bottom of my layer stack.

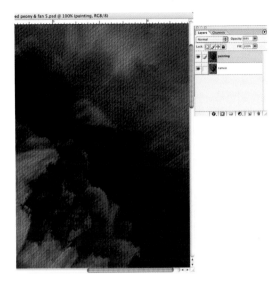

Figure 5-67
Layers are combined

Top layer is the cloned painting—set at 65% opacity
Bottom layer is the canvas version of the painting
Layers are combined (Drop) to tone down the canvas effect
The top layer named "painting" did not have the cotton canvas texture applied. It was still the painting, as I had saved it. I blended those two layers together using a 65% opacity on the painting layer, allowing some of the texture to be used, from the bottom "canvas" layer. Those two layers were condensed into one (Drop). That new version was saved with a new name that incorporated the word texture in its title. Be sure to use the "Save As" command to retain the original painting.

Draw lines, young man, many lines, from memory or from nature; it is this way that you will become a good painter.
—JEAN-AUGUSTE-
    DOMINIQUE INGRES,
    spoken to Edgar Degas,
    quoted in *Ingres*, by
    Walter Pach (1939)

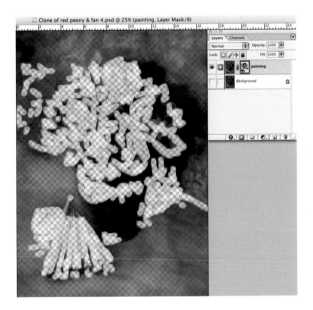

Figure 5-68
*Photoshop combination of
Painting and Painting with
Canvas*

Open both paintings in Photoshop (Painting and Painting with Canvas texture)

Use a layer mask to bring out the paint strokes and eliminate the canvas texture

The canvas texture version is the top layer with the Layer Mask

The next step was made in Photoshop. Both painted files were opened. One had a canvas texture and one was rich in impasto brush strokes. We want both things combined into one painting. Here is how I did it. I placed the canvas textured painting on top of the impasto painting (Background layer). Using a mask on the canvas painting layer, I stroked black, using the brush tool, in a light opacity, onto the mask. This reveals the impasto painting on the background layer.

Figure 5-69
Close-up view

Figure 5-69 illustrates the combination of the canvas texture and the thick impasto brush strokes in selected areas.

The completed painting in Figure 5-70 reveals a painting that uses canvas texture and brushwork texture in unison.

Figure 5-70—*"Memories of Toledo"*
Completed painting

Old Masters Inspiration

Figure 5-71
Original photo of fruit in a shoe box

Our next example began with the idea of making a still life painting similar in feel to an old Dutch composition made in the era of Rembrandt. I simply love the shape of pears and frequently photograph and draw them. I wanted a small collection of pears with a dark background and a reflective surface for them to rest on. I couldn't find anything that matched my criteria, so I improvised. I placed the pears in a shoe box and used window light for the digital photograph.

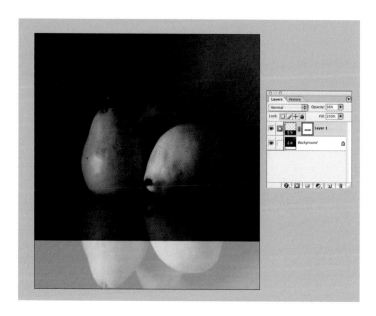

Figure 5-72
Reflection added

In Photoshop enlarge the canvas (Image—Canvas Size)
Copy lower portion of photo and flip it
Use a mask to join the two images exactly
In Photoshop I enlarged the canvas (Image—Canvas Size) and then copied the lower portion of the pears shown in Figure 5-72, placing it on a separate layer. I flipped the image to be a mirror image of the original pears. To make an exacting blend, a mask was used on the new layer.

Figure 5-73
Corrected photo is ready to go into Painter

The finished photo was ready to be transported into Painter for the actual painting process.

The secret of drawing and modeling resides in the contrasts and relationships of tone.
—PAUL CÉZANNE,
  to Emil Bernard, in *Paul Cézanne, Letters*, ed. by John Rewald (1984)

Figure 5-74
Van Gogh Cloner used

File—Clone
Use Van Gogh Cloner variant
In Painter, the photo was cloned, selected, and deleted (just as we have done on previous paintings). I used the Van Gogh Cloner all over the piece for the initial laydown of colors.

Figure 5-75
Oil Brush Cloner used

Use Oil Brush Cloner to achieve textural impasto effect and smooth the roughness of the Van Gogh Cloner
The next cloning tool that was used was the Oil Brush Cloner. This tool smoothed the color variations that resulted from the use of the Van Gogh Cloner. The Oil Brush Cloner gives an impasto brush stroke to the surface. You will notice visible texture in the quality of the brush stroke.

I never feel that it's a waste of time to make drawings. It is like being in communication with the object, with the place, which soaks up (as a sponge soaks up water) all the life that once existed there.
—ANDREW WYETH, from *Two Worlds of Andrew Wyeth*, Kuerners and Olsons, Metropolitan Museum of Art (1976)

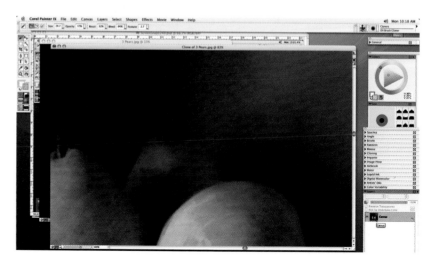

Figure 5-76
Detail

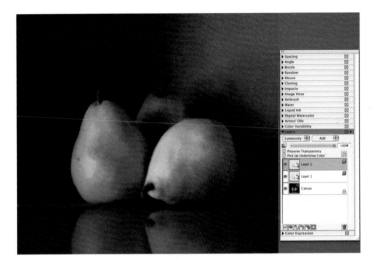

Figure 5-77
Glazing used to enhance the color

Add a new layer and use the Oil Paint—Glazing Round brush, at a low opacity, to enhance the color

Next, I wanted more color in the pears. Food photographers employ food stylists that often hand paint the blush on a peach or pear in preparation for photographing the fruit for an assignment. With Painter, you become the food stylist. The touch of your digital brush will add the desired color vibrancy and appeal. A new layer was added and additional color tones were painted on the new layer using the Oil—Glazing Round Brush, set at a low opacity. The new layer was copied and the blending mode was set to Luminosity for a bit more punch in the color.

Figure 5-78
Blending mode set to Screen

Copy the glazing layer and set the blending mode to Screen

As I continued working, I tried various blending modes and then decided to switch from Luminosity to Screen on my top layer. I highly recommend getting acquainted with the blending modes in both

Photoshop and Painter. The blending mode selected directs the software as to how the information on the selected layer will interact with the layer directly beneath it. Try a variety of different blending modes and see which one will best fulfill your intention as to how these layers will interact.

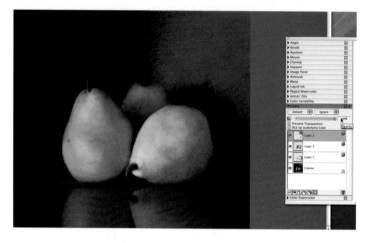

Figure 5-79
Glazing in background was added to new layer

An artist is a dreamer consenting to dream of the actual world.
—GEORGE SANTAYANA,
    The Life of Reason (1905)

Add a new layer
Add color with the Oil Paint—Glazing Round brush to the upper right-hand corner of the background
My next task was to warm the color of the background in the upper right-hand corner. A new layer was placed on top of the stack. With the Oil Paint—Glazing Round brush selected, that area was stroked with a warm brown tone.

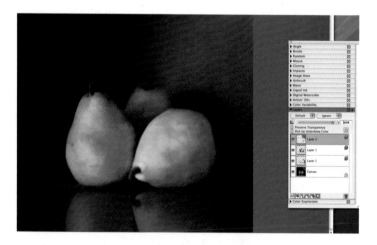

Figure 5-80
Opacity of the layer was reduced

Opacity of the glaze layer was reduced to 67%
By keeping the background on a separate layer, you can exercise more control on that specific portion of your painting, without disturbing the other brushwork (in this example, on the pears). The opacity was reduced on this overlay from 100% to 67%. This allowed for a better integration into the painting.

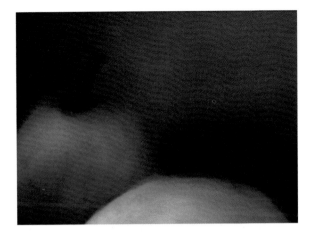

Figure 5-81
*Sfumato effect pioneered by
da Vinci*

In Figure 5-81 you can notice the soft blending of the color tones in the rear of the still life. The softening of those edges corresponds to what happens with a shallow depth of field in photography. In painting terms, it resembles a technique used by Leonardo da Vinci called sfumato. This effect gave the appearance of looking through a veil of smoke. da Vinci used this technique on his famous *"Mona Lisa,"* and other works.

Figure 5-82

Figures 5-82 and 5-83 illustrate our before and after on this Old World still life. I don't think many people would believe that it began in an empty sneakers box.

More still life paintings are included here. Figure 5-84 was made primarily with the Chalk Cloner.

Each year, when the peonies are in bloom, I put together at least one still life using these incredible blossoms. They have such large, showy blossoms. Figure 5-85 was made with the Chalk Cloner and the Oil Cloner. Notice the impasto texture of the Oil Brush Cloner's brush strokes.

Drawing is describing form and the importance of it is its veracity, not the finish.
—NED JACOB,
American Artist Magazine
(August 1975)

Figure 5-83—*"Dutch Still Life"*

Figure 5-84—*"Peonies and Lavender Still Life"*

Figure 5-85—*"Peonies Still Life"*

Figure 5-86
"Sledders"

Figure 5-86 was created for a commissioned Christmas card. Sledders are pictured in this piece. This piece was made primarily with the Chalk Cloner and the Oil Brush Cloner.

The Impressionist Cloner was the primary tool in the creation of Figure 5-87. The brush size was varied for larger or smaller strokes. It is one of my favorite pieces.

I occasionally take on a wedding assignment for clients who want a more artistic approach to their wedding photos. This painting (Figure 5-88) was made from a wedding that took place in Cape May, New Jersey, on the beach. This image used the Chalk Cloner and various watercolor cloners, including one that left telltale spots of water.

The concern of the artist is with the discrepancy between physical fact and psychic effect.
—JOSEF ALBERS,
    From *Interactions of Color* (1953)

Don't copy. Feel the forms. Feel how much it swings, how much it slants—these are big factors. The more factors you have, the simpler will be your work.
—THOMAS EAKINS,
    in *Thomas Eakins*, by Lloyd Goodrich (1987)

Figure 5-87—*"Sunday Riders"*

Sometimes you may find yourself struggling with an image and the software doesn't seem capable of giving you what you had imagined. This was the case with Figure 5-89. The whites that I desired did not seem pure enough in my digital painting. I tried painting and erasing, but I simply wasn't satisfied with the results. I printed the painting and looked at it with dismay. I was right. The whites simply were not white enough. I then took a real paintbrush and some opaque white watercolor paint and literally stroked real paint onto my print. As that was drying, I felt compelled to give a few touches to the details, with my real colored pencils. When the print was dry I scanned it back into the computer, and worked on it a little more, until I felt satisfied with this commission. The point to this story is that you have to use the tools that are appropriate to your task. Feel free to intermingle digital painting tools with real painting tools. You do not need to be a purist about the tools. It is the art that is important, not the tools that were used. Use what "feels" right. Follow your instincts.

Figure 5-88—*"Wedding Embrace, Cape May, NJ"*

Figure 5-89—*"President's House, McDaniel College"*

Photo Illustration

Photocopy-Inspired Painting

Figure 5-90
Original photograph of a "faux" priest character at a Renaissance Festival

The next example sprang from a conversation I had with an artist friend, Ann Curtis. Ann is a wonderful artist and is known throughout the United States for her work at Renaissance Festivals, making plaster body-cast sculptures. As most artists do, she dabbles in other mediums also. She showed me a few portraits that she had done with her colored pencils, working on black and white photocopies of photographs. They were lovely, but the poor quality of the photocopy paper was not going to be very long lived in archival terms. She was having such a good time with this process that I thought I could show her how she could achieve similar results digitally. The resulting prints would have a much higher archival standard. For this project I decided to use a digital photograph that I had taken at the local Renaissance Festival.

Figure 5-91
Photocopy version of the photograph

Desaturate the color photo
Copy the desaturated photo on a new layer
Use Color Dodge Blending Mode—combine those layers into a new layer
Duplicate the combined layer
Apply a curves adjustment to lighten the image
Duplicate the layer and apply the Filter—Photocopy it
Set the Photocopy layer to 78% opacity and set on the Multiply Blending Mode

My first task was to convert this color photograph to the "look" of a black and white photocopy. When I thought about what a photocopy looks like, I realized that lots of mid-tones and detail in highlights and shadows are lost. I wanted to replicate that effect, so that it would resemble a real photocopy. Here are the steps that I used. I desaturated the image, leaving a black and white rendition of the photograph. That layer was copied and the Color Dodge Blending Mode was applied to it. Those two layers were combined in another layer, and labeled Combination. By leaving the first two layers, I reserved my ability to go back into those layers, if need be, later. The Combination layer was duplicated and a curves adjustment was applied to it, lightening the image. That layer was duplicated and the Photocopy Filter was applied to it. This new layer was then set on the Multiply Blending Mode and reduced to 78%.

Choose only one
master—Nature.
—REMBRANDT,
  in *Rembrandt Drawings*,
  by Paul Nemo. trans. by
  David Macrae (c. 1975)

Figure 5-92
Hand-colored version

Save
Flatten and save this flattened version (under another name)
Using the flattened version, create a new layer
Set the blending mode on the new layer to Color Blending Mode
This is a good point in the process to save your work. I saved both a full layered version and a flattened one. The next step is the fun, artistic one. Create a new layer and set the blending mode on it to Color. This is your hand-coloring layer. I selected colors from the color palette and painted them onto this layer. You can be rather messy, loose, and imprecise in this step. Figure 5-92 shows the completed Photoshop piece. Figure 5-93 shows only the hand-painted layer set to Color Blending Mode.

Figure 5-93
Hand-colored layer only

Bring flattened colored version into Painter
File—Clone
Select all and delete
Use Chalk and Straight Cloner
Add a background using Artist Pastels and blend with Just Add Water

Mission accomplished! But, then I started thinking about what it might look like if that completed Photoshop portrait were used as the basis for a clone image in Painter. Figure 5-94 was made using the Chalk and Straight Cloner. The blue background was painted in with Artist Pastels and blended with Blender—Just Add Water.

Figure 5-94
Image cloned in Painter and a painted background was added

Figure 5-95
Painter version with solid background

One touch of nature makes the whole world kin.
—WILLIAM SHAKESPEARE,
Troilus and Cressida
(1601)

Figure 5-95 was made with the same tools. The difference was made at the beginning of the cloning process. When the portrait was cloned, and the clone was selected and deleted, the entire area was then filled with the tan color. This simulated a piece of tan charcoal paper. My little experiment yielded another way to make a photo-like illustration. In this case, it was a portrait, but this same process could be used on other subject matter.

Edges and Cloning

As a photographer, you know that some images "speak to you" immediately. Others take time to float to the surface of possibilities. The image shown in Figure 5-100 took a decade to be made. That long ago, with a long lens and from far away, I took a photograph of a Civil War re-enactor. I just liked how he was standing and waiting for someone. I did not ask permission or get a release from him. I never intended to use the image. The background was full of water coolers, ice chests, fellow soldiers, pick-up trucks, and more. It was simply awful. Looking through my slides years later, I stumbled onto the image of the soldier again. I decided to scan it into my computer and delete the objectionable background elements in Photoshop. Armed with that improved

Figure 5-96
"Doctored" original photo

"doctored" image (Figure 5-96), I returned to the site of the annual re-enactment, where I had taken the original image. Tens of thousands of re-enactors were present. How would I ever find this one man, so that I could give him his photograph and get him to sign a release form? It was a long shot at best. I showed the photo around in the re-enactors' camp. Unbelievably, fellow re-enactors recognized him and directed me to his unit. I found him, gave him his photo, and secured a release from him. He was a needle in a haystack indeed, but found.

Figure 5-97
Enlarged canvas and rubber stamped background

Duplicate the image
Use Filter—Stylize—Find Edges on the duplicate layer
Set the Find Edges layer to the Darken Blending Mode
Add a new layer and add more hand-coloring, painting with the brush tool and selecting the desired colors
Set the hand-colored layer to the Color Blending Mode
Enlarge the canvas (Image—Canvas Size)
Rubber stamp the image to expand the background
Select the rubber stamped area with a feathered lasso tool, and run a Gaussian Blur filter on it, to soften it

My first step in this photo illustration was to duplicate the layer. On the new layer I applied the Stylize—Find Edges Filter. The edges were not sharp in the original image (due to the use of a long lens with no tripod). Using the Find Edges filter provided more edge definition. The Find Edges layer was set to the Darken Blending Mode. This provided a black edge around the edges that had contrast. Another layer was added and some hand-coloring was applied to it using the Color Blending Mode. For the photo illustration I needed more ground around our re-enactor. I expanded the canvas and rubber stamped more ground in place. Those areas were selected and softened with the filter Gaussian Blur. I just wanted the color tones, no detail.

Figure 5-98
Painter Clone

Open flattened painting in Painter
File—Clone
Cloners used included Chalk Cloner, Van Gogh Cloner, and Oil Cloner
Add a new layer, set to the Gel blending mode, and paint in additional color tones

The image was saved and opened in Painter. The image was cloned with a variety of cloners, including the Chalk Cloner, Van Gogh Cloner, and Oil Cloner. I added additional layers and applied more color directly to the clone. In most instances, the blending mode was set to Gel.

A painting is a lie that tells the truth.
—PABLO PICASSO, in "Picasso Speaks," *The Arts* magazine (May 1923)

Figure 5-99
Layers are blended

Use Blenders to blend the new paint into the previous version
Various Blender brushes were used to combine the clone and the overlaying Gel layers.

Figure 5-100
Completed painting

The resulting illustration was achieved more than a decade after the original slide image was made. The background had been simply horrible and the image lacked sharpness. Despite those huge impediments, a pleasing image was made using the digital artistic tools of a modern era. Maybe we should go back through those old slide collections and find other candidates for revitalization using these techniques.

Painterly Edge Effects

One of the techniques that I love to incorporate into my digital artwork is the use of painterly edges. There are so many possibilities and so many brushes. We will explore a few here. Feel free to mix and match them as possible edge effects.

Figure 5-101
New layer filled with white and painted with the History Brush

Open photo in Photoshop
Add a new layer and fill it with white
Use the History Brush, with a rough brush type selected, to paint the photo onto the white layer

There are just tons of edge effects that are available to you. Some effects were discussed in Chapter 4. Edges are easily purchased in various third-party software packages. Many are really great. Let's look at how you can achieve painterly edge effects within Photoshop and Painter.

Figure 5-101 was created solely in Photoshop. A new layer was applied over the existing photograph and filled with white. The irregular stroke was made using the History Brush and the selection of scratchy wide brushes (located in the lower realms of the Brush selections).

The kind of photography I like to do, capturing the moment, is very much like that break in the clouds. In a flash, a wonderful picture seems to come out of nowhere.
—ELLIOTT ERWITT,
  Between the Sexes (1994)

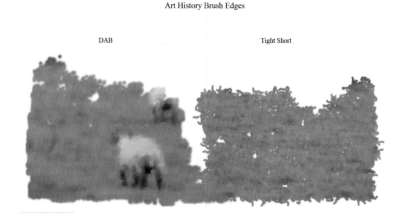

Figure 5-102
Art History Brush used

Experiment using the Art History Brush
In this example we used the Dab and Tight Short variations

The next example is two different brush stroke types found in the Art History Brush selections. The left-hand portion of the image used the Dab type of stroke. The right-hand portion of the image used the Tight Short stroke. Each brush type yields a different kind of mark.

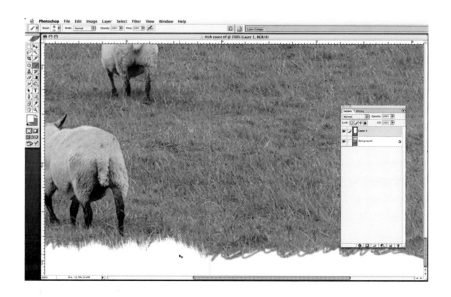

Figure 5-103
Eraser as a paint tool

Try using the brush tool to create a border effect

Don't rule out using the eraser or some white paint, if your background color is white. In Figure 5-103, the scratchy-looking brush was filled with white and stroked onto the painting. Brush marks were made from the border into the image, mimicking the grass directionality in the photograph.

Figure 5-104
The Rough Pastels filter was the dominant effect on this piece

Duplicate the image and apply the Rough Pastels filter
Stroke white around the border

Figure 5-104 illustrates the duplication of the image and the use of the Rough Pastels filter on this duplicate layer. White was stroked onto the image around the edges.

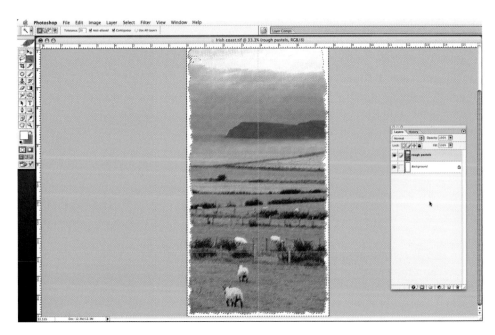

Figure 5-105
Beginning of edge effect

Fill the original photo layer with white
Use the Magic Wand tool to select the white edge of the top layer—
then delete it
The bottom layer (the original image) was filled with white. The Magic Wand tool was used to select the white border area on the top layer. This selection area was deleted. There appears to be no change. But wait . . . there is more.

It, therefore, should be possible for even the photographer—just as for the creative poet or painter—to use the object as a stepping stone to a realm of meaning completely beyond itself.
—CLARENCE JOHN
  LAUGHLIN,
  to Daniel Masclet
  (October 19, 1953)

Figure 5-106
Edge effect develops

Chose a shadow from the Layer Style effects
A torn edge effect can be achieved now by using Layer Style effects. I chose a shadow to be cast from the irregularly edged top layer. The shadow falls onto the white layer beneath. Ta-da! The settings used were:

Blend Mode: Multiply
Opacity: 49%
Angle: 47 degrees
Distance: 8
Spread: 27
Size: 16
Noise: 23

Figure 5-107 shows this simple edge effect. It is a particularly good edge for a photo illustration in a magazine or newsletter.

The effect shown in Figure 5-108, on colored paper, was created in Painter.

Figure 5-107
Completed edge effect

Figure 5-108
Painter Clone with a brown-tone paper

Open photo in Painter
File—Clone
Select all and fill with a color (a brick-red type of brown was used in our example)
Edge effects in Painter can vary widely as well. The beginning premise, once again, is the clone. We will look at a few examples. In Figure 5-108 the photograph of the Irish coastline and sheep has been cloned. The clone was selected and deleted. The space was filled with a shade of brown. The view on the right indicates the transparency of that brown layer, if the tracing paper feature is turned on.

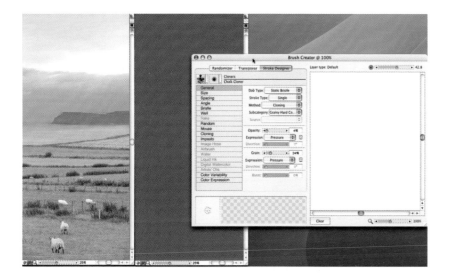

Figure 5-109
Use of Brush Creator

Window—Brush Creator
Using the Brush Creator (located in the Window options), a rough, bristle brush was created. The modifying factors were:

Dab Type: Static Bristle
Stroke type: Single
Method: Cloning
Subcategory: Grainy Hard Cover

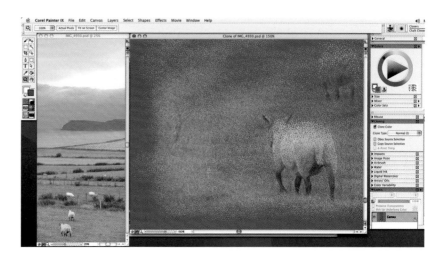

Figure 5-110
Chalk Cloner used

We must never forget that art is not a form of propaganda, it is a form of truth.
—John F. Kennedy, from an address at Amherst College, October 26, 1963

Use Chalk Cloner brush
The Chalk Cloner was the brush selected and applied onto the brown, bumpy paper. Notice the fragmentary way the color is deposited on the higher raised surfaces of the paper. This created an uneven edge effect. The look is very much like using real chalks on rough pastel paper. Additional applications of chalk over the area will yield a more solid laydown of color.

Figure 5-111
Chalk Cloner used on white paper with a large brush

I recommend experimenting with other cloner brush types. Figure 5-111 used the Chalk Cloner. Figure 5-112 used the Van Gogh Cloner. The Impressionist Cloner also gives an interesting small, rice-like, dab of paint. Experiment with many, and see what you might like.

Figure 5-112
Van Gogh Cloner used

Figure 5-113
Watercolor Run Cloner used along the edges

I especially like to use the Watercolor Run Cloner along edges. This brush is just fascinating. You can brush an area and then watch the color run down, depositing more color on the outside edge of where the color comes to rest. It is so wonderful at simulating gravity at work with a real water medium. Using this brush creates a Watercolor Layer that must be dried or dropped down on the layer beneath, before other non-wet brushes can be used.

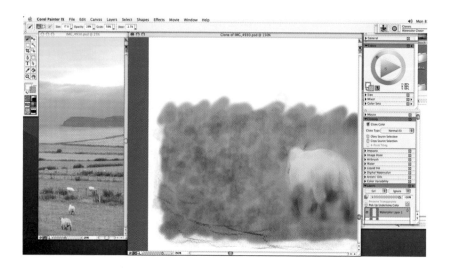

Figure 5-114
Watercolor Cloner adds a textural feel

There are always two people in every picture: the photographer and the viewer.
—Ansel Adams, interview, *Playboy* magazine (May 1983)

A cousin to the Watercolor Run Cloner is the Watercolor Cloner. This brush applies various random sizes of little drops of paint onto the canvas. They also spread and settle out. Notice the textural effect they gave in our example.

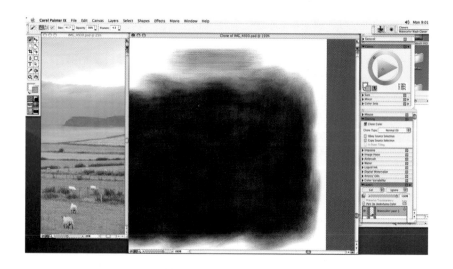

Figure 5-115
Watercolor Wash Cloner

I don't often use the Watercolor Wash Cloner, as the color is very dark when applied, even with a light opacity.

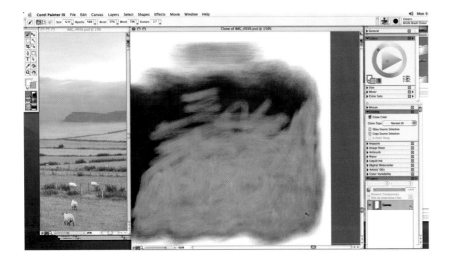

Figure 5-116
Bristle Brush Cloner used over the Watercolor Wash Cloner

One way to use the Watercolor Wash Cloner, for its edge possibilities, is to cover the area, except the extreme outside edges, with another cloner. In this example I used the Bristle Brush Cloner. That double cloner approach can yield some watercolor effect on the edges without darkening the interior of the clone.

Figure 5-117
Woodcut Filter effect

Duplicate the layer
On the duplicate layer apply Effects—Surface Control—Woodcut
Paint outside edges with Chalk—Dull Grainy Chalk
A completely different kind of look is seen in Figure 5-117. In this example I have duplicated the image and applied Effects—Surface Control—Woodcut. This look resembles a relief print carved from wood or linoleum blocks. After applying the woodcut look, the outside edge was painted with Chalk—Dull Grainy Chalk. The color of the chalk was selected from the colors used in the woodcut.

Figure 5-118
Oil Brush Cloner edge

Art is an extension of
language—an expression
of sensations too subtle
for words.
—ROBERT HENRI,
   The Art Spirit (1923)

The final edge that we will explore in this chapter is the Oil Brush Cloner. This effect will yield a thick, streaky, impasto feel to the edge.

Figure 5-119
Completed oil effect painting

Painting for the Artistically Challenged

This technique is foolproof and easy. If you feel that your artistic "skills" are a little underdeveloped, this technique is for you. Start, again, with a photo that you would like to convert into a painting. Open that image in Painter.

Figure 5-120
Original photo taken in Rome

Open photo in Painter
Effects—Surface Control—Sketch
The next step is an outlining or sketch effect. Simply go to Effects—Surface Control—Sketch. Use the dialogue box that appears, and use the sliders to achieve your desired result. You can monitor the effect in the Preview box.

Painting is for me but another word for feeling.
—John Constable, lecture, *Discourses on Art* (1836)

Figure 5-121
Sketch Effect dialogue box

When making the decisions about the quality of the sketch, keep in mind that you probably want a crisp outline without a lot of extra, stray marks throughout the picture. Experiment with the sliders until you achieve an effect that is pleasing to your eye.

Figure 5-122
Sketch Effect combined with photo, using Gel blending mode

Copy the Sketch effect
Paste it into a new layer
Return to the original photo
Set the sketch layer (on top) to the Gel blending mode
Copy the Sketch effect and paste it into a new layer. Go backward in your "undos" until you return to the original photo. Now you have both images, as separate layers. Set the sketch layer (which is on top of the original photo) to the Gel blending mode. This will combine these layers together well without the interference of a white background on your sketch layer.

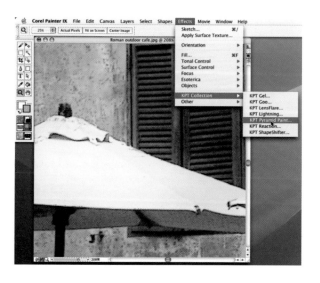

Figure 5-123
Navigating to the KPT paint effect

On the photo layer use Effects—KPT Collections—KPT Pyramid Paint

The next step creates the painting for you. Included in painter are some KPT filters. We will use one now. Go to Effects—KPT Collections—KPT Pyramid Paint. That will bring up a new dialogue box that is unique to the KPT filters and effects.

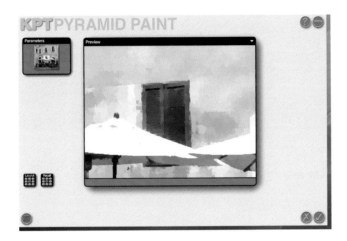

Figure 5-124
KPT Pyramid Paint dialogue box

The KPT Pyramid Paint dialogue box gives you a preview of effects.

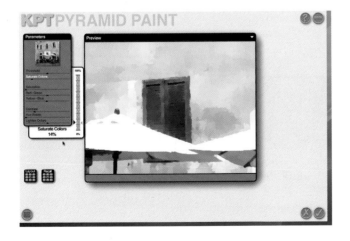

Figure 5-125
Using the sliders to modify the saturation

Use sliders to modify the effect

Use the sliders within the box, if you want to make any changes. In my example, I increased the saturation of the color.

Imagination rules the world.
—Napoleon Bonaparte,
  Epigrams (c. 1810)

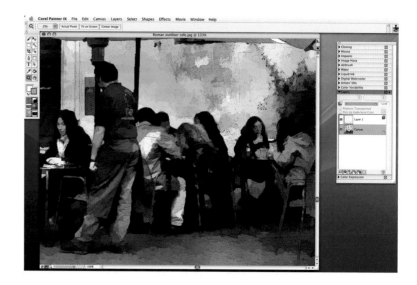

Figure 5-126
Combining the Sketch with the Painting layer

For some people, this combination of the KPT Painting layer and the Sketch layer may be sufficient. But I'm going to suggest that you take this up to a higher level by one more simple step that will allow you to "brush" the painting.

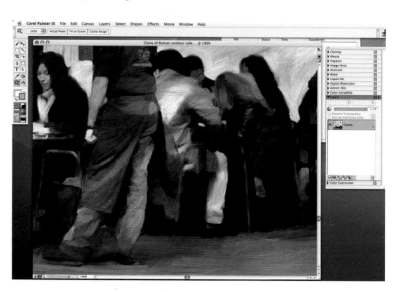

Figure 5-127
Using the Oil Cloner, to give a three-dimensional brush stroke

Clone the completed and flattened painting
Use the Oil Brush Cloner for a textural, impasto feel
Clone the completed painting. Now, on the cloned image, use the Oil Brush Cloner to "brush" the painting. Simply stroke over the entire painting, section by section, creating an active textural feel to the painting. Make your brush strokes go in the direction that seems appropriate for the object. In our example, a small brush was stroked down the legs of the chairs and across the shutters. A larger brush was used for the walls. A small brush with a light opacity worked on the faces of the patrons of the outdoor café. Too much texture on the faces could be too distracting.

Figure 5-128
Brush strokes applied to the painting

This method of painting from a photo is very easy for beginners. The color decisions on the painting were automatically made by the KPT Pyramid Paint filter. The painting was then individualized, by the artist, with the technique of applying an Oil Brush Cloner brush stroke throughout the entire painting. An inkjet canvas would be an ideal printing surface for this type of painting.

Explore the realm of possibilities available in Painter or Photoshop or a combination of both programs. Your job, as the artist, is to find the brush or mark that works best for the feel and look that you have in mind for your artwork.

This chapter is but a little taste of the art tools available in Painter. I have concentrated on the cloning tools, since they are the tools most likely to be used by a photographer. You are not restricted to those tools and should explore other tools in Painter and the combination of those tools with cloning tools. The possibilities are virtually without end.

Figure 5-129—*"Peonies and da Vinci Bust"*

6

Assembling a Collage in Photoshop

Collages are beautiful. They have the ability to combine many images and textures in a unique manner. They can have the delicacy of a butterfly's wing or the graphic nature of a wanted poster. The range is huge. We will explore various methods of assembling this type of artwork.

Collages combine a variety of images into one piece. They can combine just a couple of layers or a hundred. Each layer can be handled separately. Layers can overlap previous layers and, with transparency, reveal layers underneath. There are so many options.

The first task is to gather imagery for a collage. What is your theme? Do you want to assemble family images for a special occasion or person? A collage portraying the life of one person or their family

Figure 6-1

heritage can be interesting. A collage depicting a vacation can be a variation to the traditional album. A collage of a wedding day is a splendid way to share many photos in a work of art that can be framed and displayed.

Be sure to scan images with enough information to allow you to use them large or small, as the assembly process begins. Be open with your original concept and allow the process to dictate spacing and scale decisions. Be sure to determine, at the beginning, the ultimate size of the printed piece. Will it be printed as a 12 × 16-inch piece or something smaller or larger? For something that has a good photographic quality, plan on using a resolution of 300–360 dpi.

Select a unifying element to pull the piece together. It can be something as simple as a photo of clouds or water. A bit of texture often works well. A crumbled scrap of fabric, a rusted piece of metal, or a faded piece of wallpaper—all can be candidates for the task of uniting the entire design.

How do you want to construct this collage? Some concepts will work well with a grid structure. Guidelines can be particularly helpful in lining up these collages, since they often use many layers. Other collages will benefit from a nonlinear approach that relies on overlapping layers with transparency. The concept will dictate the best approach.

Art is an outsider, a gypsy over the face of the earth.
—ROBERT HENRI,
The Art Spirit (1923)

Photoshop is the ideal tool for making collages. In the past, collages were constructed by cutting and pasting images and objects together. With Photoshop, each element can reside on its own layer. That allows you maximum flexibility in arranging the various elements into the best composition.

Too many layers? It is easy to be overwhelmed by the sheer number of layers when working on a collage. To preserve your sanity, make a habit of naming each layer. Finding a tiny picture in a sea of layers takes lots of time. Named layers are easier to locate. If you are indeed drowning in too many layers, think about using Layer Sets to group them.

Photographs are not the only element that can be used in collages. Use your scanner as a camera and introduce other elements into your work. Try scanning a seashell, a moth wing, a leaf, a rusted key, a crumbled piece of tissue paper, etc. Scanned elements often work well as the textural layer that can unify the design. I recommend visiting your local antique mall or flea markets. Interesting old postcards, magazines, fabric, lace, and more can be collected for pennies. Be sure to protect the glass of your scanner. If the object could scratch the surface of the glass, use a piece of clear acetate between the glass and your object.

Simple Collages

Figure 6-2
Two images to combine

A good way to begin experimenting with collaging is to find two simple images that you want to combine. Our example works with different types of animals. A trip to the zoo can yield a ton of animal images. Nature is so endlessly fascinating in the variety of animal possibilities (feathers, scales, fur, etc.). Our first example comes from photos taken in Australia, where they seem to have a monopoly on animals that appear to be put together from spare parts. Our example will just keep going on that theme of really different creatures. A lizard and an emu were both photographed in profile. They appear to be somewhat compatible.

Figure 6-3

Resize objects to the correct proportion
Add canvas, if needed

The first step was to resize the emu head to be the right scale for our lizard and its background. We placed the emu head on a new layer above the lizard and used Edit—Free Transform to scale the emu head smaller. Be sure to hold down on the shift key to ensure correct proportionality. The lizard photo did not have enough headroom for the new hairdo. The canvas was extended on the lizard photo, and the rubber stamp tool was applied to the lizard layer to add on more background. Parts of the folds of skin under the lizard's mouth were rubber stamped away to allow for a smoother transition into the emu beak.

Figure 6-4
Combination creature

Use a layer mask to transition one layer into another

The final, but the most important, step was to use a layer mask to transition the emu head into the scaly lizard body. A layer mask was added (Layer—Add Layer Mask) and the mask was painted with a paintbrush loaded with black. Anywhere on the mask that is painted with black will allow the image below to show through. If you make a mistake, you can simply paint with white to restore the top layer. Subtlety is important. Be sure to vary the size of the brush and its opacity to whatever the task at hand requires. Your work is done on the mask and not on the image itself, so no harm can come to your photos. They remain intact.

Figure 6-5
Barnyard possibilities

Of course, you can go wild with this idea and start working with barnyard animals too.

Figure 6-6
Does it croak or cock-a-doodle-doo?

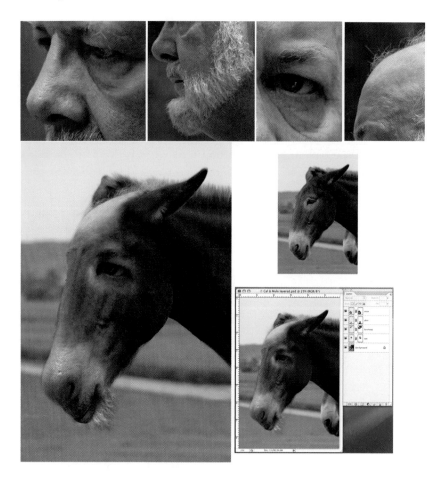

Figure 6-7
Mule-headed man?

There is no end to the trouble you can get into with this collaging technique. What if you combined an animal head with human parts? There are lots of slang animal and human combinations in our language. If someone is stubborn, they are mule-headed or bull-headed. You can have fun with this one.

Figure 6-8
A teacup and a whale to combine

The rules of nature do not apply to you as you collage. You can make elements of your collage as big as an elephant or as small as a flea. They do not have to be the size that would seem natural. The following example plays with the idea of sizing. My morning cup of tea became the playground for an exercise in scale. My first impulse was to put a breeching whale into the cup.

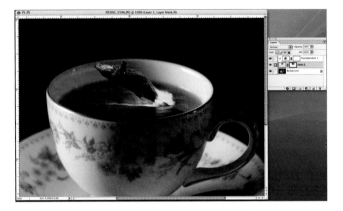

Figure 6-9
Whale breeching a teacup, showing layers

Use Free Transform to scale down a component part
The whale was scaled down using Free Transform. A layer mask worked the seawater into the tea. To correct the color, a clipping mask was used on a Hue and Saturation Layer Adjustment. The hue slider was moved to warmer tones.

Figure 6-10
Completed collage

The completed image is nonsensical and purely for fun; however, this approach is often used in advertising to grab our attention.

I love red so much that I almost want to paint everything red.
—Alexander Calder, in *The Artist's Voice*, by Katherine Kuh (1960)

Figure 6-11
Possible subjects to put in my teacup

Many photographers sit down with their contact sheets and think of various combinations and possibilities for combining images. I rely on my digital contact sheets and my file browser to explore those artistic possibilities. Using the teacup as the background, I found four more possible images for a simple collage that explores the ridiculous with the element of scale.

Figure 6-12

Figure 6-13

Figure 6-14

Figure 6-15

Figure 6-16
Fish and tea anyone?

Figure 6-12 explores the idea of a Hawaiian surfer in the cup. Figure 6-13 uses an aquatic clown (actually I think it was an otter). Figure 6-15 uses a small boat. The boat version was enhanced by the inclusion of a reflection from the boat. Figure 6-16 employs a fish on ice at a famous Seattle fish market. Notice that the body of the fish continues down into the tea. This transparency was achieved with the use of a layer mask. This is a fun exercise. Pick a photo, like my teacup, that can be the background, and look through your files for wacky or provocative combinations.

We become what we contemplate.
—Plato,
    Ion (350 B.C.)

Figure 6-17
"Bonfire of the Vanities" collage

In Figure 6-17, the collage was very simple to execute. I had been photographing the fire in our fireplace, on a snowy winter afternoon. The pattern that the fire made was really fascinating. I literally took over a hundred images that day, for later use. I started thinking about the Bonfire of the Vanities in Florence, Italy. Many painters, like Botticelli, fell under the spell of the monk, Savonarola. Their paintings, which were seen as vanities, were burned in the great Piazza della Signoria, in 1497. Later, Savonarola would be tortured and burned in that same plaza, on May 23, 1498. One can only speculate on the fabulous art that was lost to this political and religious movement.

One of the painters that burned his secular paintings was Lorenzo di Credi. I remembered that I had photographed a surviving nude, painted by him, in the Uffizi, when photography was still allowed in Florence. The painting of Venus depicts her in what is referred to as the "modest Venus" pose. Her hands are covering herself, with the help of a sheer piece of fabric. Yes, she was failing miserably at being modest. But if she were wearing a coat, no one would identify her as Venus, Goddess of Love. Remember that most people were illiterate. Stories, myths, and biblical and historic events were told through a recognized symbolic iconography in paintings.

Voilà! A collage was born. My photo of the painting was dark (due to the inability to use a tripod in the museum) and purposely taken at an angle to the painting, for a bit of distortion. I simply resized the painting image to fit with a photo of my winter afternoon fire, and combined the two using the Multiply blending mode and a little bit of a layer mask, to soften the edges. That was an easily constructed collage. Nothing else was necessary. If you know the history of that period, it will make sense to you, and is again a piece of art telling a story. If not, it is still an engaging image.

Collage with Lighting Effect

Figure 6-18
Collage component parts

The next collage began with a wonderful tile floor, photographed in Spain. The tiled corner was like a stage, calling out for actors to enter. Instead of a ceiling, a dramatic sky was selected and an antique songbook was selected for a foreground element. The component that would tie the images together was a bird (Figure 6-18).

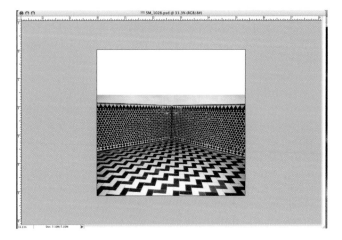

Figure 6-19
Canvas enlarged at the top

Enlarge the canvas: Edit—Canvas Size

The tiled corner was too short. The canvas needed to be enlarged. The background color was white. The canvas was extended visually, by using the crop tool. The entire image was selected and the top anchor point of the crop tool was pulled up, beyond the image. Pull it as far as you would like to enlarge your canvas. With this method you can "eyeball" the amount of enlargement you want, instead of measuring it, as you do with Edit—Canvas Size. Press Return to complete the crop. This is a quick way to extend your canvas. If you want white canvas, be sure that your background color is white.

What lives on in a painting is the personality of the painter.
—Edward Hopper, in *Edward Hopper*, by Lloyd Goodrich (1978)

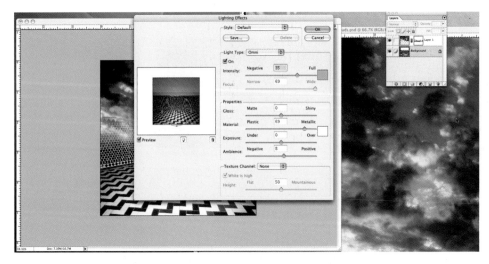

Figure 6-20
Lighting effect added

Sky area was added on another layer and a layer mask was used to integrate the sky into the floor area
Filter—Render—Lighting Effects—Omni: Omnidirectional light, with a golden color, was used for the lighting effect
The sky area was placed in the collage as another layer and a layer mask was used to blend the image into the tiled corner photo. The match was good but the color was off and the sky presented a definite source of light that did not match the floor. This was corrected by using Filter—Render—Lighting Effects. An omnidirectional light was selected and shaped by pulling on the edges of the preview image. The color of the light was changed from white to a soft golden color, to match tones in the sky.

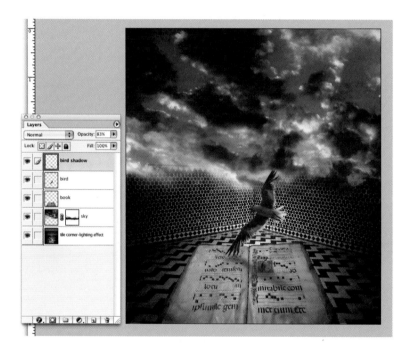

Figure 6-21

Antique songbook was added with Transform—Distort
Bird was added and color corrected with Image—Adjustments—Color Balance
A bird shadow was painted onto a separate layer
Next, the book was placed into the foreground and shaped a bit, to fit the perspective, by using Transform—Distort. All that was needed now was the bird photo to connect the sky and the book visually. The coloring of the bird was corrected, using Image—Adjustments—Color Balance, before bringing it into the collage. Notice that the bird photo that was selected was lit from behind. If the bird were really flying into this space, as depicted, it would definitely be casting a shadow. A bird shadow was needed. A new layer was created. Using a dark gray, at a low opacity setting, the shadow was painted onto the new layer. By confining the shadow to a separate layer, it can be altered and adjusted without harming the rest of the collage.

I retain in the depth of my heart the memory of all my works.
—Eugene Delacroix, *The Journals of Eugene Delacroix*, trans. by Walter Pach (1937)

Figure 6-22—*"Grace Descends"*
Completed collage

Suspend True Scale

Figure 6-23
Component parts for a collage

It is fun to push the edges of reality with collages. Suspend what is, and look for what could be. The egg has always been a symbol of birth and life potential. It is also a beautiful shape. Couple the egg with a door or portal, and add in a little girl. And then set that combination in a beautiful rural landscape. The landscape was created as a panorama from ten photos, taken in sequence (see Chapter 8).

A cast shadow was added for realistic effect
Finishing touches on this collage included an additional layer for the shadow cast by the egg. An elliptical shape with a feather of 15 was selected and filled with a 30% opacity of dark gray. Shadows were added behind the little girl. Her dress was colored a pale blue and her skin was given some flesh tones. These colors were on a separate layer with the blending mode set to Color.

Let the poses of the people and the parts of their bodies be so disposed that they display the intent of their minds.
—Leonardo da Vinci,
Treatise on Painting
(1651)

Figure 6-24
Completed panorama collage

Themed Collages

Family photos are a wonderful source for meaningful collages of family members. The collage in Figure 6-25 relied on the scan of a family quilt to be the textural element that pulled the separate pieces together. A double meaning existed with thoughts about the fabric of a family. Even Civil War muster roll records from the War Department, at the National Archives, were used to add meaningful text to the imagery. The migration of this family west was a direct result of their Quaker ancestor serving in the war and then moving his young family to Missouri. The collage tells the history of this family in a unique way.

Likewise, this technique could be employed on all types of family collages: the birth of a baby, a graduation, a marriage, or an anniversary. Pull those old photos out of the shoeboxes and the attic and see what you might creatively produce.

Figure 6-25
"Family Collage" uses a quilt as the unifying design element

Suspend Reality

Figure 6-26
Venetian gondolier

The next collage started with a photo taken in Venice of a gondolier (Figure 6-26) and a photo taken in Seville, Spain (Figure 6-27) of a grand building. That gorgeous brick path was just calling for something to be progressing toward the building. The choice of the gondolier did obscure the brick path, but opened up other imagery possibilities.

Figure 6-28 shows the selection taken from the gondolier shot and imported as a new layer into the building background. It became apparent that more water needed to be created.

I want to make of Impressionism something solid and lasting like the art in the museums.
—PAUL CÉZANNE,
  Paul Cézanne, Letters, ed.
  by John Rewald (1984)

Figure 6-27
Spanish walk and building

Figure 6-28
Combining gondolier and background

Figure 6-29
*Rubber stamped water
expanded the water around
the hedge*

Rubber stamp tool was used to "flood" the walkway
With the use of the rubber stamp tool, water was cloned to expand out
and fill the area that needed to be flooded. Water flowed between the
hedges and up to the doorway, where an old man dressed in black,
holding a newspaper under his arm, was waiting.

Figure 6-30
The waiting man's lower legs were submerged in the water, using transparency

For realism's sake, the man's sweater was lightened to separate it from the dark background, using the Dodge Tool
The water was made to be transparent on the man's legs, using a layer mask
A slight reflection of the building was added, by copying and flipping it 180 degrees
Hedge shadows were added for a realistic effect
What could be done to make this scenario more believable? Although the waiting man was a very small element in the building image, his presence created a sense of waiting for the gondola. The photo of the building was a grab shot, taken as I was touring Seville. I couldn't ask the gentleman to change his sweater, because it blended into my background, now could I? The dodge tool, which I seldom use, was great for lightening his sweater, separating him from his surroundings. I wanted him to be standing in the water, so a layer mask was used for transparency through the water. Another touch of realism was added with the reflection of the building into the water. The building was copied and flipped horizontally. Only a faint reflection was allowed to show, by using a layer mask. The hedges along the path would also create a shadow and reflection. That was added on an additional layer and painted in. Tiny little details were added for realism, including painting with white, at a very low opacity, around the man's boots and doorway. This small touch made the surface of the water surrounding him more realistic.

Figure 6-31
Close-up of details added

The sky was very blank and overcast on the day that the building was photographed. More drama was needed. A new sky was found on another image. It was imported over into the collage. The sky would come with a bit of reflection in the water. The new sky was duplicated and flipped horizontally and merged into the collage lightly, using a layer mask. It just added a little of the blue from the sky above.

Figure 6-32—*"Stray Gondola"
Completed collage in color*

The completed collage was interesting in color (Figure 6-32), but what would it look like in black and white?

Figure 6-33
*Completed collage in black
and white*

I rarely start anything that
isn't pretty clear to me
before I start. I know what
I'm going to do before
I begin and if there's
nothing in my head, I do
nothing.
—Georgia O'Keeffe,
   in *Portrait of an Artist:
   A Biography*, by Laurie
   Lisle (1980)

The whole collage was saved and then flattened. The flattened image
was desaturated to achieve our monotone version.

Pile on the Layers

Figure 6-34 is a more complex collage that evolved out of another
collage (Figure 6-35).

Figure 6-34—*"Holy City"*
A complex collage created from a previous collage

Figure 6-35
Component pieces for initial collage

Figure 6-36
Pearl Harbor failed collage— later used for texture

-Gray added 85% Overlay
-Hydrangea 30% Normal
-Rose 50% Luminosity
-Rose 50% Luminosity
-Echinachea 42% Luminosity
-Echinachea 21% Luminosity
-Iris 52% Luminosity
-Oil on water 51% Difference
-Coffee Stained Paper

The eye of imagination is dark and yet it fills with light, both from within and from without.
—ALEXANDER ELIOT,
  Sight and Insight (1959)

Sometimes you will make a collage that is simply unsatisfactory to your tastes. That is the case with Figure 6-36, which was created from the components shown in Figure 6-35. Those components included coffee-stained paper, flowers, and a blue-toned photo taken of an oil slick floating above the sunken ship at Pearl Harbor, Hawaii. The oil slick image was converted to pink tones using Photoshop's Hue Adjustment (found under Image—Adjustments—Hue/Saturation). Despite various attempts at different versions of this collage, it was an artistic failure. Despite that, it was not discarded. I suspected that the texture that it held might be useful later. And it was!

Figure 6-37
*Spanish Cathedral dome—
The inspiration for this
collage*

The dome of a Spanish cathedral was the starting point for the collage shown in Figure 6-37.

Figure 6-38
*Failed Pearl Harbor collage
combined with Spanish dome*

The dome was combined with an earlier collage made with flowers and a piece of paper containing coffee stains (see Figure 6-38). The pieces were combined using the Difference blending mode, set at 57% opacity, with the collage layer on top of the dome (Figure 6-36).

What lies behind us and what lies before us are small compared to what lies within us.
—RALPH WALDO
EMERSON,
*Essays: First Series—
Intellect* (1841)

Figure 6-39
Additional components to be added

The combined image seemed to call out for more imagery that was related to Europe and religion: additional photos (Figure 6-39) of Grenada in the fog, a lion from St. Mark's in Venice, a mosaic from St. Marks, and a statue on the face of the Cathedral in Toledo, Spain. It was a hodge-podge of origins, but I thought it might work.

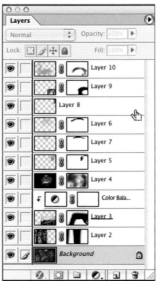

-Gold color 100% Color

-Fresco 38% Hard Light

-Grey color 61% Normal

-Gold color 55% Normal

-Gold color 97% Normal

-Lion 85% Difference

-Village segment 100% Normal

-Adjustment Layer - Color Balance

-Village 100% Overlay

-Statue 100% Hard Light

-Background Textural Collage

Figure 6-40
Layer structure of the combined collage

The collage has been dissected for you in Figure 6-40, layer by layer. Each layer is further elaborated on with the opacity it was set to and the blending mode that was used on it. Almost all the layers used a layer mask for blending precisely into the entire collage. Notice that a golden glow was added coming from the top of the dome and on the village below. The golden color helps tie the entire collage together and helps emphasize the central focal point.

The forms of a model, be they a tree or a man, are only a dictionary to which the artist goes in order to reinforce his fugitive impressions, or rather to find a sort of confirmation of them. Before nature itself, it is our imagination which makes the picture.
—CHARLES BAUDELAIRE, *Epigrams* (1860)

Shadow Power

Figure 6-41
Component pieces for wood nymph collage

Our next example began with a photo I had taken for a fashion shoot, many years ago. The model's eyes and expression had always made the photo a favorite of mine. In the original image the model was standing beside a Grecian column. I decided to turn the column into a tree and go with the feel of a wood nymph in this collage.

Figure 6-42
Collage begins

We do not see things as they are, we see things as we are.
—The Talmud

I first began by putting the model's eye into a leaf lying on a coral walk. The result was okay, but not really exciting. The next thought was to put the leaf and eye combination back into the face. That started to work better visually, and the concept became that of a wood nymph or the goddess Flora. Additional leaves were used to clothe the model. The column was replaced by a tree trunk. The other eye was festooned with flower petals and a background was imported into the composition. Notice the cast shadow from the leaf onto the face. It is a separate layer, with the color gray painted on. Shadows are the powerful component that unites this piece and creates the realistic effect.

Figure 6-43
Shadow layers turned off

He is nothing but an eye.
—Paul Cézanne,
 writing of Claude
 Monet, *Paul Cézanne,
 Letters*, ed. by John
 Rewald (1984)

This collage relies on separate layers of shadows that are painted into the piece with a low opacity of dark gray. Figure 6-43 illustrates the collage with the shadow layers turned off. It resembles pieces that were cut from magazines and glued in place.

Figure 6-44

Figure 6-44 shows the collage with the impact that shadows bring to the realistic rendering of this collage. Shadows create a modeling of light and form that was needed for a uniform, cohesive, and realistic rendering. There is a tremendous difference in the total effect.

The last step was to pull the saturation down, for a more subtle effect.

Figure 6-46 is part of a series of images that revolve around the concept of Venus. Component parts include a nautilus shell, patterned rocks, a statue, and a photo of a nude torso.

Beauty is the natural product of good order.
—FABER BIRREN,
    Principles of Color (1969)

Figure 6-45
Final collage

Figure 6-46
Nautilus Venus collage

Figure 6-47
Butterfly/woman collage

Figure 6-47 is a very simple collage combining a model (photographed at dawn) with the wings of a butterfly. Cast your restrictions to the wind. Scale in real life is not important when you are putting a collage together. Stretch your imagination!

Gridded Collages

Gridded collages in Photoshop involve a structured grid and careful placement and sizing of design elements. Decide on the output size of the final printed piece of art. For our example, we will use the 13 × 19-inch (Super B) size of paper that can be printed on many midrange printers. The size of the final piece will dictate how large the file size needs to be on each element of the collage. This type of collage does not rely on a textural layer that provides cohesion to the design. Instead, the very structure of this type of collage fits together like a jigsaw puzzle.

At the very beginning of this project, establish the size of the borders. On this project I wanted a printed area of 12 × 16 inches. That size is a standard frame size. The choice of a standard frame size can be important when the piece is finally framed. Odd sizes will require custom-made frames. Standard frame sizes are easy to work with and will ultimately prove to be more economical. Nonprintable grid lines can be brought onto the canvas with the move tool. Simply pull a grid line from the ruler area onto the canvas. To dispose of a grid, just grab it with the move tool and pull off the canvas onto the ruler area. Another way to lay down a grid is to use the automatic grid supplied by Photoshop (View—Show—Grid). It is accurate and easy.

The way to perfection is through a series of disgusts.
—WALTER PATER,
The Renaissance (1873)

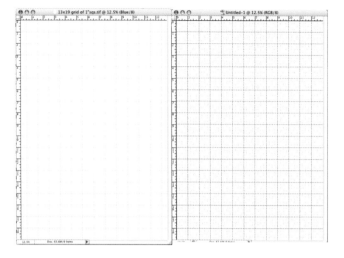

Figure 6-48
*Grid to use as the "bones"
on which to hang the images*

In this next example of a wedding collage, a centrally located large photograph will be the focal point. It will be edged with other photos from the wedding day. Additional grids were laid down, being careful to line them up with the ruler marks. If you are placing the grid system yourself, be certain that the grid lines are accurately placed. I usually enlarge my viewing area, to be sure that the grid, which I will use as my underlying armature, is not placed slightly off center to a ruler mark. You can only be accurate with this underlying grid if you carefully go over the grid placement in a greatly enlarged view. The accuracy of this step will pay off in the future, as you place your images into the grid structure. Again, you may choose to use the built-in grid system in Photoshop (pictured on the right in Figure 6-48) using View—Show—Grid.

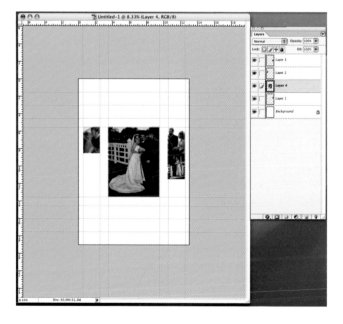

Figure 6-49
Beginning the layout

Place your focal point image first

Select more photos than you will really use. Be sure to have both vertical and horizontal images to select from. Place the large focal point image first and then work around it, adding images, as you progress.

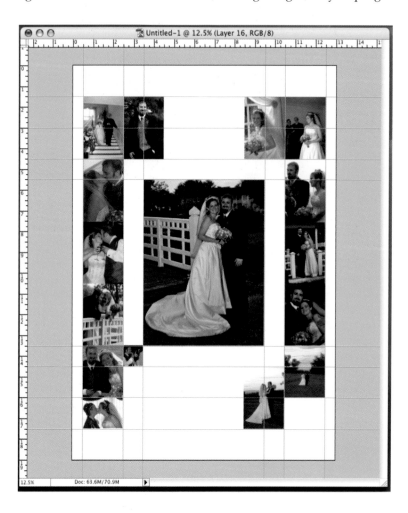

Figure 6-50
Add images into the collage

Add photos, using Edit—Free Transform to resize (cropping may be necessary)

Add photos, resizing them as you go. Using Edit—Free Transform is an easy way to size your images on the fly. You can place them exactly using your grid. Once all the photos were in place, it was time for another evaluation. The composition was too busy. The color was distracting. A decision was made to desaturate the image, converting it to a black and white image.

Figure 6-51
"Filled" collage in color

More refinement was necessary. The small frame of photos that encircled the main photo did not stand out separately as a framing device. A glow effect was applied to the edges of that "frame" of photos. The glow was also used on the outside edge of the entire collage. The image was flattened and converted to a sepia tone, and a small, thin, dark sepia border was added to the outside edge to complete the finished collage.

Figure 6-52
Collage in sepia tones with a glow effect to accentuate the small frame of photos

The grid technique is a good one for a variety of subjects.

Figure 6-53
Another wedding collage

Figure 6-54
Sequence of photos of a little girl with apples

Figure 6-55
Sequence of photos with a flower girl and bride

Figure 6-56
Collage of images from one person's life and family

There really are no limits to the subject matter for a grid collage. Likewise, there is no limit to the number or arrangement of grid lines to facilitate the placement of your photos. Remember that the grid lines do not print, so there is no need to clear the lines from your completed image before printing.

A Gridded Collage exercise has been provided for you in Chapter 11: Projects and files can be found on the accompanying web site.

. . . .

Collage Possibilities for Wedding Photography

Collage is a wonderful technique that you can really use if you photograph weddings. Although this example addresses weddings, you can certainly apply the same concepts to other purposes. I'll use the example of the wedding of Tess and Michael. Their formal collage is featured in Figure 6-53. They were a fun-loving couple that applied a sense of humor to their wedding day. After the wedding, we went out to the 50-yard line of the football field for an unusual shot with a fish-eye lens. Tess displayed her New York Giants garter belt and Mike threw his arms in the air in jubilation and machismo, while holding her bouquet. It was wacky and fun. Their humor carried through to the top of their wedding cake with a statuette of a bride pulling an unwilling groom. Why not carry that humor one step further?

I am following Nature without being able to grasp her. . . . I have gone back to things that can't possibly be done; water, with weeds waving at the bottom. It is a wonderful sight, but it drives one crazy trying to paint it. But that is the kind of thing I am always tackling.
—CLAUDE MONET,
    letter to Gustave Feffroy,
    June 2, 1890, in *La Vie de Claude Monet* (1929)

Figure 6-57
Transforming the cake topper with the actual bride and groom

I often photograph details at the wedding, such as the cake, flowers, champagne glasses, etc. The cake topper was too good to resist. I searched through the photographs that I had made of the couple and found two heads that I could use to substitute on the little statuette. I resized them using Transform and masked them into the original photo. It was easy and the couple was pleasantly surprised.

Figure 6-58
Album layout using collage techniques for a double-page spread

Staying with the same wedding, collage was used to make a double-page spread for an album. The bouquet of roses was used as the background, at a low opacity. The photos were added on top, with the help of the grid system. The photos had a drop shadow and bevel and emboss added.

Figure 6-59
Collaged close-up

I really liked the intense look in the groom's eye in one of the shots, but part of his face was obscured with the bride's hair. I decided to use her profile with this shot and cast him in the shadows for a mysterious kind of look. Extra layers were added for shadows and sepia toning.

Figure 6-60
Original photos used in the collaged composite

Figure 6-61
Fantasy collage

Taking it one step further into a fantasy kind of collage, I incorporated Tess's roses into her head. This may be over the top for some couples. You need to know your clients. It certainly will be different from their friends' conventional wedding photographs. Let your imagination loose. Follow your nose. Investigate options. Experiment. Have fun with it. Collaging can make your work unique among your peers.

In short, collage can be anything that you can imagine. Exaggerate scale, suspend reality, and let those creative juices flow. Keep in mind the need for unity to knit the piece together and you should be successful at collaging.

7

Assembling a Collage in Painter

Each piece of software has unique ways to work with pixels. Photoshop is by far the first piece of software that comes to mind when contemplating putting a collage together. It has the tools that make resizing and placement of images easy. However, don't rule out Painter as a program for collaging. Painter offers some unique possibilities, especially for textural effects.

Using Painter's Image Hose

Open all files in Painter
The completed nature-oriented collage shown in Figure 7-10 was created in Painter. The background layer was a scanned piece of art

Art is nature as seen through a temperament.
—Jean-Baptiste-Camille Corot,
in *Corot*, by Keith Roberts (1965)

Figure 7-1
Original photographs used in Painter collage

paper with a botanical feel (purchased from a bookmaking/paper store). The other photo contributions were butterfly specimens that I photographed (Figure 7-1). Figures 7-2 to 7-9 demonstrate the collage processes. All the files were opened in Painter.

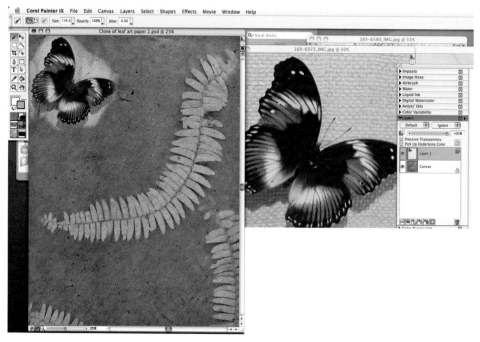

Figure 7-2
Cloning butterfly

Clone the background paper (File—Clone)
Create a new layer
Change the File—Clone source to the open butterfly file
Clone the butterfly on the new layer
You will notice that the butterfly appears in the upper left-hand corner of the image. That is the location where the cloner begins. It shifts all image files to square-up to the upper left-hand corner. If that is not where you would like the image to appear, then take the move tool and place that layer where you would like. Be sure to complete the cloning first.

Figure 7-3
Moving the butterfly

Use the move tool to reposition the butterfly

Some of the burlap cloth background, on which the butterfly was mounted, came along for the ride. That was deleted by erasing the cloth, using the eraser brush. The blending mode was set to Shadow Map, once the butterfly was in the desired location. Two more butterflies were added in a similar fashion. They were both set at the default blending mode, but the butterfly on the upper left was reduced to a 79% opacity.

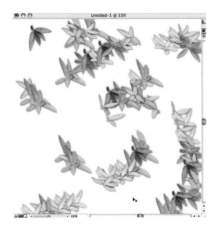

Figure 7-4
Image Hose: Swallows and Look Selector: Passionflower Leaves

Image Hose was used to "spray" on swallows and leaves

There are some really wacky images that you can spill onto the page by selecting the Image Hose Brush. The size of these randomly thrown objects is determined by your brush size. Placement is not precise. The challenge here was to use these Image Hose components in a way that integrated them into the collage. Generally speaking, the Image Hose libraries are fun, but not terribly useful, when creating art. They are digital spin-art (discussed in Chapter 9, "Filters"). I chose the swallows from the Image Hose Library and the passionflower leaves from the Look Selector. Each of those components was sprayed from the Image Hose, directly onto a new layer. Note that each upgrade of Painter has new Image Hose Libraries. Some of the old libraries have some interesting items that are worth examining.

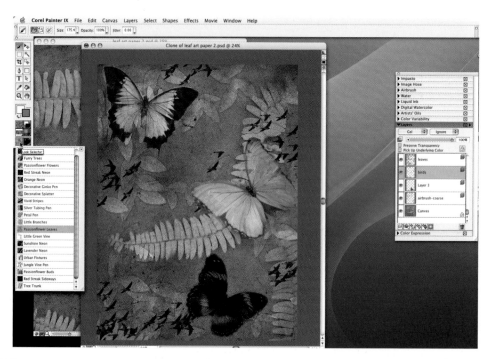

Figure 7-5
Using the Image Hose

Leaves were sprayed on a separate layer and the blending mode was set to Overlay and the opacity was reduced to 56%

The swallows were sprayed onto a separate layer and the blending mode was set to Gel

Another new layer was added and the Airbrush—Coarse Spray variant was used to spray a dark brown texture in segments of the piece, especially near edges, with a large brush; the opacity was set at 22%

The next challenge was to integrate these various components together to create a feeling of wholeness. That was achieved by varying the blending modes and spraying a coarse airbrush texture along the edges and in several locations, to vary the tone.

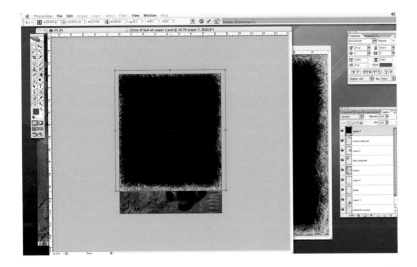

Figure 7-6
*Adding scratchboard edges
in Photoshop*

**Scratchboard File is placed on a layer above the collage and resized
with Free Transform in Photoshop**
The collage could be complete now, but I decided to save it as a Photoshop file, thus preserving all the layers, and open it in Photoshop. I
also opened a file of a scanned piece of scratchboard. Scratchboard can
be purchased from an art supply store or created on your own. Scratchboard is a board coated with a chalky-like base (several coats of gesso
will work) and covered with a layer of black ink. With a sharp stylus
or pin, the artist scrapes through the ink, revealing the white layer
beneath. The scratchboard used in Figure 7-6 was scratched around the
edges with a few random marks throughout the board. It was scanned
for my collection of edge effects (see Chapter 4). The scratchboard
image was placed on a new layer above the collage, and Free Transform
was used to resize the scratchboard to fit the edges of the collage.

Figure 7-7
*Close-up of edge effect:
Blending Mode is Difference*

Blending Mode is set to Difference

All the blending modes were tried out to arrive at the best integration of the edge effect with the Painter collage. I settled on the Difference Blending Mode. That blending mode created a turquoise color for the edge effect that worked well with the color of the butterflies.

Figure 7-8
Layer effects completed

The layers remain separate for modification at a later time

Figure 7-9
Blending Mode set to Hue

Blending Mode set to Hue

While trying out various blending modes, you may stumble on an unexpected rendition. The Hue Blending Mode created this interesting lavender version. I decided to crop out the edges, which appeared rather orange, and only use the top portion of the collage. This created an entirely different kind of look.

Figure 7-10
Completed collage

The completed Painter collage has a nature theme that was enhanced by the use of Painter's Image Hose.

Figure 7-11
Alternate version of collage, using Hue Blending Mode

Beauty is not in the face; beauty is in the heart.
—An old adage

The alternate image made from the collage would work nicely on a greeting card.

Using Painter's Unique Brushes for Texture in a Collage

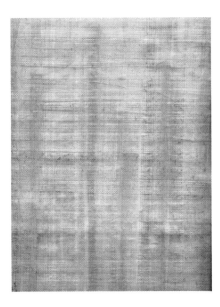 

Figure 7-12
Original images

The next Painter collage relies on the wonderful surface texture effects that Painter offers. The collage consists of just two images (Figure 7-12). The one on the left is a scan of paper made from bark. The image on the right is sunrise in Venice. The goal was to push this image combination with a rough textural feel.

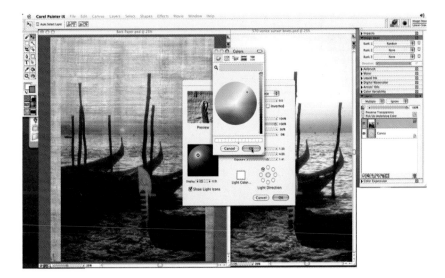

Figure 7-13
Selecting color of light

The Venetian image was placed on another layer, above the bark paper

The Blending Mode was set to Multiply

Effects—Surface Control—Apply Surface Texture dialogue box appears

The light color selected was a golden shade

The Surface Control called Apply Surface Texture offers a world of possibilities. It allows you to apply lighting effects that can be colored, like putting a colored gel over studio lighting. It can bring the texture out in the paper that you have selected. There are just tons of options and combinations. I chose Image Luminance as the type of surface texture that I wanted.

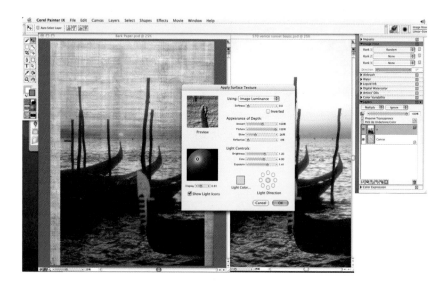

Figure 7-14
Apply Surface Texture—
Image Luminance

Figure 7-14 illustrates the settings that were applied to this image. The preview window allows a look at how the effect will appear.

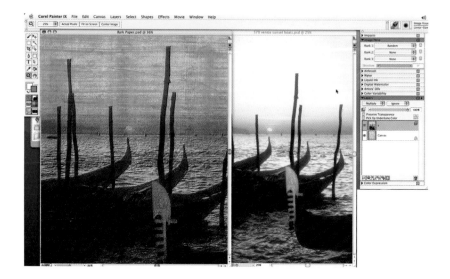

Figure 7-15
Blending Mode set to
Multiply

The Blending Mode was set to Multiply

Try all the blending modes to see which one will work best for the desired effect.

One should not pursue beauty so much as one should be open to it.
—MORTIMER ADLER, in *Six Great Ideas*, a WNET-TV broadcast (1984)

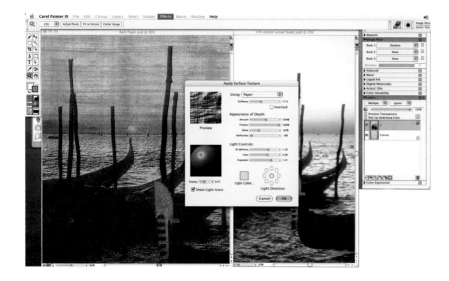

Figure 7-16
Apply Surface Texture—Paper

Apply Surface Texture—Paper

Apply Surface Texture was used a second time, using the Paper Texture option.

Figure 7-17
Edges erased

Erase sharp edges

Using the eraser brush, the straight and sharp edges were erased to create an irregular edge.

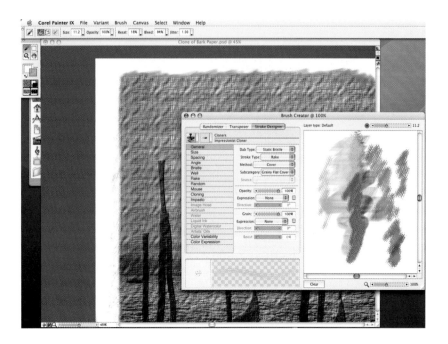

Figure 7-18
Brush Creator creates custom brushes

Window—Show Brush Creator

The Brush Creator allows you to make and test custom brushes. A custom-made Impressionist Cloner brush was created, using a Static Bristle, Rake Stroke type and a Grainy Flat Cover method of applying the strokes. Try the brush out in the area provided.

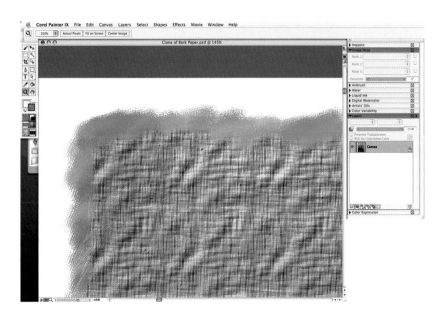

Figure 7-19
Rough edge applied with custom-made Impressionist Cloner Brush

Apply rough strokes around the edges of the collage

Rough strokes, using the custom-made Impressionist Cloner brush, created a rough-hewn edge effect.

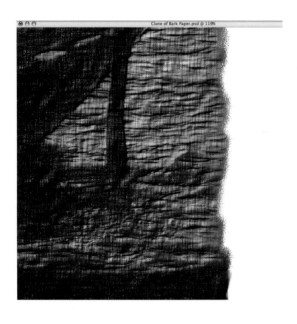

Figure 7-20
Straight Cloner "fills"
within the painterly edge

Straight Cloner used to bring the textural effect up to the rough edge

The edge created a different textural look as it made the rough edges. To bring the textural image up to the rough edges, the Straight Cloner was used.

The completed Painter collage has a rough, bumpy, deep textural feel, thanks to the textural possibilities available in Apply Surface Control.

Black is like a broken
vessel, which is deprived
of the capacity to contain
anything.
—LEONARDO DA VINCI,
Treatise on Painting
(1651)

Figure 7-21
Completed textural collage in Painter

Using Colored Paper and the Brush Creator

More Cloning

Cloning can be done on any colored paper. The paper texture can also be varied using the variety of papers that Painter offers. In the next Painter collage a soft yellow tone was used to fill the clone. This underlying tone will help unite the piece of art later.

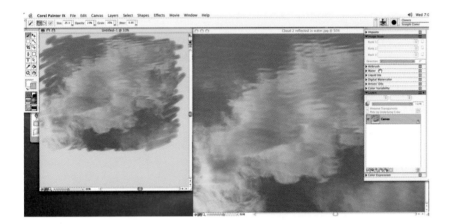

Figure 7-22
Reflected cloud in a pond is straight cloned onto the paper

Select paper color and size: File—New
Open the photo of a cloud formation reflected into the surface of a pond
Using the photo as the File—Clone Source, the Straight Cloner was used to apply the image onto the paper, using a moderately large brush

A soft butterscotch color was selected for the background color of the paper selected. A photo of clouds reflected in a pond was selected for the "sky" area of this collage. It was cloned with the Straight Cloner, using a moderately large brush.

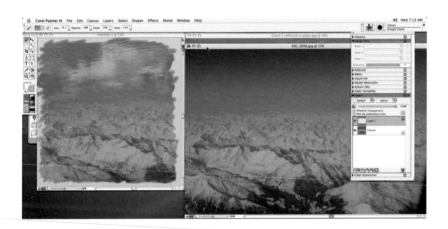

Figure 7-23
The Alps are added for the "ground"

Photo of the Alps was opened
Straight Cloner was used, with the Alps photo as the "Clone Source"
A photo of the Alps taken from the air was used to create the "ground." The Straight Cloner was set at a low opacity to blend the Alps image into the sky area.

Figure 7-24
The next addition was a portal, guarded by angels

Open portal/door photo
Set the Clone Source as the door image. Use Straight Cloner, with low opacity to blend this new image into the others. Note: each cloned image is on its own new layer
Something heavenly was starting to happen with this image, so a photo of angels at a door or portal was used to build on that theme.

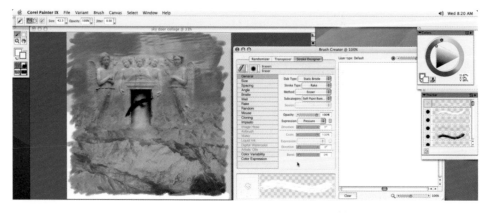

Figure 7-25
Bird in flight was added and golden glow

Open photo of flying bird: Straight Clone it into the composition
A golden glow was created with the airbrush tool, on its own layer
An eraser brush was created with the Brush Creator and began to whiten the outside edge

I tried several bird photos that I had in my files. My first thought was a white dove, but it wasn't visually or emotionally equal to the dark bird. The dark bird created a sense of foreboding or mystery. The white bird just looked too ordinary. In order to make the bird more visible and add to the mystery of what was behind that door, I added a soft golden light, spilling out from the doorway. Again, it was on its own separate layer underneath the bird. The golden glow worked well with the undertone of the paper that was lightly showing through some of the cloning. The paper worked like an underpainting, providing a soft color tone that subtly worked to unite the piece. The colored outside edges of the paper, however, distracted from the piece, and were erased with an eraser brush created with the Brush Creator.

The entire image with the layers intact was saved as a Photoshop file
In Photoshop the Color Balance was corrected and Curves were used to brighten and accentuate the contrast

Creativity can be described as letting go of certainties.
—Gail Sheehy,
   Pathfinders (1981)

Figure 7-26—*"Portal"*
Completed Painter collage

Combining the Power of Painter and Photoshop in a Collage

Figure 7-27
Out of focus: "Lens Baby" shot

The next collage began as an out of focus "Lens Baby" shot of some of my Hibiscus flowers. The Lens Baby attaches onto your SLR and has a tilt feature that can throw things out of focus. You could achieve a somewhat similar effect by using your blur filters. It is a fun lens, especially to loosen up your imagery, concentrating more on color and shapes, and less on detail.

I love to combine the potential of the two powerful programs, Painter and Photoshop. Each piece of software offers unique ways to make your creative mark. In this example we will use Photoshop for the initial collage, followed up by brushwork and textural effects in Painter.

Figure 7-28
Adding in portions of petal detail

Detailed portions of Hibiscus petals were added into the composition with a Layer Mask
The Blending Mode was set to Screen
In Photoshop, additional petals were selected from photos that were in focus. Portions of these images were added using a Layer Mask and setting the Blending Mode to Screen.

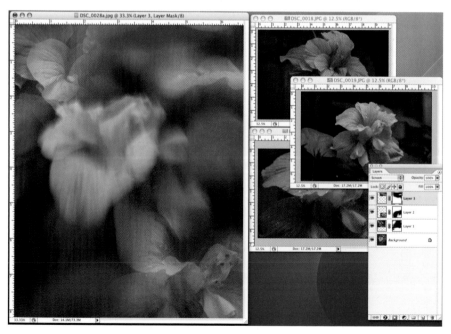

Figure 7-29
More petals added

More petals were added using a Layer Mask to blend them into the collage. Again, the Blending Mode was set to Screen on each additional petal layer.

Education for creativity is nothing short of education for living.
—ERICH FROMM,
  Creativity and Its
  Cultivation (1959)

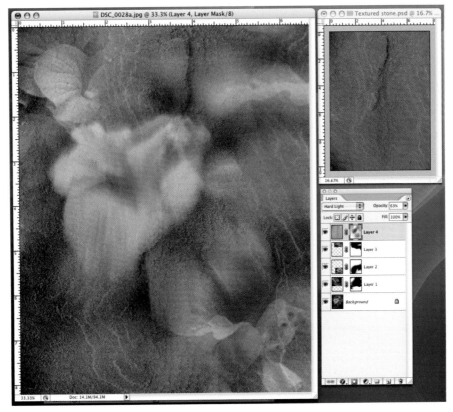

Figure 7-30
Eroded sandstone was added for texture

A new layer was added with a sandstone texture
The hue of the sandstone was changed to an aqua shade, using a Hue/Saturation adjustment
The Blending Mode was set to Hard Light

The image seemed a bit too soft, so I decided to add texture. I used a digital photo of a detail of an eroded sandstone tombstone in Scotland. I changed the color of the stone to an aqua shade by using Image—Adjustment—Hue/Saturation. The Blending Mode was set to Hard Light, allowing the texture to show with clarity.

I next opened the image in Painter and cloned it. Working on the clone, I applied some clone brushwork using brushes that gave me some depth (Wet Oils, Smeary Bristle Cloner and Flat Impasto Cloner). These brush strokes were judiciously used in small sections. I didn't want to lose the texture of the sandstone throughout the piece. The brushwork was essentially used to accent areas.

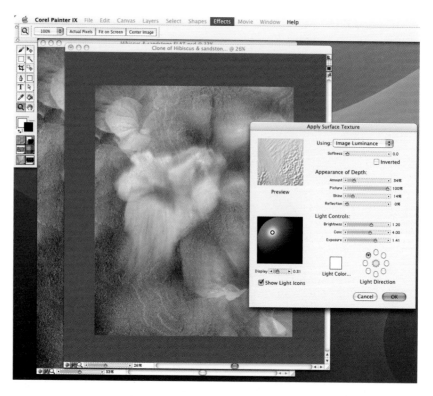

Figure 7-31
Surface texture applied

Looking at the landscape from an airplane, I began to understand Cubist painting.
—ERNEST HEMINGWAY,
The Toronto Daily Star
(1922)

Effects—Surface Control—Apply Surface Texture

Painter offers an interesting effect called Surface texture. I chose the Image Luminance type. After adjusting the sliders to my satisfaction, checking the preview throughout, I applied this effect.

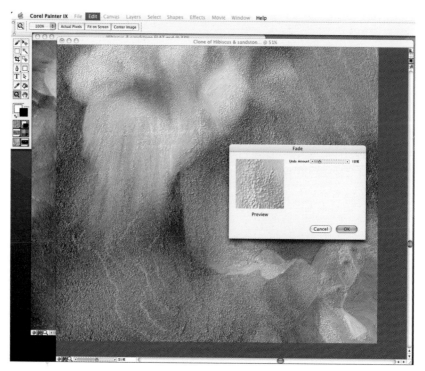

Figure 7-32
Effect was faded

Effect was faded

If the effect seems a bit too strong, you can "Fade" the effect, after it is applied. Fade is located under Edit, in the top menu.

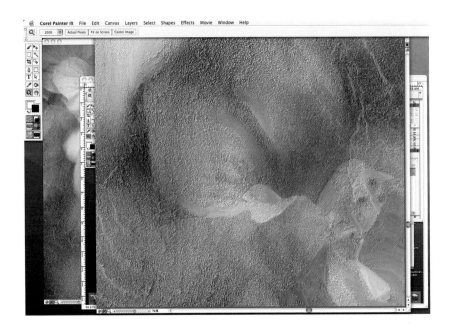

Figure 7-33
Close-up of Surface Control Effect

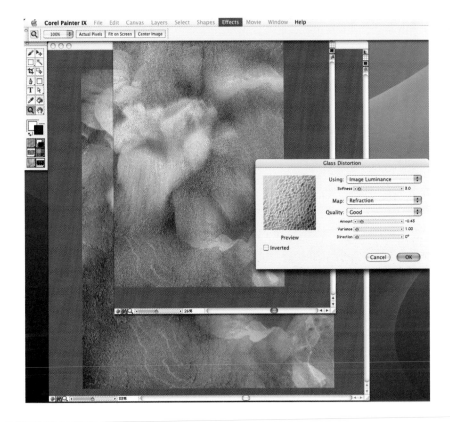

Figure 7-34
Glass Distortion was applied

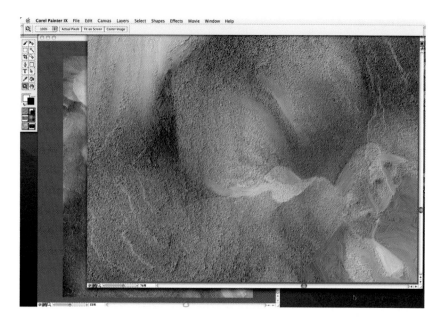

Figure 7-35
Close-up of detail in lower right-hand corner

Effect—Focus—Glass Distortion was applied also

Another Surface effect, Glass Distortion, was applied to enhance the textural quality.

When you are contemplating making a collage, remember that Painter can offer some unique effects and is especially good for a textural feel. I am constantly going back and forth between Painter and Photoshop in many pieces. Simply pick the tool that is best suited for the job at hand. Both programs offer a stunning array of options singly, but when you combine the power of both of them together, you have a greatly extended range of artistic options.

Figure 7-36
Completed abstract collage made in Photoshop and Painter

8

The Paradox: The Absolute Truth and the Exquisite Lie—Creating a Panorama in Photoshop

Concept and Preparation

A panoramic image may well be the ultimate collage. There are many ways to approach a panoramic project. There are prepackaged software programs designed to tackle this task. Photoshop even includes stitching software, called Photomerge, in their program. Photomerge is located under File—Automate. Or you can elect to stitch your photos together yourself. Although the do-it-yourself approach may take you longer to construct your image, I really like it for two reasons: quality and control.

I feel like I need to wrap this chapter in yellow tape, saying CAUTION, like you see on the television crime shows. This process

OPPOSITE PAGE FROM TOP TO BOTTOM: *"Fox Hunting, Pennsylvania;" "Boston Common;" "Cadillac Mountain, Acadia, Maine;" "St. Augustine, Florida;" "Cappadocia, Turkey;" "Capri, Italy;" "Garden Wedding, Maryland"*

401

can become addictive. You will want to make panoramas everywhere you go, from your own backyard, to exotic vacation locations. Travel spots are ideal material for this process. You know what it feels like on vacation, when you are standing in a beautiful location, and you just want to soak it all up and carry this place home with you. You want to remember what it felt like to be at this spot in this place and at this time of day. You simply want to bottle it up. Snapshots seldom bring home the feeling you had on that spot. The panoramic process will certainly come closer to the real thing.

The concept is simple. You revolve around in a complete circle, taking photographs as you go. Those images are then pieced or stitched together. The result is one very long image that reveals not only what was in front of you on that spot, but also what was at your sides and behind you. Now you can really have eyes in back of your head, just like you thought your Mom had, when you were a child.

In some ways this panoramic is the penultimate truth of that moment in space and time. You quite literally see it all. The flip side of that is that it is all an exquisite lie. Take the example shown in Figure 8-1, a panoramic taken in Florence, Italy. I had just come out of the Uffizi Art Museum in Florence, after spending many hours with some of the finest art on the planet. I walked through the colonnade (known as the Piazzale degli Uffizi) towards the Arno River. Through the colonnade I could still see, in the distance, the fake Michelangelo's *David* in the Palazzo Vecchio (remember, the real one is now in the Galleria Dell' Accademia). Behind me was the famed Arno River and to my side was the Ponte Vecchio, the bridge that dates from 1345 and is occupied by fine goldsmith shops. What a wonderful moment and place, I decided, and I proceeded to take about sixty photographs as I spun around.

In dealing with light, the photographer is dealing with one of the most fundamental, and mysterious, things in the universe. It is related, on the one hand, to the basic vital processes of all living things; on the other, to the inner nature of time. . . . We are creatures of the light, and photography is one of the most creative ways by which we can re-affirm this relationship.
—Clarence John Laughlin,
in "A Statement by the Photographer," March 1955, typescript for *Modern Photography* (never published)

Figure 8-1
Uffizi Museum in Florence, Italy

Look closely at the completed image. It is very much the truth of that moment, but it is such a lie, as well. The Uffizi Museum in the panoramic appears bowed, as you would have with a fish-eye lens. How could that be? Consider the laws of perspective. What is closest to me will appear larger. Things further away become smaller, as they recede into the distance. As I pivoted around, taking the images that I would later composite together, those same rules apply. As I joined those images, in Photoshop, they took on the bowed effect, illustrated here. Anyone that has ever visited the Museum or walked along the beautiful Arno River knows that there is no curve. It is a straight street in that vicinity. Therein is the lie. But the image is beautiful and fascinating nonetheless.

Another interesting concept, as you put together your panoramic image, is that you can juggle the pieces around to create your focal point, since it is really one long continuum that interconnects together. Picture yourself with this long print literally wrapped in a circle around your head. You choose what will be the center of interest. Consider the panoramic in Figure 8-2, which illustrates that point.

Figure 8-2
Wedding ceremony

This panoramic was taken inside a country church during a wedding ceremony. I'm standing to the rear of the main aisle. The stained glass windows are behind me. The windows, with their bright colors and shear largeness of scale, easily dwarf the bridal couple. The completed image should be about the wedding, not the windows. I split the windows in half. By delegating the stained glass windows to the edges of the finished print, I've downplayed their importance. The drapery of white tulle fabric that lined the aisle leads the viewer's eye toward the front of the sanctuary and the ensuing ceremony. Notice how the church pews appear to bow, like our previous example of the museum.

Figure 8-3
Carroll County, MD Courthouse

In Figure 8-3, a panoramic of the Carroll County Courthouse, the emphasis needed to be on the courthouse. As I stood in the middle of the street, the area behind me was really boring and contained some parked cars. In the finished piece that area was delegated to the sides as unimportant. Another way to cope with an unattractive area is simply to not show it. Instead of a three hundred and sixty degree image, you could reduce it to two hundred and eighty degrees, or whatever works for the image. You get to call the artistic shots. Include or delete what you deem appropriate.

In Figure 8-4, I'm sitting on a hillside, watching a preseason football scrimmage. This image is not quite one hundred and eighty degrees. I didn't want to include close-ups of the people to my sides or behind me. Due to the bowl-like nature of the terrain, I would have been looking up into the nostrils of the people behind me. I really didn't want to include that! I did, however, want the flag to the left and decided to balance that with the knee and the hand holding a pair of binoculars to my right. Remember that you are in charge. There aren't any digital police that will slap you with a fine for not making the image a complete three hundred and sixty degrees. Include what seems right for the completed image. In some places, a complete three hundred and sixty degrees does not make artistic sense. Use your own judgment.

Figure 8-4
Football scrimmage

Figure 8-5
Pemaquid Lighthouse, Maine

Speaking of judgment, let's play with the idea of a complete circle. Anything in the complete circle can be the center of interest. You can deconstruct your panoramic, after it is completed, and rearrange the parts if you are looking for a different effect or area of interest. In Figure 8-5, I liked making the lighthouse and buildings the central design element, and the rock strata provided a good directional line into the composition, leading you to the lighthouse. But you can change your mind later. You can rearrange the pieces of this puzzle. The huge, boulder-like, light-colored rocks could be more prominent if the panoramic was rearranged (Figure 8-6).

Figure 8-6
Pemaquid Lighthouse reformulated

Figure 8-7
Marshall's Lighthouse, Maine

Another peculiar thing that happens with panoramas, which can be really interesting, is the ability to see in front and behind, at the same time. In Figure 8-7, I was standing on the suspended walkway that leads from the shore to the lighthouse. As I pivoted around, the walkway became dissected. In a circumstance like this, you will have two large directional elements that can be used to your advantage in the composition and placement of the images. This will happen whenever you are on a road or path. You will have the path in front of you and also the path behind you.

Exposure Controls, Proper Overlap, Tripod or Not?

What do you need to know before you take those photographs for your intended panoramic? Important issues to keep in mind are exposure, overlap, and tripod usage. Let's start with exposure. Normally, we photographers abhor taking a photograph when the sun is directly above us. There are no long shadows to carve out our subject matter. But with a panoramic, it can be the ideal time of day to capture your imagery. Think about it. If the sun is not directly above you, somewhere during your time pivoting around, you will be looking into the sun. Likewise you will also be looking away from the sun, during some portion of your exposure. Sometimes the sun can be hidden behind a tree, building, or cloud. Sometimes it is simply unavoidable. You can imagine how this might wreak havoc with your exposure settings.

My rule of thumb is this: Stand with your shoulder to the sun. You are at a ninety degree angle from the sun. Take a meter reading. Make a mental or written note of the settings. If you are using the automatic exposure setting on your camera, change it to the manual mode and dial-in that suggested exposure setting. That exposure setting will be used on ALL the images that will be used for the finished panoramic. All of your photographs will be taken with the same f-stop and shutter speed setting. Why, you ask? The exposure, if it remained in the automatic mode, would create the best exposure for each and every shot, but they would vary too greatly from one another to be blended together cohesively. You would be surprised at the difference, especially in the sky areas, from one exposure to the next. Saturation will also vary. For this task we want a uniformity of tone for easier blending, as we join our pieces together.

Figure 8-9 illustrates a series of four exposures taken with the same exposure settings on all, using the manual setting. Figure 8-8 illustrates that same series taken with an automatic exposure setting.

My work is my sensuous life. . . . To make the subject become more beautiful took my full attention, the attention of a lover for his beloved.
—RUTH BERNHARD, in *Ruth Bernhard: Between Art & Life*, by Margaretta K. Mitchell (2000)

| 1/320s at f/9 | 1/250s at f/9 | 1/320s at f/10 | 1/320s at f/9 |

Figure 8-8
Automatic camera exposure

There are exceptions to this rule. A good example of this is a panoramic that I made as I entered the Scottish Highlands. The weather and sky were dramatic that day. Remember, your digital camera has a finite tonal range, just as film does. Knowing that piece of information, and sensing a huge range of tones in front of me, I actually

Figure 8-9
Manual exposure setting of
1/400s at f/10

1/400s at f/10

pivoted around three times to obtain the shots for Figure 8-10, taking in excess of 150 photographs. I used three different meter settings. On one sweep, I metered for highlights; on another sweep, I metered for mid-tones, and on the final sweep, I metered for shadowed or dark areas. I knew that was the only way I would come close to the tonal range I saw that day. I wouldn't recommend this technique for the first dozen or so panoramas that you contruct, as it can be quite a challenge. But once you are a seasoned panoramic photographer, you may want to try it for those difficult scenes that exhibit an enormous amount of tonal variation.

Figure 8-10—*"Scottish Highlands"*

Let's look at the issue of overlap. I always overlap at least a third, sometimes more. I need a large area of overlap to blend one image into the next one. Some subjects are trickier than others. If there is a vertical element in my series of photographs, such as a pole or tree, I make sure that the vertical element is in the middle of at least one exposure. Curvature of the lens will bow the vertical element as it progresses to the edge of your photographs (see Figure 8-11). You need at least one exposure where that flagpole or tree is standing straight upright.

Figure 8-11
Curvature of the lens will bow vertical objects on the edges

To use a tripod or not, is the question. The answer should be—"Yes, always!" But, alas the real world intervenes and I don't always walk around with one. I especially don't carry them in cities, when I travel. There is only so much I can carry anymore. Short of hiring an assistant or Sherpa, I'm on my own, and I would rather carry an assortment of lenses. Are the images sharp, you ask? They probably could be a little bit better if I used the tripod, especially in low light situations. But, I've made literally hundreds of panoramas without a tripod that I consider to be rather nice indeed. So, don't dismay if you find yourself somewhere without your trusty tripod. You are only using a sliver of each image in the total compilation. When those slivers are amassed together, you will discover that you will have a huge image file. Those slivers add up quickly and the result is an image that can easily be 400–500 MB, or more.

Another tip is to always hold your camera vertically. This gives you more image area to work with. You can include more sky and ground. It also covers a multitude of sins, so to speak. Because you may be taking these images without a tripod, the extra headroom afforded by a vertical orientation can be helpful. You will need to eventually crop the final image, due to the slight variations, due to hand-holding the camera. That is especially true if you are standing on an incline, as you make the circular sweep of the area. Some people go really nuts with this tripod thing and use levels and precise incremental overlaps, etc. That is fine, if that is how your mind works. I don't work that way. I can work fast and move on to another interesting area, before my photo friends have set up their tripod, leveled it out, and gotten their meter readings. I've done so many, that I have it down to a science now. You may need that extra piece of time and patience later, to wait until that distracting person, who stepped into your picture frame, moves on.

Beware of moving people. If you are panning in the direction that someone is walking, you will have him/her in multiple shots. Sometimes you can put them in one spot and delete them from others. It depends on the surroundings. This is always an issue when shooting in a crowded area, where people are moving about. Take extra shots to be sure that you will be "covered" when you make the panoramic.

Making panoramas has also made me more aware of the sky. I am now constantly amazed at how different the sky is in front of me,

There is no best way or only way. We learn from the past, in order to understand the present. The past is our foundation, the springboard into the future. Tradition and past ideas are important bases to begin with, but can be traps if misunderstood.
—Arnold Newman,
   in *Arnold Newman*, by
   Philip Brookman (2001)

compared to behind me, at any given moment. There doesn't have to be an approaching storm to see a vast difference in sky from front to rear. The colors of the sky and the cloud formations are much more variable than I would have suspected. Take a look around.

Relying on Layer Transparency and Layer Masking

Step-By-Step Panorama Instructions Using Collaging Techniques

I usually take about sixty photographs to make a single panoramic image. That is a lot of photographs to merge into one image. But remember that we will only be using a sliver of each frame that was shot. To begin, I open about five to six images in succession. I miniaturize the images on my desktop and place them off to the edges of my monitor.

Figure 8-12
Sequential overlapping photos

Open 5 or 6 sequential shots, with a generous overlap, in Photoshop
Starting with the first image in this photographic sweep, I immediately add canvas (Image—Canvas Size). Be sure to have white as your background color. The canvas will be the color of your background.

Figure 8-13
Adding canvas to your image

Add canvas width to the first image, in the direction that you will be adding images

I add canvas in the direction that I moved while taking the photos. If I pivoted to the right, as I was photographing, the canvas is added to the right side of the current picture. I usually add a little room on the top and bottom also. It will be cropped later.

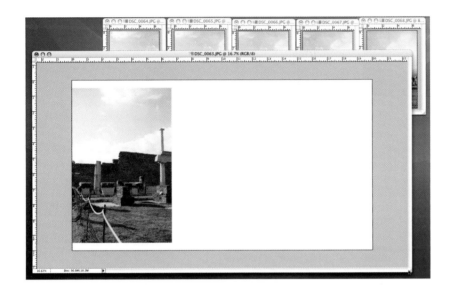

Figure 8-14
Additional canvas allows room for more photos to be included

Figure 8-14 illustrates the expanded canvas. The extra canvas will allow room for the inclusion of successive photos to the right.

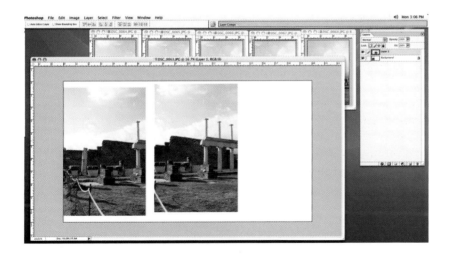

Figure 8-15
Second photo added

Add the next layer

You can copy it and paste it onto the panorama, or simply use your move tool and drag the image onto the panorama.

Look for the whole thing, the ensemble.
—William Merritt
  Chase,
  In the Company of Friends
  (1979)

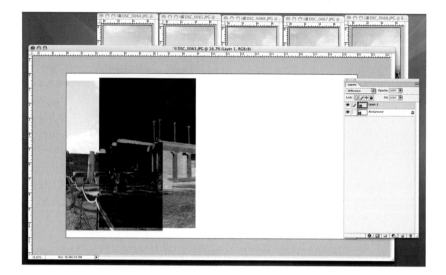

Figure 8-16
*Difference blending mode
used to position the added
layer*

Set the blending mode to Difference, to precisely line up the photographs

There are a couple ways to position the new layer in place. You can lower the opacity on the new layer and use that transparency effect to exactly position the new layer. I prefer to switch the blending mode to Difference. This blending mode will look for the differences between the layers. You want a solid laydown of black. That means that where the black occurs, the new layer is in perfect synchronization with the previous one. This technique allows for precise positioning. Remember there is a built-in curvature of your lens that will not allow all portions of the new layer to be in exact sync with the previous layer. Move the new layer until the middle section of it matches up correctly with the lower layer.

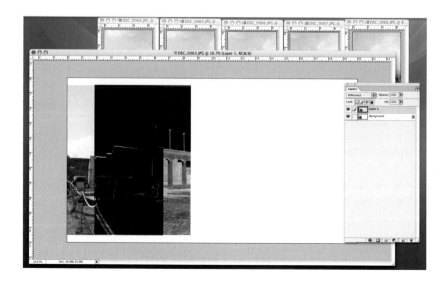

Figure 8-17
*Align photos for a solid area
of black to appear*

After aligning the images, return the blending mode to Normal

When the positioning of the new layer seems that it is as precise as possible, return the blending mode to Normal. At this point, add a layer mask. We will use a layer mask on every new layer to blend the new photo into the one beneath.

Figure 8-18
Adding a layer mask

Add a layer mask to blend the two images together

Use black as your foreground color. Using the layer mask, paint black into the mask to reveal the area beneath. Use the layer mask and the colors black and white on that mask, to fine-tune the integration of that layer into the previous one. By using the layer mask, everything you do is reversible. If you were to use the eraser instead, areas could possibly be lost. Remember, using white restores any areas that you have deleted by using the color black.

Figure 8-19
Using the layer mask to blend one image into the next

Whatever you can do or dream you can, begin it. Boldness has genius, power and magic in it.
—JOHANN WOLFGANG VON GOETHE, *Proverbs in Prose* (1819)

Continue to add layers and layer masks for each layer
Continue this process by adding the next layer. Use the Difference blending mode again for accurate placement of the new layer.

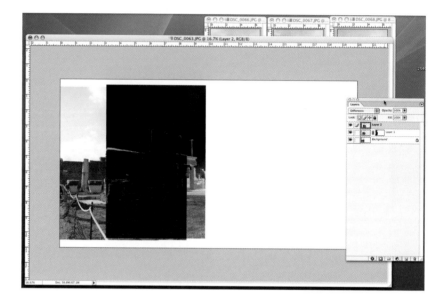

Figure 8-20
Adding the third image, using the Difference blending mode

Figure 8-21
Six layers composited together

Figure 8-21 illustrates the compilation of six layers. Review the panorama closely before you merge those layers together.

After close examination for any flaws, merge those layers

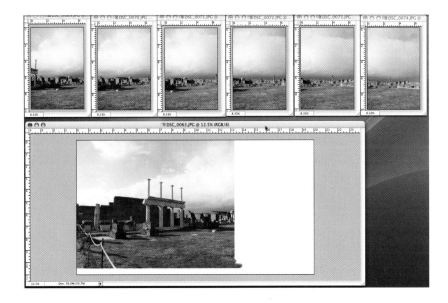

Figure 8-22
Grass is cloned with the rubber stamp tool

Continue opening additional photos, in sequence, and repeating the steps listed above

Collapse those layers together and open five or six more photographs that will be added into the composite. To compensate for the difference in height in the lower grass area, the grass was cloned to fill in the empty space. This stair-step effect is due to a slight difference in the position of the camera, as the images were taken without a tripod. Using a tripod would have been helpful. Ground and sky areas can usually be cloned easily, for the sake of size and unity.

Five more layers were added and more canvas was needed. There was no more room to add more photographs.

Figure 8-23
More layers are added

Add more canvas, as needed

You can add more canvas by going to Image—Canvas Size again.

Figure 8-24
Adding canvas by using the crop tool

If I have been able to see farther than others, it is because I have stood on the shoulders of giants.
—SIR ISAAC NEWTON,
   Isaac Newton's Papers and Letters (1958)

A neat trick to add more canvas is to use the crop tool. Pull the handle beyond the image, in the direction you are going
You can also add more canvas by using the crop tool. Select the whole panoramic. Notice the handles on the bounding box. Pull the handle on the right to extend it beyond the image edge. Hit the Return key, and you automatically have additional canvas. It is a neat trick that is quick and easy.

Figure 8-25
More layers added

More layers were added. Each one used a layer mask for blending.

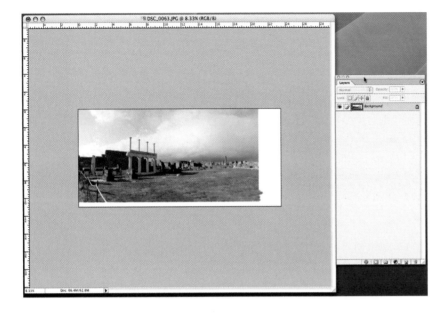

Figure 8-26
Grass was cloned for uniformity

If there are voids in the panorama, such as gaps in the grass or sky area, you can rubber stamp the area to clone more grass or sky
The layers were merged and new grass areas were cloned to fill in the empty spots.

Figure 8-27
Entire image is cropped

Crop, as needed

As the panoramic progressed, it became evident that the lower grass area that had been partially cloned was really not essential to the feel of the overall image. A crop was made to shorten the entire image and extend the canvas again on the right-hand side.

Figure 8-28
Completed panorama of Pompeii

The completed panoramic, in Figure 8-28, was made from forty-nine photographs.

Creating panoramas is like sitting at a movie with a box of popcorn. You can't just eat one piece. One piece leads to another, time and again. You can't wait to see how it will turn out.

Figure 8-29 *Venice at dawn (see insert)*

Figure 8-30 *Pemaquid, Maine (see insert)*

Figure 8-31 *The Gates, NYC bridge (see insert)*

Figure 8-32 *Bryce Canyon, Utah (see insert)*

Figure 8-33 *Grand Canyon, Arizona (see insert)*

Figure 8-34 *Pantheon, Rome, Italy*

Figure 8-35 *Inside the Colosseum, Rome, Italy*

Figure 8-36 *Cherry Blossom Festival, Washington, DC*

Figure 8-37 *Small cove in Maine at dusk*

Figure 8-38 *Sepia tone: Cimetiere du Pere Lachaise, Paris, France*

Figure 8-39 *Olympia, Greece*

Figure 8-40 *Longboat Key wedding*

Figure 8-41 *Capri*

Figure 8-42 *Outside Colosseum, Rome, Italy*

Figure 8-43 *Spanish Steps, Rome, Italy*

Figure 8-44 *Baltimore Ravens game*

Figure 8-45 *McDaniel College, Maryland*

Figure 8-32 *Bryce C*

Figure 8-33 *Grand Ca*

dawn (see page 417)

Maine (see page 417)

bridge (see page 417)

Figure 8-29 *Venice a*

Figure 8-30 *Pemaquid*

Figure 8-31 *The Gates*

nyon, Utah (see page 417)

yon, Arizona (see page 417)

Some panoramas will work better if they are not a complete three hundred and sixty degrees. Usually that determination is made on the spot. That was true of the panoramas shown in Figures 8-41 to 8-45. A distracting background, clutter, and moving people can be some of the many reasons. It is up to you, as the artist, to determine how much you will choose to include in your final panoramic.

Man's environment becomes his mirror. A person comes to know himself by expressing himself.
—JOSEPH CAMPBELL, *Hero with a Thousand Faces* (1949)

"Grab Shot" Panoramas

Figure 8-46
Individual photos made from a moving car

Occasionally you may find yourself at a disadvantage in your ability to achieve proximity to your subject. In the case of Figure 8-46, I was in a moving car, traveling through the Scottish Highlands with friends. We had stopped frequently to allow for making photographs. But where does it end? Around each bend there were new and beautiful vistas! Instead of asking the driver for yet another pull-over, I simply made these quick "grab" shots through the window as we were traveling. I never intended to make anything of them. Later, when I was looking through my contact sheets, it occurred to me that a combination of these two images might just work.

The secret of "Fusion" is the fact that the artist's eye sees in nature . . . an inexhaustible wealth of tension, rhythms, continuities, and contrasts which can be rendered in line and color; and those are the "internal forms" which the "external forms"—paintings, musical or poetic compositions or any other works of art—express for it.
—SUSANNE K. LANGER, *Mind: An Essay on Human Feeling* (1967–1982)

Figure 8-47
Simple panorama made from just two photos

In Figure 8-47, those two photos, with different exposure settings, were combined using a layer mask and adjustment layers to correct the color and contrast.

Figure 8-48
Small Irish panorama

Figure 8-48 is a small panorama made from just six photographs. This small-size panorama could easily be done with Photoshop's Photomerge ability. The photos were taken at the ruins of an Irish castle.

Figure 8-49
Individual photos used in Figure 8-48

Faux Panoramas

If you are feeling ambitious and want to really stretch your ability to integrate one photo into another, you might try making a faux panorama. Figure 8-50 was created from just eight separate images (Figure 8-51). These were taken from a moving tourist bus on a Scottish island. Although the exposures were not the same, the overcast and sometimes rainy day lent a similar lighting feel to all the pictures. This faux panorama was created from separate photos taken in different places throughout the bus trip. This scene does not exist in reality. It is utterly and completely false.

Figure 8-50
Faux panorama on a Scottish island

Figure 8-51
Separate photos that were combined

If an image exists in your mind, perhaps you can bring about its creation. I began with the side of the cottage and the clothes hanging out to dry. I blended those together in Figure 8-52. The opacity was lowered on the top layer to accurately place the clothes. The bus I was on had been moving, so my perspective had changed. I had fired off several shots in passing. I needed to transform the clothes to make them the right scale. Adjustment layers were used to correct color and contrast.

Figure 8-52
Combining clothes on the line

I began to work on the right-hand side of the panorama, adding in a cove and some boats. The image began to take shape as additional layers were added.

Figure 8-53
Adding in a little cove and some boats

There is a right physical size for every idea.
—HENRY MOORE,
  The Sculptor's Aims
  (1966)

The tone in the sky was a big problem above the boats. And a foreground with grass detail was needed for the middle of the panorama.

Figure 8-54
Vegetation added in foreground

Vegetation was brought in using additional photos, shown in Figures 8-55 and 8-56.

Figure 8-55
Hedge row

Figure 8-56
More local vegetation was added from additional photographs

The sky was cloned, using the rubber stamp tool, to even out the tone and color of the sky. And one last group of vegetation was added to complete the composite.

Figure 8-57
Last bit of vegetation is scaled using the transform command

Everything is impossible. And yet . . . I have all the more desire to work.
—Alberto Giacometti, *Alberto Giacometti*, by Peter Selz (1965)

The completed piece relied heavily on changing the scale of various components and altering the tonal qualities and color balance for an even-looking integration. Although all of these images were made on the same day, on the same island, it certainly could be possible to construct a faux panorama from various pieces taken around the world. There is no limit to what you can imagine. You could transport an igloo to a desert vista. You could put lions in Central Park. It is simply the horizontal length of this collage that puts it into our discussions on making panoramas. In reality, panoramas are simply another technique for collaging images together.

Themed Panorama-Style Linear Collages

Figure 8-58
A different type of collaging that relies on the panoramic format

With the idea of collaging in mind, why not make a long, linear, pano-like piece that uses images that are not meant to form a continuum of one particular image? Figure 8-58 illustrates three such pieces. You can throw scale out the window. Close-up details of a sculpture can be used with rural vistas. Here, one image was blended into the next with layer masks. These are fun to put together, especially using favorite photos from trip, as seen here.

*Tip: This type of collage could be used well as a ribbon of images that frame a newsletter or magazine article.

Figure 8-59
Bridal panoramic collage

The same idea can be used for a collection of family images or bridal photographs, as shown in Figure 8-59.

Hurry-Up Panoramas—Using Photoshop's Photomerge

Photoshop has a marvelous process called Photomerge that can be used to stitch panoramas together. It is especially good for smaller, less complex panoramas. Figure 8-60 shows four photos taken in succession, using the same exposure settings. The location is Dolphin Encounters on Blue Lagoon Island, Nassau, Bahamas.

Figure 8-60
Four images to combine in Photomerge

You can access Photomerge through File—Automate—Photomerge. If you own Photoshop CS you can also access Photomerge through the File Browser. Simply select the images that you want to merge together and use Automate—Photomerge from the menu available in the File Browser.

Figure 8-61
Photomerge selections from the File Browser

If you own Photoshop CS2 and Bridge, you can enter the Photomerge window through the Bridge application, using Tools—Photoshop—Photomerge. The third way to open Photomerge is in Photoshop through File—Automate—Photomerge. Photomerge will open up a new window dedicated to the Photomerge operation. Checking the Snap To box will make elements of the photos appear to magnetically jump in alignment with one another. Checking the Save Layers box will preserve each image on a separate layer.

Figure 8-62
Photomerge using Snap To command only (layers are not saved separately)

Often, this technique will be sufficient to make a very fine panorama. In our example the sky area suffered from diagonal banding streaks.

The great use of life is to spend it for something that outlasts it.
—WILLIAM JAMES,
Thought Character (1900)

Figure 8-63
*Results of Photomerge:
Notice diagonal streaking in
the sky area*

If you find that streaking happens to your panoramas in Photomerge, try clicking on the box labeled Save as Layers. This will give you more options to correct any flaws that you notice in the resulting panorama.

Figure 8-64
*Photomerge screen with the
Save as Layers command
checked*

The resulting panorama will come with all the layers intact and separate. In this technique you will notice a stair-step feel to the finished image. The Photomerge operation has placed the photo layers for you but has left the blending to you.

Figure 8-65
Results of Photomerge—
Saved as Layers: Notice the
stair-step sky area

It is not always necessary to proceed to the next step, but in this case it would be wise to apply layer masks to each layer. It is a relatively quick process to add a layer mask and quickly paint with black on the mask to blend one layer into the next. The layers have already been placed correctly in the Photomerge operation.

Figure 8-66
Layer masks applied to each
layer for smooth blending

If you have a very large panorama that requires extensive stitching/blending, you could choose to create the panorama in small sections. Try combining the photos in groups of four layers each, using Photomerge. These small panoramas can then be combined for a larger image, as seen in Figure 8-68.

I have far more images than I shall ever be able to do.
—FRANCIS BACON,
in *Francis Bacon*, by John Shepley (1975)

Figure 8-67
Small panorama units, containing four images each

After each small panorama is checked for any flaws and corrected, proceed to merge those four layers together, to reduce the file size, as we later combine these units together. The resulting large panorama was created from small panoramic units.

Figure 8-68
Completed panorama made from smaller Photomerge unit

Printing Panoramas

Printing panoramas requires roll paper. There are so many different surfaces available now. You can print on luster, matte, watercolor, gloss, canvas, and more. I often find that I can purchase the odd ends of paper rolls on clearance sale. Short rolls work quite well with this type of image. The images are long, but not very tall. Search for a bargain on your favorite paper surface.

Fractured Panoramas

Figure 8-69
"Fractured panorama" of Rockport Harbor, Maine

Normally when I'm photographing component parts for a panorama, I want the images to go together seamlessly, as if they were taken in one shot. That is not true in our next example, which I call a fractured panorama. These resemble the photographic collages made by the painter David Hockney. The images vary in tone, color, and scale. There is no attempt to make a seamless sky. Variations in tone can be quite appealing in this type of work. You can almost haphazardly photograph these images, twisting and turning your camera. You can vary the white balance, ISO, shutter speed, and more. You can let the camera make the decisions by setting it on the automatic or program setting. It is a virtual free-for-all. Have fun with this one. It is stress free.

The master of this technique is Pep Ventosa, who is one of our featured artists in Chapter 3. His sense of color and composition is superb. Be sure to look at his work and web site.

Panoramas are quite simply addicting. They present another way of documenting our world. They are time consuming but worth the effort. They hold an inexplicable fascination. I hope you jump in with both feet and explore your hometown and beyond.

III

Artistic Considerations

9 *Filters*

Using All the Great Filters Available in Photoshop

Do you remember as a child going to the local carnival or fair? Remember the booth that offered "Spin Art"? It consisted of a turntable from an old record player, some mustard and catsup squeeze bottles filled with paint, and a piece of tagboard. The concept was a simple one. Anyone could be an "artist." You stepped up to the turntable, placed the tagboard on the spindle, and with the board whirling quickly around, you proceeded to squirt paint onto the board. You were finished in seconds. Voila! An interesting random spin pattern emerged. It was destined to hang on Mom's refrigerator as your artwork. It was mindless and fun.

OPPOSITE PAGE: *"Graceful Waterlily"*

437

Today we have digital spin art in the name of filters. Don't get me wrong ... filters are fun and many are very useful. Some are really wacky, some are artsy, and some are ridiculous. You need to play with all of them. Explore what they do. Move those dialogue box sliders, Try one on top of another. Change the blending modes. Spend time just playing with filters.

My word of caution is this: filters do not make photos "art." Putting a photo through a watercolor filter does not make it a watercolor painting. You may end up with digital spin art. Just because a filter is available doesn't mean that it is right for your image or concept.

When the Macintosh computer was first introduced, several of my friends and I loosely formed an informal Macintosh Users Group. We pictured ourselves as the brave pioneers. In those early days, everyone got excited about the variety of fonts available. Because most people had never studied typography, they made horrendous mistakes in their written documents. They used so many fonts (in various sizes, bold, italic, underlined, etc.) that the written page looked like a ransom note, cut from magazine pages. The sheer joy of using all those fonts and their variations overrode what their eyes were seeing. Filters can be as seductive as those early fonts. Just because they exist doesn't mean that you should use them.

Picture yourself with a large tool belt around your waist. That tool belt contains all those filters, art tools, etc. As a carpenter would pick the right tool for the job, you need to think about the selection of your digital tools. Don't fall in love with a filter and render all your images through it, like meat being pushed through a meat grinder for hamburger. Just because that filter gave you a great effect on one image doesn't mean that it is appropriate for all your images.

With that word of caution declared, let's have fun!

Photoshop ships with a huge variety of plug-in filters. Despite that enormous range of options, there is a market for more filter plug-ins. Various software companies offer more plug-ins that can be added into your Photoshop plug-in folder. On top of that, there are also plug-ins for different edge effects for your images. I've shown you how to make your own edges in Chapters 4 and 5. There are also free shareware filters that can be downloaded from the web. The range of options is overwhelming and more filters are on the market every day.

In Chapter 4 we looked at the use of various Artistic Filters, available in Photoshop, that could be used alone or in combination for a painterly effect. Some of my favorite filters are the Watercolor, Underpainting, Colored Pencil, and Rough Pastels filters. They tend to have the ability to render brush-like applications of color. And of course the art materials available in Painter are virtually endless.

It almost always happens that true, but exaggerated, coloring is more agreeable than absolute coloring.
—MICHEL-EUGENE
  CHEVREUL,
  The Principles of
  Harmony and Color
  (1839)

Figure 9-1
*Original water lily photo
and close-up*

Let's start with the original photograph of a water lily on a local pond (Figure 9-1). We will experiment with filter-like effects from both Photoshop and Painter.

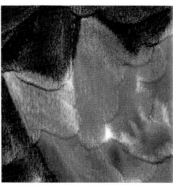

Figure 9-2
*Painter: Watercolor Runny
Cloner*

In Painter, the water lily was cloned using the Watercolor Runny Cloner and saved as a Photoshop file and re-opened in Photoshop. In Photoshop this runny watercolor version can be used with other filter effects, on its own separate layer. (See Chapter 5 for painterly cloning in Corel's Painter.)

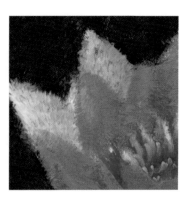

Figure 9-3
Painter: Impressionist Cloner

Figure 9-3 illustrates the use of the Impressionist Cloner in Painter. This was also saved in a Photoshop format and re-opened in Photoshop.

Figure 9-4
Photoshop:
Filter—Underpainting

Figure 9-4 shows the use of Photoshop's Underpainting filter. Notice in the close-up how this filter affects the edges of objects.

Figure 9-5
*Photoshop: Filter—Stylize—
Find Edges*

The most impressive edge tool in Photoshop is the Filter—Stylize—
Find Edges filter. This tool looks for contrast differences on edges. It
often gives the effect of a pen contour drawing. The filter was used
twice for a stronger look.

One becomes in time so
sensitive to color harmony
that the instant one puts
on a false spot of color it
hurts, like the wrong note
in music.
—WILLIAM MERRITT
  CHASE,
  In the Company of Friends
  (1979)

Figure 9-6
*Finished water lily, made
from bits and pieces of all
the previous filters and clone
effects*

The final compilation of all these filters working together is Figure
9-6. It uses a little sampling from each of the filter effects that were
applied to the water lily. You can vary the types of filters used in your
artwork. They can come from a variety of software options. You can
combine the filters in Photoshop with cloners in Painter or third-party
filters. You are the artist, you decide what is appropriate. Remember,

we are selecting how we will make marks. The quality of those marks and how the effect will work with the final image are the important considerations.

Most software will allow you to save and open your image in Photoshop. If you have been consistent in the size of the original image, in every effect or filter that you have used, you can put each version on a separate Photoshop layer and use Layer masks on each layer to determine how much of that layer will be used or hidden. If you couple that range of options with the ability to vary the blending modes on each layer, the possibilities become mind-boggling.

Favorite Photoshop Filters

Find Edges

Figure 9-7
Completed photo illustration

Filter—Stylize—Find Edges
There is a wonderful filter that is located under Filter—Stylize in Photoshop. It is called Find Edges. You may recall seeing it in Chapter 4 (Figure 4-62). This filter is wonderful to use in connection with another layer or two. It creates a line drawing around the contours of anything that exhibits contrast.

Figure 9-8
Original photograph

Figure 9-9
Photoshop: Filter—Stylize—Find Edges

In the most "commonplace" objects marvelous new realities lie hidden, ordinarily unperceived relationships of forms, new combinations or psychological connotations, new aggregates of symbolic meaning.

—CLARENCE JOHN LAUGHLIN,

typescript for a lecture, *Some Observations on the Functions of Photography* (1939)

Using the Find Edges filter creates a line drawing everywhere that contrast exists. It is as if you had outlined the edges with a fine-point pen. Some color remains and can even appear somewhat bizarre in tone.

Figure 9-10

Adjustment made to desaturate this filter effect

Image—Adjustment—Desaturate

All color was eliminated by using Image—Adjustment—Desaturate. This allowed only the line drawing effect to remain.

Figure 9-11

Layers used on completed photo illustration

In the completed illustration, the Find Edges layer was masked to allow some of the underlying image of the original photo to show through. A duplicate of the original photo was placed on top at a 37% opacity. This yielded a colored version of the line drawing.

Experimenting with Blending Modes, when using filters

Figure 9-12
Original photo, taken in Venice

Continuing to experiment with the Find Edges filter takes us to an example that kicks this concept up a notch or two. The original photo was duplicated and the Find Edges command was used to create an outline sketch effect.

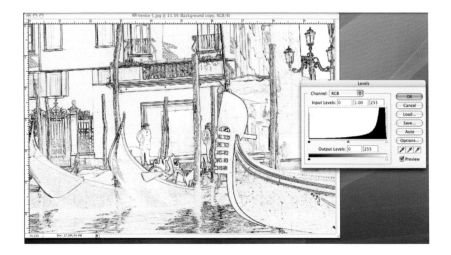

Figure 9-13
Photoshop: Filter—Stylize— Find Edges effect taken into Levels

Filter—Stylize—Find Edges
Image—Adjustments—Levels
After using the Find Edges filter you may find many small areas that are gray-like whorls of tone. They make the effect appear dirty. The next step is to eliminate those pesky areas.

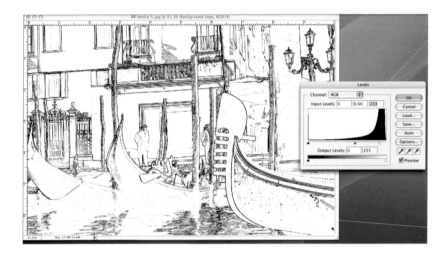

Figure 9-14
Level sliders used to get rid of unwanted gray mid-tones

A clean-looking black and white outline sketch was achieved by using a Levels Layer Adjustment on the Find Edges layer.

Figure 9-15
Find Edges layer applied over the original photo, using Exclusion blending mode

The blending mode was changed from Normal to Exclusion
Make a habit of trying out different blending modes. Remember that blending mode determines how the selected layer will interact with the layer beneath it. I tried several before I arrived at the right one for this image.

Blending mode was set to Difference

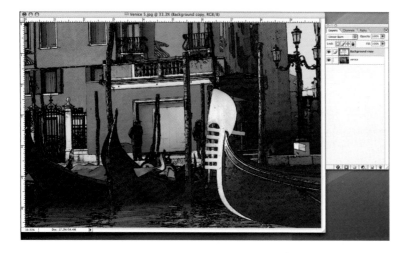

Blending mode was set to Linear Burn

The great artists never really stopped experimenting. . . . Titian continued to use different techniques until the end of his long life. . . . Renoir grew even more experimental as he grew older.
—KIMON NICOLAIDES,
  The Natural Way to Draw (1941)

Blending mode was set to Overlay
The Overlay blending mode appeared to have the most potential for this image.

Figure 9-19
Layer mask is added, to fine-tune the edge effect on the photo

Layer mask was added for selective effects

Figure 9-20—*Waiting in Venice*
Completed photo illustration

Isolate and Blur

Figure 9-21
Original color photograph

If you have ever tried to capture children at a wedding, you know the perils and joys that ensue. The little flower girl in Figure 9-21, Josie, was posing with her parents and young baby brother. As often happens, as the parents struggled to position the baby, little Josie was quietly trying to independently do her part. She was the only redeemable portion of this photo. But why not use her alone? Josie was cropped out onto her own photo page.

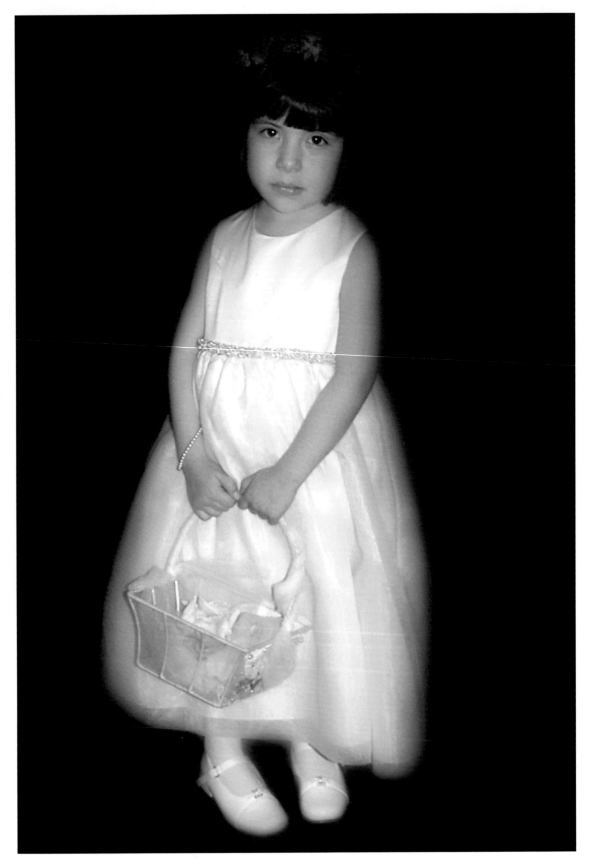

Figure 9-22
Completed sepia-toned image

Photo was cropped
Image—Adjustments—Desaturate
Image—Adjustments—Color Balance (yellow and red added)
Layer was duplicated
New layer used a Filter—Blur—Gaussian Blur
New layer added a layer mask to allow the crisp photo to appear through the blurred image in selected areas
Background was painted a soft, dark brown tone

After the photo was cropped and copied onto a new canvas, the color was converted. First the photograph was desaturated into a black and white image. Next, color was applied back in, by adding red and yellow in all three of the tonal areas (highlights, mid-tones, and shadows). That layer was then duplicated. The duplicate layer was blurred using the Gaussian Blur filter. This step gave us that soft, ethereal effect on the edges. Josie was a fairy princess that day, in her flower girl role—why not increase that sense of a magical, romantic moment in time? The original photo was allowed to peep through by using a layer mask on the blurred layer. Finally, the background was painted a soft, dark brown.

The independence or detachment of the creative individual is at the heart of his capacity to take risks and to expose himself to the probability of criticism from his fellows.
—JOHN W. GARDNER, *Self-Renewal* (1963)

Photoshop Photo Filters

Photoshop comes loaded with several photo filters, like the ones you would attach onto your lens. Of course, these are digital ones that you apply, after the photograph has been taken.

Figure 9-23
Original bullriding photograph

Our bullriding photograph was taken at the Battle of the Beast with a long lens in late evening. The action was great but the color proved to be distracting. I find these types of venues to be quite challenging. It is often impossible to rid yourself of poles, gates, and stray elements, if you want to capture the action. Although the expression on the clown's face to the right was good, as was the body language, I wanted to emphasize the bull. Here is what I did.

Figure 9-24
Channel Mixer used to desaturate the image

An adjustment layer was created to use the channel mixer
The Channel Mixer is a great way to desaturate your photos. Try it! It can take care of contrast problems at the same time.

Figure 9-25
Image—Adjustments—Photo Filter was selected

Access the Photoshop photo filters through Image—Adjustments—
Photo Filter

Figure 9-26
Sepia photo filter

Choose Sepia from the Photo Filter options
I love the look of sepia. Many of my wet darkroom prints have a bit
of warming, due to selenium toning. I just like the look. It is so easy
to do in Photoshop.

Figure 9-27
Fade sepia photo filter

Edit—Fade sepia filter

Immediately after you render a filter you have the opportunity to fade the effect. If the color is a little too vivid, as it was for my tastes, in our example, go immediately to the Edit—Fade command. Don't wait until several steps later: you will lose the opportunity, unless you work backward in your history palette.

Motion Blur

Figure 9-28
Motion Blur filter—Radial

Duplicate the image on another layer; the Radial Blur filter is applied to the new copy layer
Filter—Blur—Radial Blur
Edit—Fade—Radial Blur (56%)
Motion Blur is a filter that I seldom use. Radial Blur, however, was the perfect filter to call attention to the bull and minimize the rest of the image. I then faded the blur effect a bit.

Figure 9-29
A layer mask is applied

Apply a layer mask to bring back the sharpness on the bull, on the underlying image

The only portion of the image that I want to be crisp and tonally correct is the bull. The rest of the image can be fuzzy. This was achieved by applying a layer mask and only painting in the area of the bull. Notice how the mask also appears in the channel dialogue box that is currently open.

Figure 9-30
Completed "Battle of the Beast" bullriding photograph

Creating a Black and White Pencil Sketch Effect Using Filters

If you are artistically challenged and want a pencil sketch feel from a favorite photograph, this is the trick for you. It can be used as a line drawing or in combination with other images. Give it a whirl. It is different than the previous effect of Find Edges.

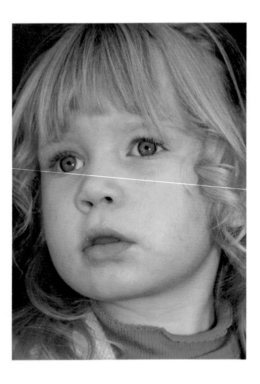

Figure 9-31
Original photograph of Simone

The supreme misfortune is when theory outstrips performance.
—LEONARDO DA VINCI,
Treatise on Painting
(1651)

Desaturate the photograph (Image—Adjustments—Desaturate)
Duplicate the desaturated layer
On the new layer, apply Image—Adjustments—Invert (it will appear as a negative)
Set the blending mode to Color Dodge. Surprise! The image should now be entirely white!
This is like a magician's hat trick. You will soon be pulling the bunny out of the hat. If you are the kind of person that has to know why this magic happens, think about it. The images have cancelled each other out.

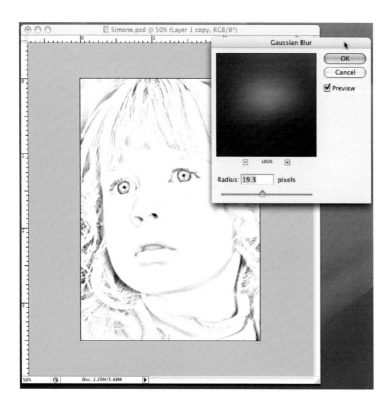

Figure 9-32
Apply Gaussian Blur in inverted layer

Apply the Gaussian Blur Filter to the inverted image
Voilà! The rabbit has come out of the magician's hat! The trick on this step is to disregard the preview window on the Gaussian Blur. Look only at the image itself. Adjust the slider to the look that you like for the sketch.

Figure 9-33
Apply Filter—Artistic— Rough Pastels

Filter—Artistic—Rough Pastels

To accentuate the sketch effect, we applied the Rough Pastels filter. Other candidates would have included the Cross Hatch filter. You decide which look you would like. You could stop now, if you like. The sketch has a neat look. But, what if you took it a little further?

Figure 9-34

Setting the Clone Source in Painter

With both files open in Painter, set the Clone Source to the original photo

The pencil sketch can act as the underlying structure for a painting. You can choose to let the original sketch remain intact, by cloning it, or you can paint directly on top. Now open Painter and open two files there: the new outline sketch and the original photograph. Make the outline sketch file your active file, and set the Clone Source to the original photo. That means the brushes that you will use will be pulling their colors from the source file of the original photo.

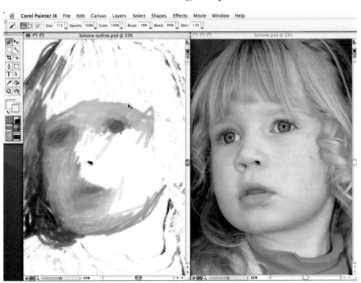

Figure 9-35

Chalk cloning: using a grainy brush made in Brush Creator

Clone Brush—Chalk

Try out a variety of cloning brushes. I generally work from loose strokes to tighter detail, back and forth, using a variety of different brush sizes and types of media. Use the Brush Creator to customize the brush.

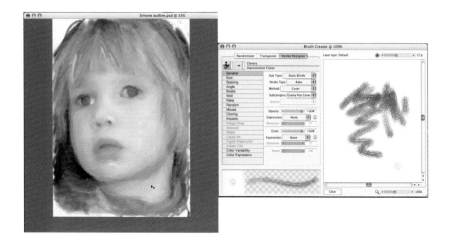

Figure 9-36
Chalk cloning: using a soft cover brush made in Brush Creator

Figure 9-37
Brush Creator making a new Impressionist Brush

Clone—Straight Cloner to selectively bring back detail in eyes, nostrils, etc.; use 2% opacity

Clone—Impressionist Brush (custom designed with the Brush Creator)

Create a new Impressionist Brush with the Brush Creator. This brush used a Static Bristle, a Rake stroke, and a Flat Grainy Cover. This custom brush avoided the usual look of the Impressionist rice-like strokes of color.

Figure 9-38
Checking the painting against the photo

There are no days in life so memorable as those which vibrate to some stroke of the imagination.
—RALPH WALDO EMERSON, *Conduct of Life: Beauty* (1860)

Evaluate

Be sure to use your photograph occasionally for reference. Are there details that you still want to capture or are there areas you want to eliminate?

Figure 9-39
Completed digital painting of Simone

Figure 9-40
*Using the sketch in
combination with the photo*

Another artistic possibility for the sketch is to use it in combination
with the original photograph. Figure 9-40 illustrates the original photo,
the sketch version, and two ways to combine them. The bottom left lays
the sketch layer on top of the photograph, with the blending mode set
to Multiply, creating an outline effect that is strong on contrast. The
illustration in the lower right lowered the opacity of the photograph
and employed a layer mask, to remove color from some areas. This
yielded a softer, pastel look.

Similar Effects in Photoshop and Painter

Occasionally you will notice that an effect in Photoshop is similar to
one in Painter. Good examples are the similar effects shown in Figure
9-41. The carousel horse had the Cutout filter in Photoshop applied

Original Photo   PhotoShop Cut Out Filter   Painter Woodcut Effect

Figure 9-41
Similar, yet different, effects:
Original photo, Photoshop
Cutout filter, and Painter
Woodcut effect

for an effect that resembles silk-screening. A similar effect, Woodcut, is found in Painter. Both effects are great for photo illustration work.

Third-Party Filter Plug-Ins

Inspiration is to work
every day.
—CHARLES BAUDELAIRE,
  Epigram (1860)

There are many companies that offer third-party plug-ins or stand-alone programs with a myriad of filters and edges. You can find most of them on the Internet. Some sites offer free filters. It would be impossible to address all of them in this chapter. We will just give a brief glimpse at two of the more popular ones that are on the market. Keep in mind that a snazzy filter does not make up for a poor photograph. Use these filters to create a mood or graphic effect that is appropriate to the photograph that you want to enhance. Be careful not to overdose on filters. They can be seductive and fun. I've seen some photographers go overboard on these effects, like a child in a candy store with all of their allowance to spend. Try them out. Find the effects that work with your own personal imagery. There are so many options. Have fun with it but maintain your photographic and artistic equilibrium.

nik Color Efex Pro Filters

One of the most popular third-party plug-in filter offerings is the nik Color Efex Pro 2. It offers a huge range of filters that simulate the filters that are normally applied directly onto your camera, as well as many unusual special effects filters. The same company also makes a wonderful piece of software that sharpens your images. The nik Sharpener will modify the amount of sharpening needed on your image according to your printer and paper types. It can also be brushed on in selective areas.

The idyllic look of the photo shown in Figure 9-42, taken near dusk, as children had deserted their bug catching efforts, suggested nostalgia to me. I wanted a softer, moodier feel to the image.

Figure 9-42
Original photograph

Figure 9-43
Completed image, "Catching Fireflies"

The completed image yields the look I was aiming for.

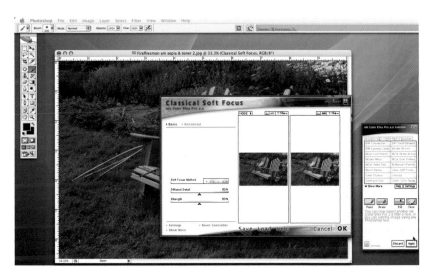

Figure 9-44
Choosing Classical Soft Focus Filter

Filter—Plug-in—nik Color Efex Pro 2—Classical Soft Focus Filter
Although the Monday Morning filter that was used later on this image will give a soft look, I wanted even more. As a result, the first filter I chose was the Classical Soft Focus filter. One of the viewing options in the dialogue box of nik Color Efex Pro allows you to view the image and its corrected version at the same time. This side-by-side comparison is very helpful.

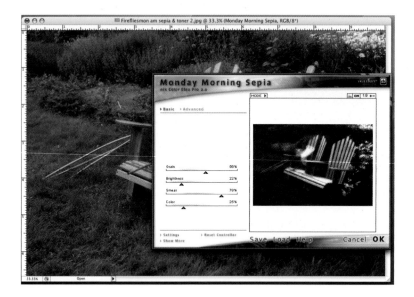

Figure 9-45
Choosing a Monday Morning filter

Filter—Plug-in—nik Color Efex Pro 2—Monday Morning Sepia
The second filter that was applied was the Monday Morning Sepia filter (it also comes in Blue, Green, and Violet). I love this filter! It gives a soft, romantic feel, similar to infrared film, with a grainy feel. Again, you can move those sliders to modify different aspects of the filter.

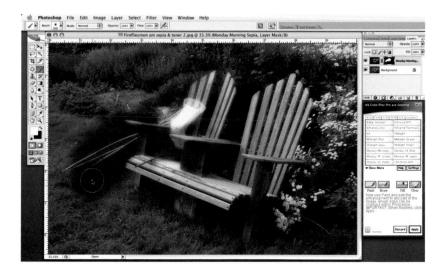

Figure 9-46
Using the layer mask to paint on the filter effect

Once you press OK on the filter, the effect is rendered on a separate layer with a built-in mask. You can then paint (with white) the filter effect in segments of your photo, or over the whole image, as I did here.

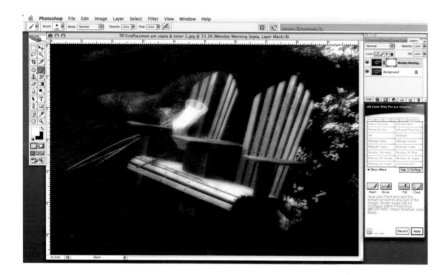

Figure 9-47
Completed Monday Morning filter

In Figure 9-47 the entire mask was painted with white, revealing the filter effect over the whole photograph. A touch of color remained, especially in the butterfly nets, which I liked. However, I wanted a warmer feel, with a stronger sepia effect.

When your demon is in charge, do not try to think consciously. Drift, wait, obey.
—RUDYARD KIPLING, *Something of Myself* (1937)

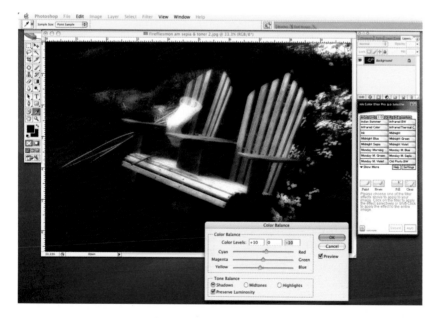

Figure 9-48
Creating a stronger sepia tint in Photoshop using Image—Adjustment—Color Balance

Image—Adjustment—Color Balance was used to increase red and yellow
A stronger sepia effect could be achieved many ways. I'll share two here. The first way is to simply go to the Color Balance adjustment in Photoshop and pull in more reds and yellows.

Figure 9-49
Sepia paper tone created using nik Color Efex Pro 2 Paper Toner Filter #2

Filter—Plug-in—nik Color Efex Pro 2—Paper Toner Filter
The second way to add a sepia tone is to use another filter effect by nik. Several different toning effects are options with the Paper Toner Filter. Select the one you like from the examples shown (we chose #2) and presto, you have the look of a toned photo, straight from the darkroom.

Increasing depth of field by using two images
Several filters applied

Figure 9-50
Image made from two photographs

This photograph was made from two images, in the Amish farm area of Lancaster, PA. One had the foreground in focus, the other had the background in focus. They were combined in Photoshop, using a layer mask. That certainly worked but the image needed more vibrant colors also.

Figure 9-51
Completed image with three filters applied

The completed image had three nik filters applied to it: Foliage filter, Polarizer, and Blue Gradient filter. The colors are more saturated and the whole image is more vibrant.

Instinct preceded wisdom.
—GEORGE LILLO,
Fatal Curiosity (1736)

Black and white conversion

Figure 9-52
Original color image of Amish buggy

The image of the Amish buggy in Figure 9-52 was rather flat in contrast and the color was dull, except for the neon red caution sign that all buggies are required to have on the rear of the carriage.

Figure 9-53
nik Black and White Tonal Enhancer filter was applied

Filters: nik Color Efex Pro—Black and White Tonal Enhancer filter applied
The answer to enhancing this image was to convert it to black and white and increase the contrast. There are three different black and white conversion filters in the nik selection. Again, choose the one that is right for your image. The Black and White Tonal Enhancer offers three different contrast possibilities with sliders for refinement. This filter solves the problem of contrast that usually comes with desaturating a color image.

Applying Filters Selectively

Figure 9-54
Original photo taken at the doorway of a mosque in Istanbul

Funny thing about painting, you don't know what makes it right, but you know when it's wrong.
—Charles Hawthorne,
Hawthorne on Painting
(1938)

Sometimes you only want a filter to be applied to a portion of the image, not the entire photograph. The original photograph in Figure 9-54 was inviting, but the color of the rolled up doorway did not complement the blue rug.

Figure 9-55
nik Color Efex Filter—Paper Toner #2 applied selectively

Filter—nik Color Efex Pro—Paper Toner #2
My favorite color of toner (Paper Toner #2) was applied to the image, but not everywhere. Using a layer mask and a low opacity on the brush, areas of color were allowed to appear slightly.

Figure 9-56
nik Color Efex Pro Indian Summer Filter added selectively

Filter—nik Color Efex Pro—Indian Summer
To warm up the overall look, a second filter (Indian Summer) was applied selectively in some areas, especially the wooden door. Again, a layer mask was used to apply the effect in specific areas only.

Auto FX Filters

Another popular series of third-party filters is the Auto FX series. The series includes several separate programs: DreamSuite, Mystical Lighting, Mystical Tint Tone & Color, Auto Eye, and Photo/Graphic Edges. They can be purchased separately or in package sets. We will take a look at a few of the huge array of options these effects offer.

DreamSuite: Deckle, Cubism, Photo Depth, Crease, and Mesh

Figure 9-57
Original photo of flower-bedecked cottage

This photograph seemed to call for an Impressionist touch. A piece like this would be a great candidate for a greeting card illustration.

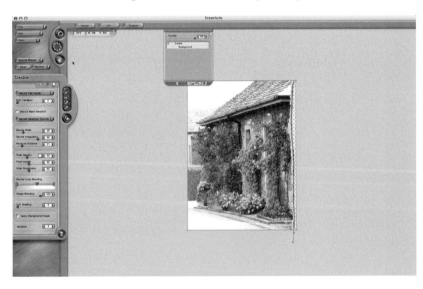

Figure 9-58
DreamSuite: Deckle effect

I perhaps owe having become a painter to flowers.
—CLAUDE MONET,
in *Monet*, by William C.
Seitz (1982)

First DreamSuite filter: Deckle
The DreamSuite was initiated and the Deckle effect was chosen to produce a deckle edge on the right side of the image. True deckle edges are produced in the manufacture of some types of paper, as the fibers thin out at the edges of the sheet, during manufacturing.

Figure 9-59
Cubism filter

The next filter was the Cubism filter: Shapes: Triangles
This is a curious little filter that breaks up the image into triangular
patches. I picked a small size and it gave a bit of an Impressionist effect,
with splotches of color.

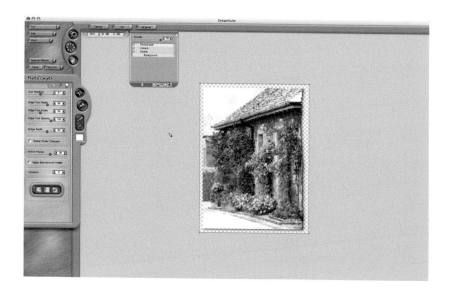

Figure 9-60
Photo Depth

The next filter was Photo Depth
This filter was a bit more predictable and added a shadowy depth to
the image.

Figure 9-61
Deckle again

The Deckle filter was used on the left side
We went back to the Deckle filter and added a Deckle on the left side.

Figure 9-62
Color was brushed onto the path, yielding a watercolor effect

The best way to learn is to learn from the best.
—Margaret Mead,
Blackberry Winter (1971)

Cool shades were selected and painted onto the pathway with a light opacity

Figure 9-63
Completed flower-covered cottage

DreamSuite: Crease

Normally we strive to keep our cherished photos from becoming creased and dog-eared. This filter purposely distresses our photos. How much damage is up to you. You determine where the folds and creases will develop.

Figure 9-64
Original wooded pathway

Figure 9-65
Crease filter used

Crease filter used

Experiment with the modifiers and pull and drag the folds and creases into your image. This filter relies heavily on shadows for a convincing folded effect.

In carrying on my humble creative effort, I depend greatly upon that which I do not yet know, and upon that which I have not yet done.
—Max Weber,
in *Three American Modernist Painters*, by James Johnson Sweeny (1969)

Figure 9-66
Completed "creased" photograph

DreamSuite: Mesh

This filter, found in the DreamSuite collection, makes a mock weave of your photo. You can even determine the dimensions on each strip of the mesh.

Figure 9-67
Original rose photograph

Figure 9-68
Using the Mesh filter

Mesh filter used

Experiment with the size and spacing of the strips that make up the mesh. This filter is a lot easier than actually cutting a photo apart and weaving it back together (see Chapter 10, "Experimentation").

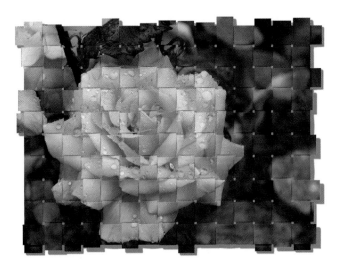

Figure 9-69
Completed rose mesh

Mystical Lighting: Mist and Wispy Mist

Figure 9-70
Original photograph of Loch Ness ruin

Mystical Lighting is a stand-alone piece of software. As the name infers, it is all about lighting effects. These lighting effects are quite different from the ones available to you in either Photoshop or Painter.

Figure 9-71
Mystical Lighting filter: Mist

Apply Mist filter
Since Loch Ness is known for one of the world's great mysteries, it seemed appropriate to enshroud it in a heavy mist. You can place the mist where you would like and control its intensity.

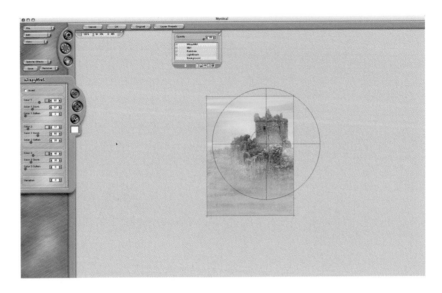

Figure 9-72
Wispy Mist

There's a time when
what you're creating
and the environment
you're creating it in come
together.
—GRACE HARTIGAN,
  Art Talk magazine (1975)

Wispy Mist applied
I decided to go for broke and really bring in a heavy mist. Wispy Mist
was the perfect answer.

Figure 9-73
Hue/Saturation adjustment

Image—Adjustment—Hue/Saturation
The image was still too cheerfully green. I needed solemn. Most, but
not all, color was deleted, using the Hue/Saturation adjustment.

Figure 9-74
nik Infrared: Black and White filter

Apply nik Infrared: Black and White filter

There is absolutely no reason that you cannot mix and match your plug-in filters. So, although we started with an Auto FX filter we have continued with a nik filter. You are the artist, you determine the look that you are pursuing. Experiment with the sliders, see where it might go. The setting applied in Figure 9-74 yielded a very dark and ominous image, suitable for a horror film.

Figure 9-75
Completed dark infrared effect

Figure 9-76
Lighter effect with the same filter

The dream of reason produces monsters.
—FRANCISCO GOYA,
in *Goya*, by Xavier de Salas (1978)

Apply nik Infrared: Black and White using lighter settings
That same filter also produced a light, ethereal look. Moving the slider modifiers was the sole difference.

Figure 9-77
Light Infrared filter effect

How far should we push this look? Just to see where this might go, we applied a layer of indigo color. The only difference in each of the six images (Figures 9-78–9-83) was the blending mode that was selected. See how different they can look, just with the change of a blending mode. Pretty neat, huh?

Figure 9-78
Overlay mode

Figure 9-79
Color mode

Figure 9-80
Multiply mode

Figure 9-81
Color Burn mode

Figure 9-82
Lighten mode

Figure 9-83
Difference mode

Photographic edges

Figure 9-84
Original fruit market

You have already learned how to make your own photographic edges. There are, however, many companies that have great edges for sale. We will look at a couple of interesting edge effects.

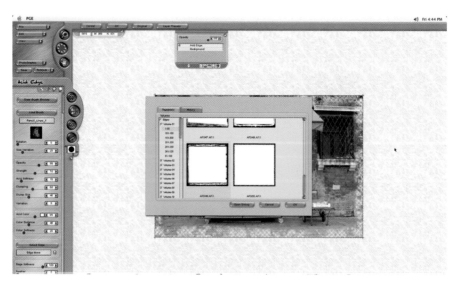

Figure 9-85
Acid Edge

Photo/Graphic Edges: Acid Edge
If you have a hard time making up your mind, don't buy the Auto FX package, Photo/Graphic Edges, because it has a ton of options. Otherwise, jump in and try it out. If you don't like one effect, there will be six more that you love.

Figure 9-86
Acid Edge applied

Figure 9-87
Completed edge effect

This distressed edge is appropriate to the weathered look of this local Italian market.

Combining the effects of different third-party plug-ins

Let's give another example of combining different third-party plug-ins.

I long ago came to the conclusion that, even if I could put down accurately the thing I saw and enjoyed, it would not give the observer the kind of feeling it gave me. I had to create an equivalent for what I felt about what I was looking at, not copy it.

—GEORGIA O'KEEFFE, in *Georgia O'Keeffe: Portrait of an Artist*, by Laurie Lisle (1980)

Photo/Graphic Edges: Burn, and nik Duplex: Monchrome

Figure 9-88
Original color photograph

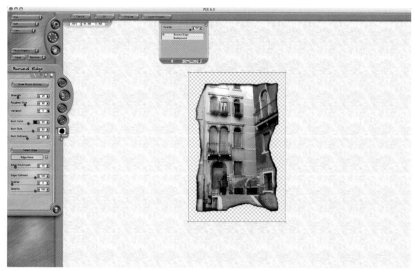

Figure 9-89
Photo/Graphic Edges: Burn filter

Burn filter applied

This is so much safer than taking a match to your favorite photograph, and the burn effect is more controllable, and of course, it is reversible. You determine where the burn will occur. It is completely controllable.

Figure 9-90
Burn completed

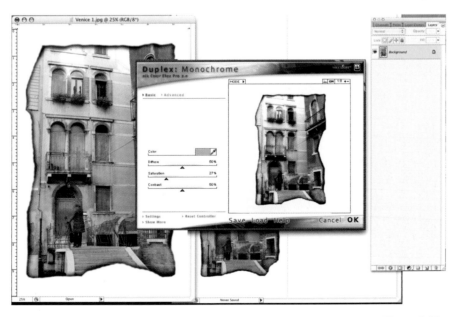

Figure 9-91
nik: Duplex: Monochrome filter

Form is the shape of
content in art and life.
—BEN SHAHN,
The Shape of Content
(1957)

Apply nik: Duplex: Monochrome

Sometimes color is distracting. It takes away the power of the composition, or lighting effect, or some other design element. This image is much stronger to me, with this monochrome look. The buttery shade evokes nostalgia and images from the 1930s and 1940s. Too bad the woman is wearing a coat that is distinctively more modern in design.

In conclusion, filters are fabulous tools that can bring great creativity to your work. But they are tools, like any other. As the artist, you must be the arbitrator of what is appropriate for your imagery. It is important to know your tools well. Know their limitations as well as their positive attributes. Filters can easily be overdone. Try not to fall in love with a filter and use it on your work indiscriminately. Filters work when they truly enhance the image, and only then.

Figure 9-93, "*Jaime*," is a bridal portrait enhanced with the nik Midnight Sepia filter.

Figure 9-92
*Completed combination filter
project*

Figure 9-93—"Jaime"

10 *Experimentation*

Chapter 10 takes the restrictions off where you might go with your digitally produced artwork. There is every opportunity available to combine various mediums. Some of the artists featured in Chapter 3 employ a variety of traditional art mediums in their digital work.

I would encourage you to keep a scrap bin of discarded prints that can be used for experimentation. Feel free to tear them up and collage them with other elements or draw and paint on them—in short, have fun with the imagery and see where it might lead you. We'll begin by recapping traditional printmaking processes.

Combining Traditional Media with Digital

Printmaking: Woodcuts, Intaglio and Lithography, and Silk-Screening

Artists, throughout time, have been fascinated with the idea of making more than one copy of a piece of art. In the example of an oil painting, only one patron or client can own the work. This exclusivity comes with a high price tag to compensate the artist for his time and talents. Over the centuries, many processes have been developed to allow artists to make multiple copies of their work.

In the woodcut printmaking technique a design is chiseled or gouged out of a piece of flat wood. The areas to be inked and printed are the remaining sections of the wood that have not been removed. Gaugin used this technique often. A modern version of this technique could use a piece of linoleum to substitute for the wood. Painter offers a technique that resembles a woodcut.

Figure 10-1
Woodcut in Painter

Engravings, or intaglio, use a metal plate that is coated with a tar-like substance (to protect the plate). That covering is then scratched with a stylus of some type, revealing a line of bare metal. When the drawing is completed, an acid is applied to "etch" the drawing into the plate. In turn, the plate is inked, and run through a press that pushes the soft printmaking paper into the inked areas, resulting in a print. Many editions can be made from the plate, as evidenced by the fine engravings by Albrecht Dürer.

The lithography process is similar to the intaglio process, but instead of a plate of metal, a thick, flat stone is used. In this technique the drawing is made directly onto the stone with a greasy pencil. The stone is etched, inked, and an edition is made. A good example is the beautiful art nouveau work of Alphonse Mucha.

Both intaglio and lithography can be made with more than one plate or stone, multiplying the effect. It was also very common in the past to employ artists to hand-color the black and white prints. The coloring was sometimes done with stencils for each color added, or with hand-painted watercolors.

Other printmaking techniques that have been popular over time include silk-screening, as seen in the work of Toulouse-Lautrec. Modern uses of silk screen are more confined to T-shirts and mass commercial productions, but the process is still used in artwork today. A modern example would be the work of Andy Warhol. A separate screen of silk is made into a stencil for each color used in the completed work.

What does all that have to do with digital printing? We are, of course, making prints. We can make multiple copies of our work, creating an edition. We determine how large or small that edition will be. The fewer the copies produced, technically the more rare the print. The more rare print can command a higher price.

Historically, in lithography, after the images had been pulled for an edition, the stone was ground down, removing the drawing and preparing the surface for the next drawing to be made on that stone. In intaglio the plate would be destroyed by slashing through the image area, marring the drawing, or actually melting the metal down. The ethics of the digital artist are perhaps not so clear-cut. The master digital file could be destroyed to ensure collectors that no more than the stated edition number will be made of that print. The waters get a little muddy as artists make another edition of that image at a different size or on a different type of paper. I will leave it to you and your own personal ethics and business practices to work out a system that works for you and your clients and that is fair to all concerned.

As we are making prints, there is no reason that we cannot make mono-prints. "Mono-print" is a term used to describe an image that is only made once. Be sure to look at the work of Bobbi Doyle-Maher in Chapter 3. Ms. Doyle-Maher makes mono-prints on top of her digital prints.

No person is real until he has been transmitted into a work of art.
—George Bernhard Shaw,
The Sanity of Art (1893)

Overprinting and Collaging

For our uses in the digital print arena, we can make a drawing on a piece of paper and then feed that drawing through our printer, applying a digital overprint. We could reverse that concept and draw or paint on our digital prints, creating one-of-a-kind artwork. We could apply translucent layers of rice paper or fabric onto our prints. There is no end to the possibilities of digital printmaking, especially if we open our minds to include other art materials.

Encaustics

When you hear the term encaustics—think wax. Pigment is joined with wax and damar varnish. Wax, as you know, is affected by heat. Encaustic paints are applied with the use of heat. Heat can be supplied in a number of ways, from a hot plate to a hand-held heat gun, to a tjanting tool, used in the art of batik. And of course, wax varies also from white paraffin, used to cover jellies in canning, to soft, buttery, smooth beeswax. You can even achieve an encaustic effect by using crayons and heat. Heat and wax can be quite dangerous, so always use precautions and have a fire extinguisher handy.

One of our digital artist contributors in Chapter 3, Leslye Bloom, uses encaustics in combination with her digital prints, in a type of art she calls encaustic computage. Be sure to look at her work.

Lazertran onto Marble, Glass, Tile, Fabric, and Silk

There are times that you do not want your image to be on paper. You may want the image to be on glass, tile, metal, or marble. What do you do? You can be sure that your warranty would be void if you tried to put a piece of marble or glass through your printer. The answer can be found by putting your image onto a material that transfers that piece of art over onto the substrate that you desire. You will in essence be creating a decal. This can be a lot of fun to explore.

A company called Lazertran, based in the United Kingdom (see Chapter 13, "Resources"), has developed a product that will allow you to put your digital image on all sorts of surfaces. One of their products goes directly into your inkjet printer to create the transfers. Another type relies on the use of a color laser copier. The company also carries separate types of materials for transferring your images onto cloth, including silk and even dark fabrics.

Don't try to learn a formula, but to become sensitive, to feel deeply.
—KIMON NICOLAIDES,
 The Natural Way to Draw
 (1941)

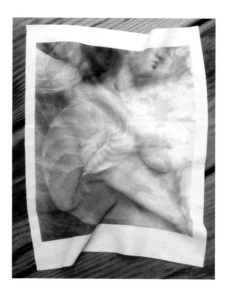

Figure 10-2
Lazertran for silk

Figure 10-3
Digital images transferred to marble and ceramic tile

inkAID—Making Your Own Inkjet Paper

Figure 10-4
Inkjet coated print, using inkAID on charcoal paper

inkAID is a product that allows you to paint an inkjet coating onto your favorite charcoal, watercolor, or drawing papers. Like most artists, I have favorite types of papers that I like to use. Sometimes I want a soft paper with a high rag content; sometimes I like a paper with embedded flecks. And, of course, I always look for a paper that is archival, that will resist decay by acid.

In Figure 10-4, charcoal paper was coated with two coats of inkAID. Use good ventilation and observe the safety precautions listed on the product. I found using inkAID to be quite simple. I allowed time for the applications to dry and then treated the sheet of paper like any other paper going through my printer. Remember, there is no white-colored ink in your inkjet printer, so the lightest areas of your image will be the color of the paper. Choose your image wisely for printing on toned paper. Darker images stand a better chance of making good use of this process.

Japanese Inkjet Coated Papers

Figure 10-5
Sampler test sheets printed on a variety of Japanese papers

The most important education you get is your own—the one you learn in solitude.
—ERICA JONG,
The Artist as Housewife
(1972)

If you like the look of your work on paper that is not the standard inkjet paper offerings, you might like to try some of the exotic Japanese papers offered by Digital Art Supplies. They offer a range of Japanese papers that are unique in texture, composition, and transparency. You can purchase a sample pack that has two sheets of each type of paper that is offered. When I get a sample pack of new papers I run a test image on one sheet of each. Your test image should be representative of the type and color of images that you typically make. You might want to include flesh tones, bright colors and subtle colors, or a black and white image on your test page. Print that same test page on all of the different types of papers. Does the ink bleed out more on some papers (excessive dot gain)? Do the dark areas block up? Does the texture overwhelm the image? Consider all these factors and more. This will help you decide what paper is best for your needs and imagery. Be sure to label your experiments for future reference.

Thinking Creatively: Paint It, Draw On It, Tear It, Glue It, and More

Add pastels, watercolors, colored pencils, gouache, and more

For those of you who like to draw and paint with traditional materials, you should feel free to use those materials on your digital prints. You may need to spray a protective coating onto the digital print to keep the inks from becoming soluble. That will depend on what printer and inks you are using. An example of a digital print on which drawing and painting has been applied can be found in Figure 5-89.

Figure 10-6
Two photos the same size

Weave two images together

It is always liberating to experiment. We often hold our art in a way that is too precious. What would happen if we tore it up or cut it into strips? In an experiment, I selected two photos that were the same dimensions. The photo on the left in Figure 10-6 was taken from a boat circling a heather-covered Scottish island. The photo on the right, taken at Pearl Harbor, Hawaii, was of the water above the memorial (the sunken vessel still leaks oil that creates these marvelous rainbow patterns on the water surface). I cut the first image into horizontal strips and second image into vertical strips and then wove them together.

Figure 10-7
Woven photos

After the photos were woven together, I scanned them on my flatbed scanner. I liked the idea of weaving but wanted to soften the effect a little.

Art seems to me to be a state of soul, more than anything else. The soul of all is sacred.
—Marc Chagall,
My Life (1947)

Figure 10-8
Sponge applied paint in Painter

In Painter, apply paint with the sponge tool
The woven photo scan was opened in Painter and colors of paint were selected and applied with the sponge tool to soften the look and provide a bit more color continuity.

Figure 10-9
The final image combined the woven image with a straight photograph

The completed image was layered together in Photoshop using layer masks. The bottom layer was the straight photo of a gondolier in Venice. The next layer was the woven piece. That layer supplied color and texture. The top layer was a blue tone reduced to 49% opacity and selectively used with the use of a layer mask.

Some forms of success are indistinguishable from panic.
—EDGAR DEGAS,
The Notebooks of Edgar Degas, trans. by T. Reff (1976)

Combining Drawing and Photography

Figure 10-10
Combining drawing of leaves with the actual leaves

I'm fond of experimenting with the combination of several art mediums used together. I'm always looking for new avenues of expression. Figure 10-14 began in such a manner. I found a cluster of leaves on the sidewalk. I decided to draw them and then to photograph the drawing with the actual leaves. On a piece of drawing paper I made a sketch of the leaves with a simple, soft, 4B drawing pencil. I made the drawing in such a way as to allow space for the actual leaves later. I then positioned the leaves on the drawing so that they and their shadows interacted with the drawing. I liked the interplay of the two different ways to capture the leaves. I especially liked how light worked with me compositionally, as the shadows became a design element in both the drawing and the photo.

My students are often told to ask "What-if?" questions. What if you combine this with that, etc.? Following that questioning philosophy, what would this image look like solarized, or inverted? How far can you push an idea or an image? Be willing to make lots of mistakes. The ride is fantastic as you open yourself to artistic experimentation.

In my wet darkroom, images with strong contrast, especially on the edges, are always good candidates for solarization. In Photoshop we can solarize predictably (something that cannot be said of that crazy and often chancy process in the darkroom).

Figure 10-11
Leaves were solarized and inverted

Photo was scanned in on the flatbed scanner
Image was used with the Filters—Stylize—Solarize
Next, the image used Image—Adjustments—Invert
I like what happens on the edges with this process. The question remains "What if?"

Figure 10-12
Combination of steps, using Transform

The canvas was doubled, in both width and height (Image—Canvas Size)
The various steps of alteration were rotated using the Transform command
One way to approach this idea of "where could it go from here?" would be using the various steps, joining them into one piece. In this posi-

tive–negative experiment, that gives a checkerboard effect and starts to create a center area that is almost forming a circle. If I still possessed the real leaf cluster, I would rephotograph it on top of this digital print. Alas, it is long gone. Too bad! The original drawing and photo were done on film over a dozen years ago, while working with legendary photographer Ruth Bernhard. Could we push this idea still further?

Figure 10-13
Central elements added

Scanned in guinea feather and scaled and rotated it with the Transform command
Single drawn leaf was added
Soft white circle was added (feathered circular marquee tool with white fill)
The leaf didn't exist anymore, but I had a guinea feather in my studio that had the same shape and similar veining structure. Why not use it? I scanned the feather in and adjusted its size. I copied a drawn leaf onto its own layer and transformed its scale. I added a soft, feathered circle that I filled with white. It was starting to go somewhere. It needed refinement.

It doesn't make much difference how the paint is put on as long as something has been said. Technique is just a means of arriving at a statement.
—JACKSON POLLOCK,
My Painting (1947)

Figure 10-14
Completed piece with its layers

Saturation on the feather was reduced
Leaf was transformed to make an X shape with the feather
Leaf had color added faintly (Color blending mode)
Gradient (radial shape) was used to darken the background gradually
It was an interesting experiment. There is nothing to keep you from drawing on your prints, or printing over a drawing. Try experimenting with mixing your media, if that is an avenue that seems intriguing for you artistically.

Creative Use of Papers for Albums

Something is happening now with albums, handmade books, and journals. Paper arts, calligraphy, and handmade books are rising swiftly in popularity. Scrapbooking is a huge hobby, and for some, an art form. I believe that scrapbooking has added to the interest in personalized books that can present visual and verbal information in a unique manner. The publishing industry caught a whiff of this trend to self-publish and now has small book-on-demand printing operations, even at the large publishing houses such as Random House.

A very nice array of companies now offer beautiful album components. The wedding photography business is changing how companies look at albums also. In the past, wedding albums were primarily constructed of pages that had inserted mattes that were die-cut in particular shapes (rectangles, squares, ovals, etc.). Now, brides want photojournalistic photography, in addition to the standard portraits. They want those images in a book that is personal to them. Some of the high-end books look like slick coffee-table books. The handmade book is being reborn and it is very exciting.

The following discussions present a few examples of book-making tools that are currently available.

iPhoto Books

Figure 10-15
Medium-sized, soft-cover iPhoto books

Apple came out with a book-on-demand service with their iPhoto program. That program allows you to download and organize your images, order prints, create slide shows (you can even add music), and publish small books. These books can be soft cover or hard cover. There are three sizes, ranging from a little book that is $3.5'' \times 2\frac{5}{8}''$, to $6'' \times 8''$, to $8.5'' \times 11''$. The prices are economical. There are easy templates to follow. You just drag and drop your images into the page format. There is also quite a bit of flexibility to customize your book to your needs.

There are companies such as Asuka Books (see Chapter 13, "Resources") that create lovely bound books in a variety of sizes on magazine glossy stock. These can be used for weddings or slick-looking portfolios.

The object isn't to make art, it's to be in that wonderful state which makes art inevitable.
—Robert Henri,
The Art Spirit (1923).

Epson StoryTeller Photo Book Creator Kits

Figure 10-16
Epson's StoryTeller Book

Epson has entered the fray with a kit that comes in two sizes (5″ × 7″ and 8″ × 10″). It can be purchased at the super office supply stores. It contains Epson's high-end premium glossy paper, a bound book, software (only for PC, not Mac), and a glossy cover. The kits contain 10 or 20 pages. You print the book, you assemble it. It is easy and very attractive.

Kolo Albums

Figure 10-17
The Kolo album has a distinctive photo window in the cover

You may have noticed Kolo albums at art supply stores, book stores, and fine stationers. This company makes a huge array of albums. They have itty-bitty, really tiny paperback ones, up to luxurious leather-bound albums with a post construction. These albums can have inkjet printed pages (they sell their own brand of double-sided inkjet paper that corresponds to the size of the album selected), scrapbook pages (even the old-fashioned black pages with photo corners), and journal pages. They are versatile for many different needs. They even sell protective sleeves to cover the pages (see Chapter 13, "Resources").

Other Album/Book Possibilities

I'm always on the prowl for a neat album cover that I can use with my own "insides." I've found lovely wooden-inlay covers at import shops. They had flimsy plastic pages for inserting 4" × 6" photos. I took those out and printed my own pages, customized to the size of the cover. Printing your own albums or books can be a rewarding experience. There are a few tools that you probably will want to have (bone folder, good scissors or knives, archival glue or spray adhesive, etc.). If you print your own, you can choose the paper type, texture, and weight that you prefer. You can print on double-sided paper also for a real book feel.

> Everyone wants to understand painting. Why don't they try to understand the song of the birds? Why do they love a night, a flower, everything which surrounds man, without attempting to understand them? Whereas where painting is concerned, they want to understand.
> —Pablo Picasso, "Conversation avec Picasso," in *Cahiers d'Art* magazine, nos. 7–10 (1935)

Figure 10-18
Hinges added to printed page, converting it for album use

Depending on the album or cover that you have chosen, the binding procedure can be a little tricky. Post-bound albums usually work well, but you will notice in the high-end, manufactured pages that there is a scored bend in the paper, to allow the page to lay flat. You can try to mimic that effect by scoring and bending with a bone folder. Another possibility is to try flexible hinge binding strips that are prescored, hole-punched, and archival. These strips come in several popular album sizes. Your paper attaches with the removal of a covering over an adhesive portion of the hinge. These provide a sturdy, archival way to use your favorite papers without physically creasing the paper (see Lineco in Chapter 13, "Resources").

Hand-made books, portfolios, and albums are definitely a practical way to display your digital artwork. These methods are a wonderful way of packaging a body of work. Perhaps you have a collection of photographs taken in parks and gardens, or a series of images made abroad. With these options you can create a book for each series of art that you produce. There are just so many materials and options available now—your own coffee-table book is just waiting around the corner.

Figure 10-19 was constructed from two separate sheep photographs and was primarily rendered with the Painter Woodcut option.

Figure 10-19—*Sheep Illustration*

11

Projects for You

This chapter is devoted to supplying you with five exercises that will allow you to try some of your new skills. The related files can be downloaded from our web site, http://www.focalpress.com/companions/digitalcollageandpainting. Three exercises are devoted to collage and two are designed for painting. It's time to get your hands dirty (digitally, of course).

Project 1: Gridded Collage Exercise

This exercise uses Photoshop to make a collage that relies on an underlying grid system. At our web site, we have supplied for you a file that

Creation lives as genius under the visible surface of the work. All those touched by the spirit see this in retrospect, but only the creative see it looking forward.
—PAUL KLEE,
  The Thinking Eye (1961)

measures 13 inches by 19 inches, with guidelines (pre-laid) of 1-inch squares. The guidelines are the guides supplied in Photoshop under View—Extras—Show—Grid. You can eliminate them later by going to View—Extras—Show—None. If you pull out your own nonprintable blue guidelines from the rulers on the top and side, using the move tool, you can eliminate them by going to View—Clear Guides.

There are also 33 photographs of flowers that are pre-cropped, for easy insertion. Feel free to use the flowers in any pattern that you desire. You do not need to follow my placement. Insert some of your own, if you like. Move the photographs until they snap in place along the guidelines.

When you are making a collage from your own images you will find that it might be easiest to pre-size them using the crop tool. You can set the crop to a certain size (e.g., 2 × 3 inches) and be sure that your photo is exactly correct.

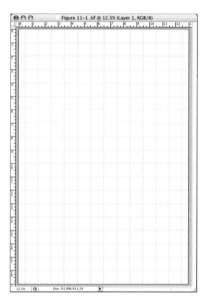

Figure 11-1
Blank grid template

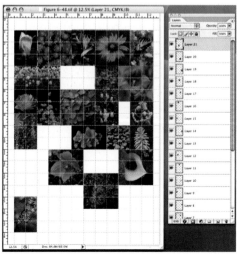

Figure 11-2
Adding flowers using the grid system

Move a photo of a flower over and make sure it "snaps" to the guideline. The easiest way to nudge the image into exact placement is to use the arrow keys on your keyboard, while your move tool is selected. It will get complicated very quickly as the number of layers mounts up. If you begin to search for an earlier layer, try turning off the "eye" symbol on that layer, to see if it is the correct one. Mix up the sizes of the photos and the colors of the flowers. If you inadvertently move a guide, you may want to lock your guides in place, by using View—Lock Guides.

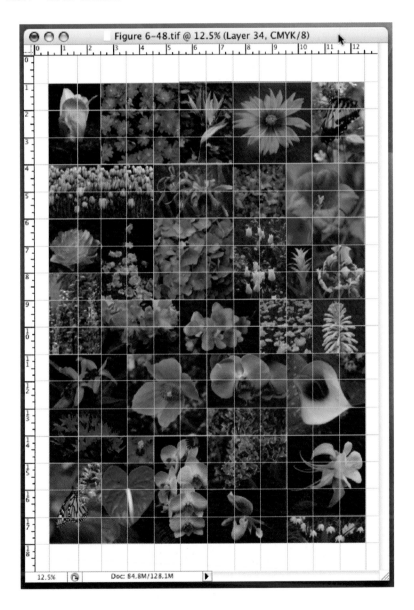

Figure 11-3
All photos are deposited into the grid

Once all your photos are in place, zoom in and check them out before removing the guides. Slowly examine the entire collage in a very close-up view format, to be sure there are no gaps present.

Figure 11-4—*"Flower Collage"*
Completed flower collage

You may find that once you remove the guides that there are tiny areas that do not meet properly. Simply nudge them closer, with your move tool. The guidelines may have obscured the fact that they were not in proper alignment. On rare instances you may need to add a little more width or height to an image. You can use free transform, to lightly stretch an image, or the rubber stamp tool to invent a few more pixels.

Creativity is looking at a problem or a situation in a different way from everyone else, and seeing something they have missed. The trail can be cultivated by refusing to accept the obvious.
—YURIKO YAMAMOTO, *Creativity: Journal of Counseling Psychology* (1965)

Project 2: Masks and Transparency Exercise

Reveal and conceal—that is the heart of masking. This exercise combines a famous nautical-theme statue in Piazza della Signoria in Florence with a school of fish from Seattle. We will use masking to set the statue into the sea and then a little transparency to add a coating of water.

Figure 11-5
Original photos for collage

Our statue from Neptune's Fountain has a green patina and a beige background. We will eliminate the background first.

Figure 11-6
The fish layer is masked to reveal the statue

Place the fish layer over the statue
Apply a layer mask—paint black over the shape of the statue, revealing it
This mask will take a little while. Vary the size of the brush as needed. Make it a small brush to give sharp edges and precise masking. Don't worry if you make a mistake. Just switch your color to white and you will be restoring the fish layer.

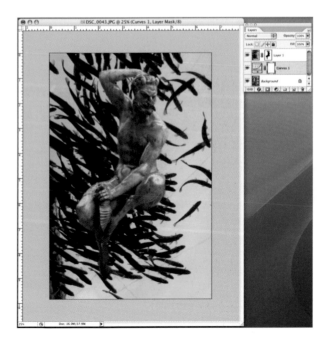

Figure 11-7
A Curves adjustment layer was used to provide contrast

Add a Curves adjustment layer to the statue—increase highlights and shadows, just a little bit

Blending the statue into the sea is our next task. A boost in contrast, using the Curves adjustment layer, helps the statue belong. Remember that if the light tones are increased a little and the dark tones are also increased, producing a slight S-curve in Curves, you will in effect have increased contrast. Be subtle.

Drawing is . . . not an exercise of particular dexterity, but above all a means of expressing intimate feelings and moods.
—Henri Matisse, in *Matisse: His Art and His Public*, by Alfred H. Bart (1951)

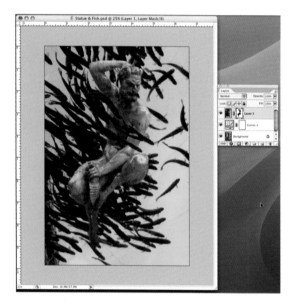

Figure 11-8
Masking fish to swim in front of the statue

Use white to restore some fish in front of the statue

We can make the fish layer go behind the statue and in front of it at the same time, using masking. Be precise in your masking by using smaller brushes.

Figure 11-9
Close-up of masked fish layer

The last remaining step is to add some transparent aqua-colored water over the entire piece.

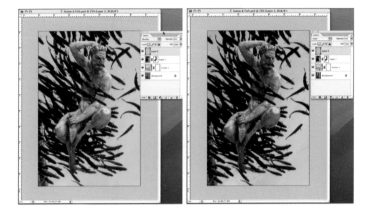

Figure 11-10
Overlay blending mode is on the left, Color blending mode is on the right

An attractive study is made from experience and calculations.
—Thomas Eakins,
   in *Thomas Eakins*, by
   Lloyd Goodrich (1987)

There are two blending modes (Overlay and Color) that would work well with this effect. Try them both. It is your choice. They both tint the statue, creating the feel that it is in water. Remember that color is one of the basic design elements, mentioned in Chapter 2, that can help bring a cohesive feel to a collage.

Figure 11-11
Completed nautical collage

Project 3: Panorama Exercise

A good way to start making panoramas is to start with a small one. This example uses twelve photos to combine in one linear image. The camera was held vertically, for more image area. The images were taken on a trip to Maine, without a tripod. *Note: If you use a tripod, there will be less variance in the placement of your photos, thus less work cropping images later in the process. But don't worry if you don't have a tripod with you. I've been quite successful making panoramas, by hand-holding the camera, trying to keep the camera level. The exposure needs to be exactly the same on all your exposures. Ours was taken with a 25 mm lens at f/8 and 1/320 second. Meter the light situation and set the camera to manual, on the proper exposure.

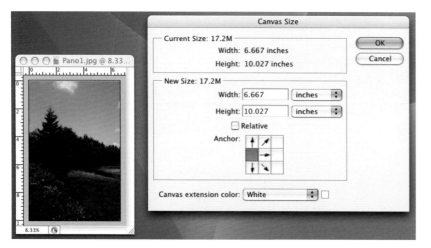

Figure 11-12
*Adding canvas onto your
first photograph*

**Image—Canvas Size (place the gray square to the side where you
began the panorama)**
The gray square represents the current photo. Make sure that white is your currently selected background color. Your background color will be the color of the added canvas.

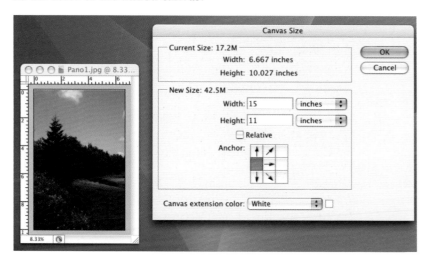

Figure 11-13
*Canvas adjusted more than
double for width, and a bit
for height*

Ability to correlate lines, shapes, tones is the rare and necessary quality of the artist.
—ROBERT HENRI, *The Art Spirit* (1923)

Increase the width to 15 and the height to 11

Figure 11-14
Canvas added

Figure 11-15
Second layer added with the Difference blending mode, for placement

Drag the next layer over onto the first image
Set the blending mode to Difference to precisely place the photo. You want to move the new layer until you get as much black as possible in the overlap
Return the blending mode to Normal
Add a layer mask
Paint on your layer mask with black on your brush, on the areas to the left that need to be blended in
You will repeat these steps for each layer.

Figure 11-16
Two layers combined

Figure 11-17
Eight layers fill the current canvas size

You will need to continue adding canvas periodically. Eight photos filled up our 15-inch width.

The greatest defect in a painter is to repeat the same attitudes and the same expressions.
—Leonardo da Vinci,
    Treatise on Painting
    (1651)

Figure 11-18
An easy way to add canvas is with the Crop tool

Select the Crop tool and pull in the direction where more canvas is needed

This is a quick and easy way to add canvas. You can "eyeball" the length that you need instead of entering specific numbers.

Figure 11-19
All twelve layers are in place

The first things to study are form and values. For me, these are the basics of what is serious in art. Color and finish put charm into one's work.
—JEAN-BAPTISTE-CAMILLE
   COROT,
   in *Corot*, by Keith
   Roberts (1965)

When all your layers are added, review the seams or joins for problem areas that need fixing. If they pass a close inspection, then flatten the image. This needs to be done several times when you are making a large panorama, which can hold 50 to 60 images.

Figure 11-20
Panorama is cropped

Crop the panorama

A crop was needed because of the variance in the images, due to the lack of a tripod during shooting. By holding the camera vertically, you gave yourself more image area to sacrifice, if need be. Just standing on a slight incline can cause a substantial shift. If you are using a tripod, use the level bubble to accurately keep the camera level throughout the exposures.

Figure 11-21
Assembled panorama

Although the assembled panorama is true to the exposure under which it was taken, I think we can expand on the tonal range available to us. Some areas are too dark.

Figure 11-22
Layer duplicated and blending mode set to Screen

Duplicate the layer
Set the blending mode to Screen
The panorama can be lightened with this technique. Some areas are improved, but other areas start to be blown out. The answer, of course, is a layer mask.

Figure 11-23
Layer masked image: Increases tonal range

It's good to have limits.
—DUKE ELLINGTON,
Music Is My Mistress
(1973)

A layer mask was used to restore some of the areas on the bottom layer, while incorporating some of the desired lighter tones. It is the best of both worlds.

Figure 11-24
*Completed small
twelve-photo panorama*

The completed image successfully combines twelve photos and increases the tonal range too. If you enjoyed assembling this small panorama, you may want to shoot some of your own.

Project 4: Painting in Photoshop

For this exercise we will use the Art History Brush and the Emboss filter. We will start off with a horizontal shot of some Scottish sheep.

Figure 11-25
Original photo of sheep

This exercise will work on most photographs. If you copy and paste a photo, please be sure to make a snapshot of it in the History Palette. Just click on the camera at the bottom of the History Palette.

Figure 11-26
Sheep roughed-in with a size 50 Dab Style Art History Brush

Create a new layer and fill it with white

Select the Art History Brush (bundled with the History Brush, it has a curly-cue on the top). In the History Palette, click on the box to the left of the thumbnail of your image. If you started with a white or transparent background, this will not work, unless you took a snapshot of the photo layer. You need to be using the photograph for the digital color information. A white or transparent layer will not give you the colored pixels that you need.

Use the Dab Style with a rough brush (size 50 pixels)

This will yield a rough laydown of color.

I'm always trying to disrupt what I can do with ease.
—FRANCIS BACON, interview, *Connoisseur* magazine (September 1984)

Figure 11-27
Brush size used at size 30 and size 10

Switch to a smaller brush (size 30 and then size 10)

The smaller the brush, the more color accuracy and detail.

Figure 11-28
Layer mask applied to pull in a little detail

Apply a layer mask to the painted layer
Use black with a light opacity (10% or less) to paint on the mask, revealing a touch of the original image below.

Figure 11-29
Desaturated copy layer with Emboss applied

Merge the layers
Duplicate the layer and desaturate it
Filter—Stylize—Emboss filter applied to this new layer

Figure 11-30
Emboss filter set to Hard Light

I paint things as I think them, not as I see them.
—PABLO PICASSO
in "Picasso Speaks," *The Arts* magazine (May 1923)

Set the blending mode to Hard Light
Using the Emboss filter will give a three-dimensional look. The dark cast shadow effect was too dark and distracting.

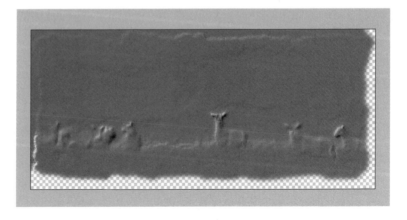

Figure 11-31
Edge of gray layer is erased

Erase the edge of the gray layer
This removes the dark area that looks out of place.

Figure 11-32
*Close-up of Art History
Brush—Emboss painting*

Figure 11-33
Finished Photoshop painting

Project 5: Painting in Painter

It is so incredible to be painting without the smell of turpentine, or dabs of paint on your clothes and surroundings. Painter allows the photographer to create a painterly rendition of a photograph, using tools that truly mimic the real art materials. In this exercise we will use a chalk cloner and a bristle oil cloner on our photograph.

The original image is never touched. It is the source of the colored pixels that we will draw from. With this method, you will never harm your original image.

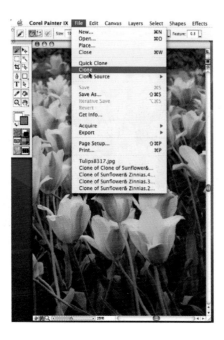

Figure 11-34
*Original photograph is
cloned*

Nature is the art of God.
—DANTE,
   De Monarchia (1321)

File—Clone

The command of Clone (under File) will create a duplicate that we will work on.

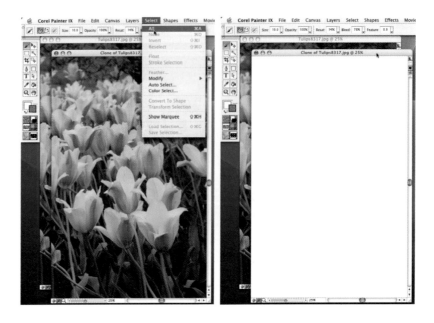

Figure 11-35
Select—All then delete

Select—All—Delete

It sounds crazy to delete the clone that you just made, but do it anyway. We will be drawing color information from the original and depositing it on this new piece of white paper. The paper doesn't need to be white, however. You could fill this clone layer with a solid fill of any color. We will stick with white for our exercise, though.

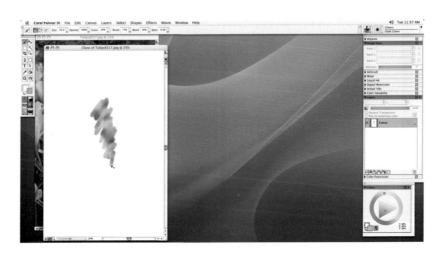

Figure 11-36
*Chalk Cloner selected:
cloning started*

Cloners—Chalk Cloner—Brush size 59 selected

Simply begin to stroke away on the cloned layer.

Figure 11-37
Chalk Cloner painted on the cloned layer

The size 59 brush—Chalk Cloner was used throughout the layer.

I cannot live without painting.
—MICHELANGELO,
   in *Michelangelo's Theory of Art*, by Robert C. Clements (1961)

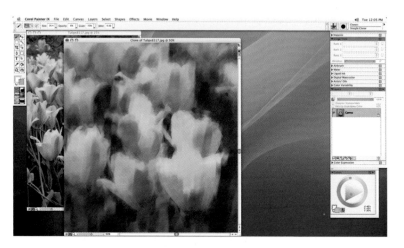

Figure 11-38
Straight Cloner is applied very lightly in selected areas

Cloners—Straight Cloner, set at 6% opacity and brushed over some edges

A little more definition was needed on some edges. The Straight Cloner restores the original photo very lightly in some areas. Be careful to not overdo it. You need a delicate balance of loose strokes and small areas of tight definition implied. It is a slender tightrope that you want to walk—a walk with a fluid, painterly feel, and yet enough detail for believability.

Figure 11-39
A Bristle Oil Cloner applied for a visible stroke

Cloner—Bristle Oil Cloner 15

This brush will pull the pigment nicely for visible brush strokes. It is not as harsh as some of the other oil brushes that give a thick impasto feel. This brush was used in much of the painting.

Figure 11-40
The Straight Cloner was applied very lightly in just a few places

Cloner—Straight Cloner, set at 65% opacity

Just a little more detail in a few spots, especially the foreground flowers. The flowers in the rear were purposely left very loose.

Figure 11-41
Completed tulip painting

The completed tulip painting is true to the breeze that was blowing throughout the tulip bed. It is rendered with the feel of the soft colors and waving tulips. Some of the tulips in the foreground are more differentiated, to lead the viewer into the scene.

These examples are meant to be a first step into some of the variety of techniques that are now available to you with the Photoshop and Painter. Enjoy the journey.

12

Essential Photoshop and Painter Techniques to Master

Although this book is not meant for absolute beginners in Photoshop and Painter, I realize that you may still need to improve some of your basic skills. What are the essential skills that are necessary to be proficient in these programs? This chapter will address the most basic techniques that will form the foundation of your digital knowledge base.

If you pare Photoshop down to its barest essentials it does two things: it allows the selection of an area of pixels to change and then the action that changes those selected pixels. That's it!

Novices are frequently overwhelmed by all the tools and options. What tool should I use and when? The answer is to use the tool most suited to the task at hand. In order to make that determination, you need to be thoroughly acquainted with your options. Be methodical

A picture is something which requires as much knavery, trickery, and deceit as the perpetration of a crime. Paint falsely, and then add the accent of nature.
—EDGAR DEGAS,
    in *The Notebooks of Edgar Degas*, trans. by T. Reff (1976)

in trying out the tools and making notes to yourself. Keep a notebook next to your computer, and keep notes. Also, buy a few books by the leaders in the field, or go to a workshop for hands-on instruction. Some folks learn best by actually seeing someone do it. You know best how you learn effectively.

My "Soapbox Lecture": Another strong recommendation is to set aside a certain number of hours each week devoted to learning this new digital artistic medium. Perhaps a Tuesday evening would work each week. Whatever fits in your schedule is right, whether you can devote three hours or twenty hours a week. Be focused and hold yourself to it. Discipline yourself to hold that time for your digital learning. Too often folks will do some productive work and then let weeks or months slip by, and they forget what they knew. Learning any new discipline requires practice. Compare it to a sport, such as biking. Lance Armstrong didn't pick up a bike and immediately win international races. Practice was required. A concert pianist has spent countless hours learning to play. You, too, need to be serious about learning these new skills and need to be focused in your approach. Success awaits the well-prepared person.

While I'm on my soapbox, I would really recommend taking a drawing class in your local area. Learning to draw will teach you so many things. It trains the eye to slow down and be attentive to line, light, shapes, contours, shadows, and more. It is all about seeing and recording what you see, whether it is with a camera or a pencil. Increase your sensitivity to your environment by drawing it and photographing it.

Additionally, while I'm on this soapbox, try to go to museums regularly. Learn at the feet of the masters. Degas, da Vinci, and van Gogh are no longer here to sit beside you and tell you their techniques, but they left a body of work to speak for them. If you make it a ritual to go to museums regularly, you will be surprised by the inspiration and technical tips you can pick up. Stand in front of a painting in two different ways: close-up, to look at brushwork, and from afar, to see the overall composition and design. From a distance you can see how the artist decided to use the four edges of the canvas. What was the "crop" used in this piece? How did that aid in the composition? What is the overall color impression? Although we often love a painting for its emotional impact on us, we will stick to basic techniques for those practical lessons. A close-up view can reveal traces of underpainting, layering, glazing, the size of the brushes used, the amount of paint used, the directionality of the strokes, and, most importantly, the colors used. In short, there is a gold mine of tips awaiting you in your local museums.

One more plea for developing your knowledge base is to take art history classes. So much can be learned. A class on the era of Impressionism will teach you so much about color usage. A class devoted to Japanese painting will be sure to affect your sense of design and composition. It is all related. Life is short; learn as much as you can as fast as you can.

I'll step down from the soapbox now to address some of the basic skills you should have tucked into your digital art tool belt.

Photoshop Selection Tools

There are many ways to select an area. The tool you choose to use depends on the nature of the selection at hand. Honestly, it is just common sense. Is the selection a large global one or a tight, precise one? Pick the tool that will do the job.

Figure 12-1
Rectangular, square, and feathered square marquee tool selections

Large global selections are most frequently made with the marquee tool. The rectangular marquee tool will make a precise rectangular selection. If you feather the selection, you will get a soft edge (the higher the number of pixels that are feathered, the softer and more gradual the edge). If you want a perfectly square selection, hold down the shift key to "constrain" the selection to a square.

Figure 12-2
Elliptical, circle, and feathered circle marquee tool selections

Nested with the rectangular marquee tool is the elliptical marquee tool. You can make an oval-shaped selection, a circular one (holding down the shift key), and a feathered selection. The feathered oval shape is great for the traditional vignette used in portraiture.

Figure 12-3
Lassoed selection

If you need to make an irregular-shaped selection you can use the lasso tool or magnetic lasso. It is nearly impossible to make a careful selection in one move. Instead, make a preliminary, rough selection. Then, modify the selection by adding to it (using the Shift key) or deleting from the selection (with the Option key held down).

Figure 12-4
Magic wand selection with a tolerance of 30, completed selection, and inversed selection

If the background is sufficiently different from the object to be selected, you might decide to use the magic wand tool to make your selection. This tool would not have been a good choice with our previous example of the sculpture because the background was too similar to the object (in color and tone). In our example in Figure 12-4 the background grassy area is sufficiently different from the statue. The tolerance of the magic wand tool was set at 30. That did not quite get all of the area. The missing sections were added to the selection with the help of the lasso. What was now selected was the grass, not the statue, so the selection was inverted. With the statue selected, it could be easily copied and pasted on to a transparent or white background.

If it is easier to paint with the brush tool, you might choose to use the Quick Mask option of making a selection.

Painting is for me but
another word for feeling.
—JOHN CONSTABLE,
  lecture, *Discoveries on
  Art* (1836)

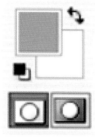

Figure 12-5
*Quick Mask mode located
on the right under the fore-
ground/background colors*

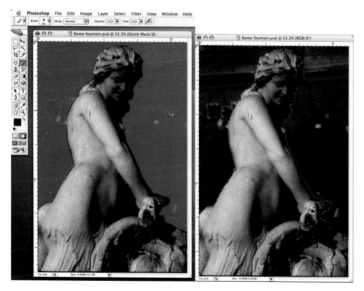

Figure 12-6
*Painting the Quick Mask
mode onto the image*

Select the Quick Mask mode (shown in Figure 12-5), and paint with your brush, using black. It will appear red on the screen, simulating the old rubylith material that was used for masking in the printing industry. If you make a mistake, use white to correct it. A soft-edge brush will yield a feathered selection. A hard-edge brush will give you a selection with precise edges. You are actually selecting the area you did not paint. Click back onto the button to the left of the Quick Mask mode button, and you will now be back to normal with your selection complete.

Photoshop: Transforming for Scale

You will often need to resize an object, especially when you are making a collage. The easiest way will most likely be to use the Transform command, located under Edit. Note: Transform will not work on a background layer. You can bypass that dead end by simply renaming the background layer to any other name. The shortcut is Command (the key with the apple icon on it on a Mac) + T. Memorize this shortcut, as you will use it a lot.

Figures 12-7–12-22 demonstrate a simple exercise for working with layers and the Transform tool.

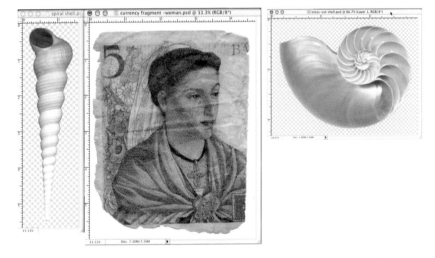

Figure 12-7
Component parts for scale exercise

This project began with a shred of old foreign currency, bought at an antique market, and two scans of seashells. The idea involved incorporating the long shell as a framing device and using the cross-cut shell as a kind of headdress for the woman on the currency. As the project evolved, more fine-tuning was done.

Figure 12-8
Long shell added

Long shell was placed on a new layer

The long shell was moved over onto the currency fragment. It occupies another layer. You can use the move tool to drag the shell onto the currency image (easiest) or copy and paste it.

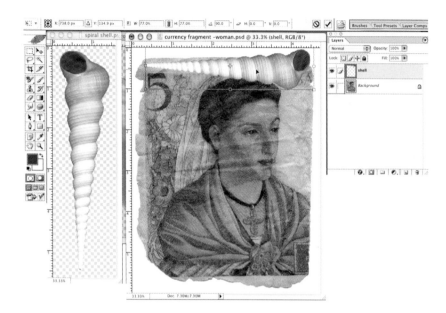

Figure 12-9
Long shell rotated and resized

Edit—Transform

Using the Edit—Transform command, the shell was rotated and scaled smaller. If you want to keep the proportions the same, hold down on the Shift key as you transform.

Figure 12-10
Second long shell added on third layer

Duplicate the shell layer by dragging that layer icon to the new layer icon at the bottom of the Layers palette
Flip horizontally
The shell layer was duplicated by dragging that layer icon to the new layer icon at the bottom of the Layers palette. The new shell was then transformed, flipping horizontally.

Figure 12-11
More shells added

Create two more layers and rotate the shells to create a frame
Two more shell layers were added, rotating and flipping them vertically to complete the framing effect.

You know a painting is finished when it no longer says, "Do something." Do something different, change that color. If it sits there mute, leave it alone.
—BERNARD ARNEST, in *Colorado Springs Gazette Telegraph* (April 28, 1984)

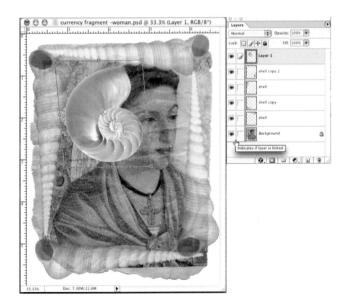

Figure 12-12
Cross-cut nautilus shell is added

New shell added, rotated, and scaled
Transform tool also was used in its Distort version to slant the new shell
The round cross-cut shell was added on yet another layer. It was rotated, scaled, and distorted using the Transform command.

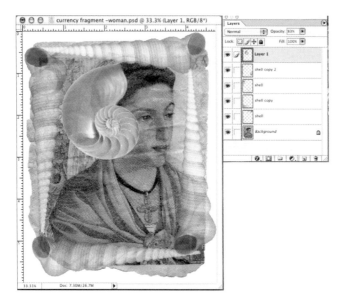

Figure 12-13
Opacity is adjusted for transparency

Adjust opacity on each layer
The long shells were each set at 68% opacity. The cross-cut shell was set at 83%.

Now we will digress from the Transform commands to finish the collage, using some other essential skills.

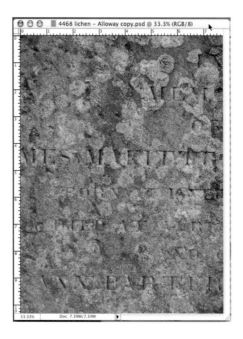

Figure 12-14
Additional element added

At this point I felt I needed a more cohesive element to pull all the components together and introduce more texture. I tried several, and decided on an image of a rough tombstone with lichen growth, photographed in Scotland. I decided to use it as the bottom layer.

Figure 12-15
Layers palette was condensed, by merging layers

Merge layers

It was time to clean up the Layers palette. I merged all the long shells into one layer. Layers were also named for ease of use. Opacity was lowered on the cross-cut shell and the blending mode was changed to Luminosity. This gave a more monotone effect.

Figure 12-16
Color increased

Currency layer duplicated, to add color
Layer mask used to dull-down the pointed ends of the long shells
Fine-tuning for optimum look and feel were now the task at hand. This often takes several hours and many different small changes for enhancement. Although I liked the monotone, muted color feel, I still wanted the currency fragment to have a slight bit more color punch. The currency layer was duplicated and the blending mode was set to normal and the opacity level was set to only 34%. The pointed ends of the long shells on the border were too bright for my tastes. To reduce their effect I used a layer mask to lessen their brightness.

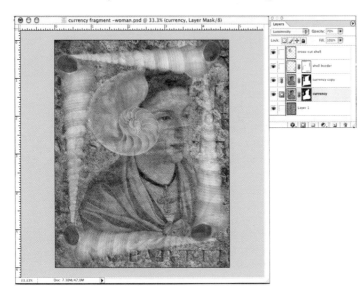

Figure 12-17
Layer mask added to both currency layers

Layer masks added and opacity was adjusted
A mask was added to both currency layers to eliminate the overhang beyond the shell border. Opacity was set at 70%.

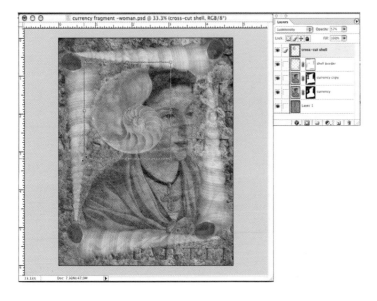

Figure 12-18
Cross-cut shell was transformed to a smaller size

Trifles make perfection
and perfection is no trifle.
—MICHELANGELO,
  in *Michelangelo's Theory
  of Art*, by Robert C.
  Clements (1961)

The round cross-cut shell now appeared too large. Transform was used again to resize that layer.

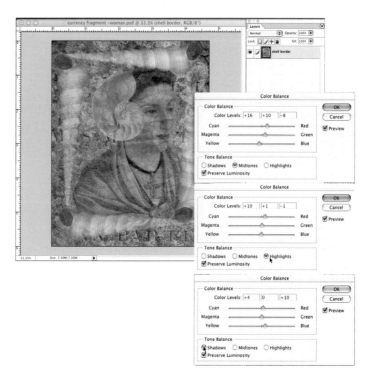

Figure 12-19
*Color Balance used to warm
up the entire image*

All layers merged
Image—Adjustment—Color Balance applied to warm up the entire image
The layered image was saved and then all layers were merged. The total image needed a little warming up in color. Color Balance was used to fine-tune the desired color feel.

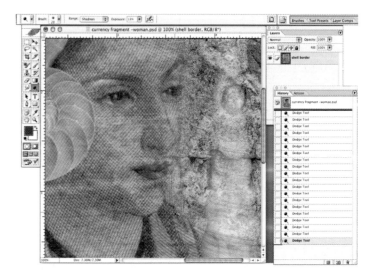

Figure 12-20
*Dodge tool used on currency
wrinkles*

Dodge tool was used on dark wrinkles of currency

The folds in the old wrinkled currency were a little too apparent in the almost finished piece. The Dodge tool was used at a low (13%) exposure. The affected areas appeared too milky in color. More color was needed. The eyedropper was used to get the approximate color needed.

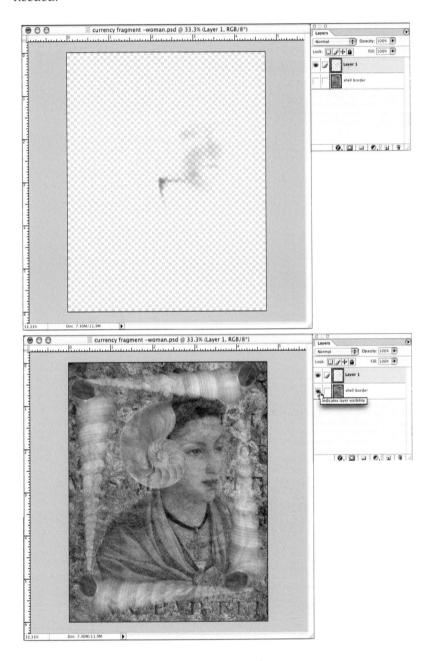

Figure 12-21
Colored brushed on new transparent layer

Add a new layer and paint color on it

A new transparent layer was added and color was brushed onto this new layer with the paintbrush set at a very low opacity. Any mistakes can be corrected on that layer. The original layer is not harmed with any brush strokes that go astray.

The finished piece, as you can see, relied heavily on the use of blending modes, layer masks, and adjustment layers.

Figure 12-22
Finished collage

Photoshop: Layer Adjustments

Figure 12-23
Original photograph: requesting a layer adjustment

There are two locations where you might select a layer adjustment. One is located under Image—Adjustments (in the top menu bar). If you use this method, the adjustment cannot be changed much later in the process. If, however, you choose the symbol that looks like a yin-yang, at the bottom of the Layers palette, you can always go back and change the adjustment later.

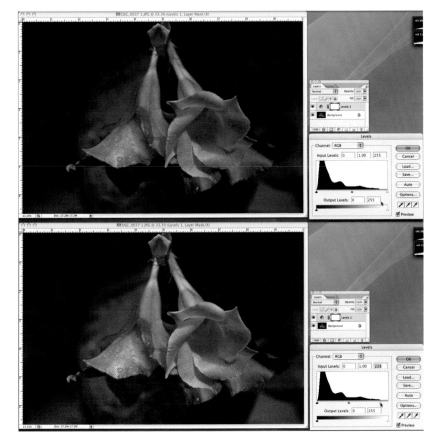

Figure 12-24
Levels adjustment

The Levels adjustment layer is helpful describing the file. There is a histogram that tells you where the pixels are located. In Figure 12-24, the preponderance of pixels are dark (located to the left of the middle gray slider). There are not very many light tones and no pure white. By moving the right-hand, white slider slightly to the left we managed to push more pixels to be lighter in tone. By doing this, you are reassigning your pixels, giving them a new address. By moving the sliders you are pushing pixels to be lighter or darker.

One of my favorite adjustment layers is Curves—I love it. It is practical for lots of different tasks but particularly good for improving contrast.

Figure 12-25
Curves adjustment

In the Curves dialogue box, black is at the lower left and white is at the upper right. If you slightly lift the light tones and drag down the dark areas, by placing a dot along the diagonal line and nudging a little, the resulting S-curve will yield an increase in contrast.

You can alter a color cast in Color Balance. If a photo is too yellow, magenta, or blue, you can move those pixels into a different color range by applying Color Balance to three areas: Highlights, Midtones, and Shadows.

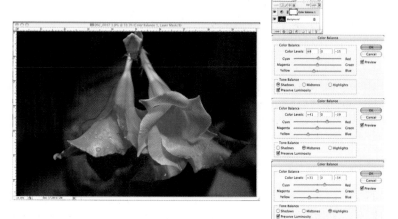

Figure 12-26
Color Balance adjustment

In our example (Figure 12-26) we have moved the pixels to be more yellow and red in all three areas. The resulting image yields a cluster of flowers that is more coral in color. Notice, however, that the adjustment was global and affected the color of the foliage also. We could have limited the affects to only the flower, if we had selected it.

The Hue/Saturation Adjustment is a good one if your image needs a stronger dose of color.

Figure 12-27
Saturation adjustment

If a photo is taken on a gray and cloudy day and the color was not vibrant enough, you may want to increase the saturation of the image, for punchier color.

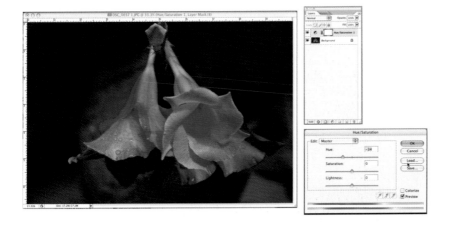

Figure 12-28
Hue adjustment

We can completely shift the hue of the image by pulling the Hue slider. In our example, we have turned our mandevilla flowers into purple blossoms. I don't think you will find that in any seed catalog!

Photoshop: Layer Masks

I often say to my students "Layer masks are your friend." I use a layer mask on almost every project that I work on. For some unknown reason, this technique seems to be the least understood of all the basic skills. Make the effort to understand layer masks and you will be amazed at how wonderful they are.

Figure 12-29
Black and white original photo

Think of a layer mask as a way of blending one image into another. With a layer mask you can choose to reveal or conceal any portion of the layer beneath. For this exercise we will start with a black and white photo, as our background image.

Figure 12-30
Sepia-colored layer added with Multiply mode, opacity set at 67%

Add a new layer and fill with brown tone
Set the blending mode to Multiply and the opacity to 67%

Our intentions were to blend the black and white image into an earth tone textured image. To make a better color match we created a new layer and filled it with a soft brown tone, setting the blending mode to multiply and the opacity at 67%.

When love and skill work together, expect a masterpiece.
—John Ruskin,
Art and Life (1886)

Figure 12-31
Coffee-stained watercolor paper

Scan a textured paper

The watercolor paper shown in Figure 12-31 was stained with coffee and the color was supplemented with pastels. Use your imagination to create a library of textural images that you can use in your collage work. Experiment!

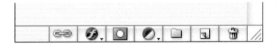

Figure 12-32
The layer mask icon is the square with a circle inside

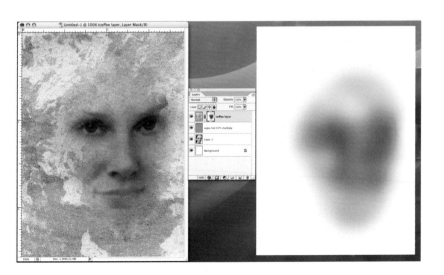

Figure 12-33
Layer mask (left) applied to the textured layer

Now add the layer mask

You can add the layer mask using the icon (looks like a circle in a square) from the bottom of the Layers palette, or from the menu (Layer—Layer Mask).

Add the coffee-stained watercolor paper layer

Add the layer mask

Use the brush tool with the color black and paint on the mask (located beside the thumbnail). Any area that has black on the mask will allow you to see the image layer beneath. In our example we wanted to see a portion of the face underneath. We wanted a soft blend, so we used a soft-edged brush and a low opacity of black. We built up a higher concentration of black on the eye area, revealing more of the image underneath. The other areas were softly brushed with a light opacity of black. If you make a mistake, simply switch the color from black to white and you will restore the image. It is fool-proof. A layer mask, unlike the eraser tool, allows you to custom fit the top layer onto the one beneath. It is reversible! Erasers actually remove pixels that you can't restore. The layer mask conceals or reveals pixels, but does not eliminate them forever. You have to love this tool!

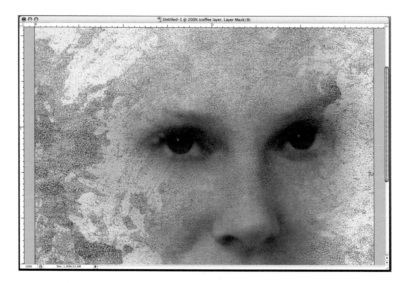

Figure 12-34

Close-up of face with a "feathered" mask

　　Notice the soft, gradual blend of the face into the textured layer. The layer mask allows you the ultimate control of opacity.

　　We took this collage a step further by adding handwritten text, stamps, and an image from a vintage postcard from Paris.

Figure 12-35
"Paris Collage" completed

Photoshop: Art History Brush

The Art History Brush allows you to lay down the pixels from your photo in a unique manner, depending on the brush you have selected.

Figure 12-36
*Original photo of boat,
selecting a new layer*

Good painting is like good cooking: it can be tasted, but not explained.
—MAURICE DE VLAMINCK,
   On Painting (c. 1901)

**Open your photo
Select a new layer**

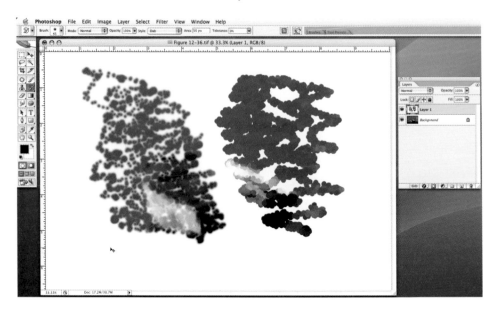

Figure 12-37
*Using the Dab Art History
Brush, size 45*

Fill the new layer with White (Edit—Fill)
Select the Art History Brush (has a curly-cue top on the icon and is
bundled with the History Brush)
Under Style (in the top modifier menu bar) select Dab
In Figure 12-37, brush size 45 was used. On the left-hand side a soft-edge brush was used; on the right hand side a hard-edge brush was used. There are lots of different brush styles to choose from; some effects resemble strands of lint from your clothes dryer—try them out. They are quite simply wild!

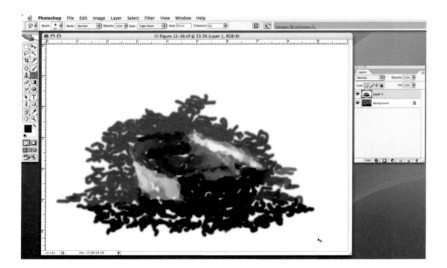

Figure 12-38
This style of brush stroke is called the Tight Short

Painting with the Tight Short style of brush, using a size 45.

Figure 12-39
A Spatter (46 pixels) brush selected from the lower end of the brush selections

Try out various brushes. This spatter brush alters the look of the Dab stroke.

Build Your Own Brush

Although there are loads of great brushes available to you, you can make more and it is easy.

Figure 12-40
Scratchy Brush marks made to construct a new brush

Make marks on a white layer to simulate the effect you want your brush to have
I wanted a rough-edged, scratchy brush.

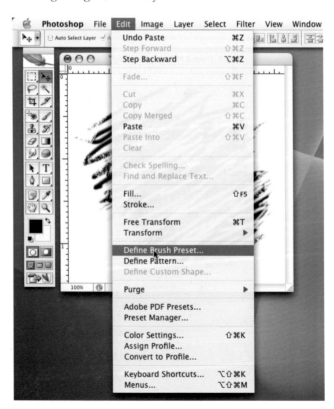

Figure 12-41
Define the brush preset

Simply go to Edit—Define Brush Preset

Figure 12-42
Give your brush a name

Name your brush; mine is Sue's Scratchy Brush 1. It is 384 pixels large—very big.

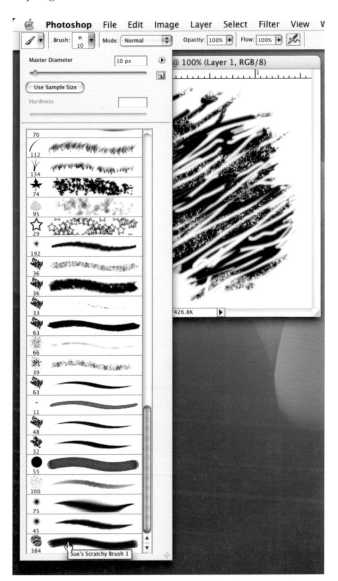

Figure 12-43
Your personalized brush will appear at the bottom of your brush menu

Your very own personalized brush will appear at the bottom of the brush menu. Doesn't that make you want to make more brushes?

Now back to our little boat. Let's use that scratchy brush.

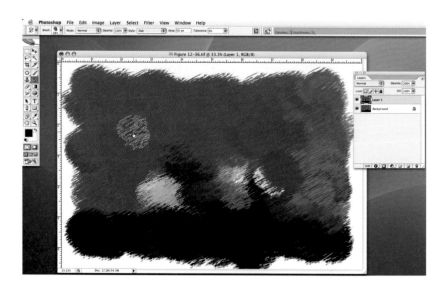

Figure 12-44
*Large custom-made scratchy
brush makes a quick painting*

Use the large brush to establish the scratchy edges that you desire for your artwork. It is, however, way too big to create any detail. Simply lower the brush size. The smaller the brush that you use, the more detail that will appear.

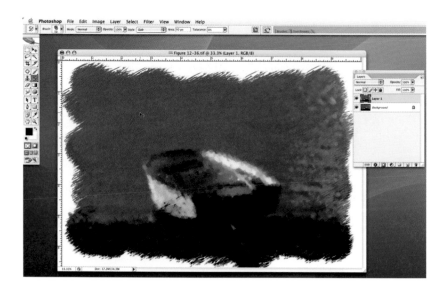

Figure 12-45
*A smaller brush size (50
pixels) was used on the
interior of the image*

Use a smaller brush to bring out more detail. It will still be somewhat clumpy, because it is a Dab stroke. The colors will be more true to the original photo, because the brush is smaller and isn't sampling a larger area. You are laying deposits of colored pixels.

Figure 12-46
A layer mask is added to bring back details

Add a layer mask if you want more detail

If the image does not have enough detail for you, use a layer mask on your painted layer, and with a light opacity black brush, stroke back some details, from the original, into your painting.

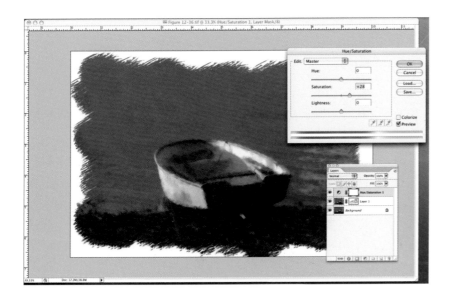

Figure 12-47
A Hue/Saturation adjustment layer was added to boost the saturation

Add a little saturation (if needed) using a Hue/Saturation adjustment layer

Our image was a little light in the saturation of colors, as it was taken at dusk. It needed a little boost in color.

Figure 12-48
Another new layer was added for some hand-coloring accents

Sculpture is the art of the hole and the lump.
—AUGUSTE RODIN,
   in *Art*, trans. by Paul
   Gsell (1912)

If you want to add some additional color accents, as we did, add another layer, setting it's blending mode to Color
With a light opacity brush, paint in your color accents. It is like glazing additional color on in an oil painting.

Figure 12-49
Completed Art History Scratchy Brush rendition painting

Note: The regular History Brush was described in Chapter 4.

Photoshop: Blending Modes

I know folks who have worked with Photoshop for years and have never taken the blending mode off the default, normal setting. Strange, but true. Blending modes are powerful ways to determine how two layers will interact. There are loads of blending modes. I'll discuss the ones that I use most frequently.

Screen

Figure 12-50
Screen blending mode used to lighten a photograph

Screen is absolutely invaluable! A quick fix for an underexposed photo is to duplicate the image and set the blending mode on Screen. It feels like you used a fill flash.

Multiply

Figure 12-51
Line art and photo combined

Multiply is a very versatile blending mode. In this mode, white disappears. The line art of the fish in Figure 12-51 was placed on top of the aerial photo. It is a bit of a pun on flying fish. The white background of the line art magically disappeared.

Figure 12-52
Multiply mode used to correct an overexposed image

If you have a photo that is overexposed (too light), simply duplicate the image and set the blending mode to Multiply. Voilà! If the effect is too strong, just lower the opacity of the duplicate layer. This trick may increase your saturation a little and it may have to be reduced separately.

Color

Figure 12-53
Color blending mode used to hand-color

Color is the ideal blending mode to use for hand-coloring. It will work on every area that is not pure white. Hand-coloring is performed on a separate transparent layer, where corrections can be made without altering the actual photograph. Color will appear on any area that is not pure white.

Overlay

Figure 12-54
Original black and white image of bride, Natalie, and her Dad

The Overlay mode is a great way to make consistent sepia-toned prints. And it is so easy. Select a black and white photo (it must be an RGB or CMYK image, not a grayscale image. It must have color channels to work with the color we will add.

A sketch is successful if it achieves its purpose by elimination and understatement and also, by suggesting what is left out.
—LEON GASPARD,
in *Leon Gaspard*, by Frank Waters (1964)

Figure 12-55
A color-filled layer, set to Overlay mode

Select a shade of brown that you like and use it to fill a new layer
Often the tone is too much. To tone it down, just lower the opacity. The color will not affect pure white at all.

Figure 12-56
Color-filled Overlay layer is reduced to 40% opacity

Reduce opacity to 40% on the Overlay layer
If you write down the numbers for the fill color (ours was Red 241, Green 155, and Blue 71) and use it exclusively, you will have consistent sepia-toned prints. Hint: You could write an action for this task, if you repeat it frequently.

Photoshop: Using Layer Adjustments, Layer Masks, and Blending Modes Together

Since we have just learned some uses for blending modes and a little layer masking, let's take all of the techniques out for a spin.

Figure 12-57
Original photo of a young mother's tombstone

I was touched when walking through a New England cemetery to spot the simple tombstone of a young mother who had been preceded in death by two young daughters. The gesture of the hand holding a rose in full bloom was symbolic and tender. Upon looking at the image later, I thought I should bring the flower to life, using a real rose.

Things are not difficult to make; what is difficult is to put oneself in a state to make them.
—Constantin Brancusi, in *Brancusi: A Study of the Sculpture*, by Sidney Geist (1968)

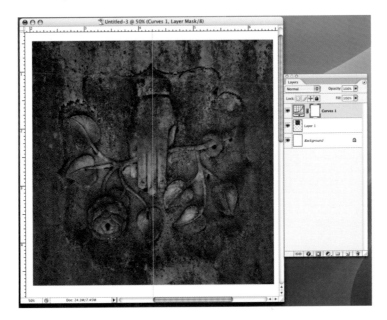

Figure 12-58
A Curves adjustment layer was made to increase the contrast

A Curves adjustment layer was added for contrast
The photograph was flat tonally. It had been taken in heavy shade. A slight S-curve was added with a Curves adjustment layer to increase the contrast.

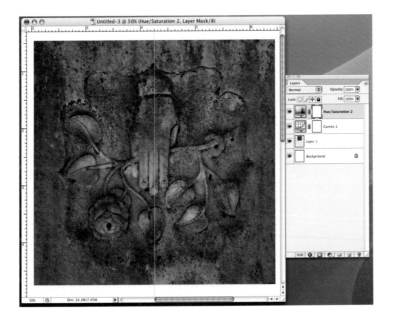

Figure 12-59
Hue/Saturation adjustment layer

Saturation was increased with an adjustment layer
Color Saturation was increased with an Adjustment Layer.

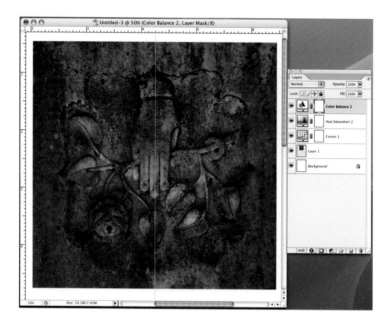

Figure 12-60
Color Balance adjustment layer

Color was shifted to warmer tones using another adjustment layer: Color Balance
The image was too green. Green was lessened and warmer tones (reds, and a touch of magenta) were added.

We need no instincts but our own.
—LA FONTAINE,
  Tables (1664)

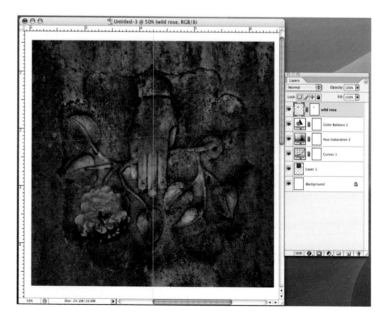

Figure 12-61
A real rose layer was added with an accompanying Layer Mask

A photo of a real red rose was added
A layer mask was placed on the rose layer to carefully mask the edges of the rose

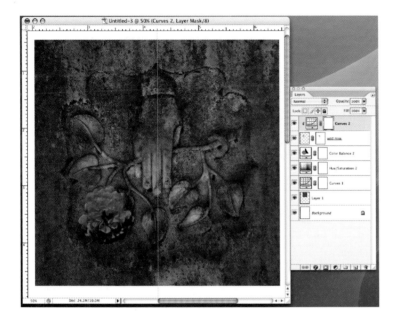

Figure 12-62
*Curves adjustment layer
with a Clipping Mask*

Curves adjustment layer was added and the effect was confined to just the rose layer by using a Clipping Mask
The rose was a bit too bright for the entire image. A Curves adjustment layer lowered the contrast and brightness. A Clipping Mask was used to confine that effect to just the rose layer.

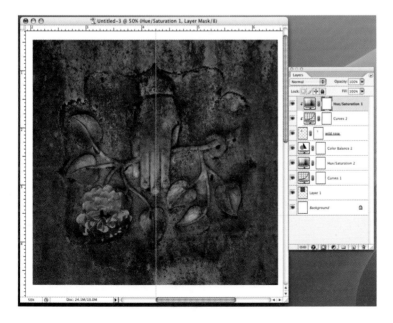

Figure 12-63
*Hue/Saturation adjustment
layer with a Clipping Mask*

**The color was too strong so the saturation was lowered using a Hue/
Saturation adjustment layer**
The saturation on the rose was lowered to a softer tone. But the color
was still not correct for the overall image.

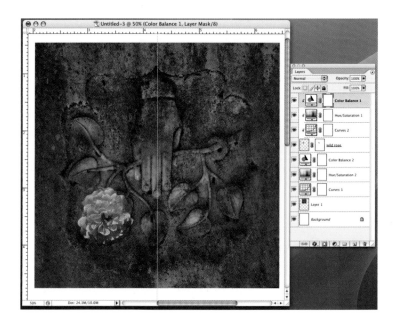

Figure 12-64
*Color Balance adjustment
layer with a Clipping Mask*

The Color was changed with a Color Balance Adjustment Layer
The softer apricot color was better suited to the overall image.

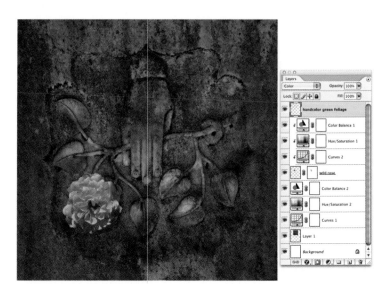

Figure 12-65
*Shades of green were painted
onto a new layer, using the
Color blending mode*

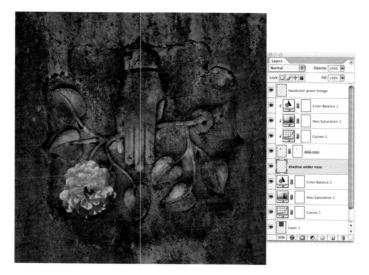

Figure 12-66
A light shadow was added under the rose

A new transparent layer was added: the blending mode was set to Color
Various shades of green were selected and painted onto the new layer with a low-opacity brush
In an effort to tie the sculptural relief on the stone to the rose layer, the leaves and vines were hand-colored.

A new layer was added for a slight shadow under the rose layer
A brownish-gray color was painted onto the new layer, to create a shadow

Beauty is the sense of life and the awe one has in its presence.
—WILLA CATHER,
  Song of the Lark (1917)

Figure 12-67
Completed "Hand and Flower Collage"

Editing Your Images: Retouching—Cover-Girl Skin, Brightening Teeth and Eyes

Retouching

Retouching can be a great way to put your Photoshop skills to good use. Our example (Figure 12-68) features a bridesmaid, my daughter, Emily at age 25, photographed in natural light, under the edge of a pavilion.

Figure 12-68

Before and after the retouching job

Although Emily is still quite young, several summers of working as a lifeguard had taken a toll on her skin. She has, in this photo, light lines on her forehead, and wrinkling near her eyes. Retouching will even out the skin tone.

Figure 12-69

Patch tool selection of eye area

Select the area you would like to correct with the patch tool
Move the patch tool to a good section of skin tone (it doesn't need
to be the same coloring)
This is such a fabulous tool! It is so much easier than matching up skin
tones using the rubber stamp tool.

Figure 12-70
*Patch area "implanted," and
later, faded a little*

The patch was too much of a difference. Edit—Fade was used to
restore some of the original
Remember, you don't want to eliminate the natural lines of the face,
just lessen their impact. You still want the image to look like the person,
just a bit more refreshed.

Figure 12-71
*Patch tool selecting a line on
the forehead*

The patch tool was used on the forehead to decrease the appearance
of lines

The sense of the beautiful
is God's best gift to the
human soul.
—William Henry
    Hudson, *Green Mansions*
    (1937)

Figure 12-72
Smooth forehead after patch tool work

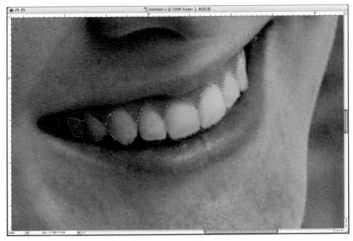

Figure 12-73
Lasso tool selection of the teeth, with a feather of two

Lasso the teeth with a feather of 2
Use an Adjustment Layer of Curves to brighten the teeth

Teeth whitening is all the rage. This one doesn't cost a penny. Simply lighten the teeth using a Curves Adjustment layer.

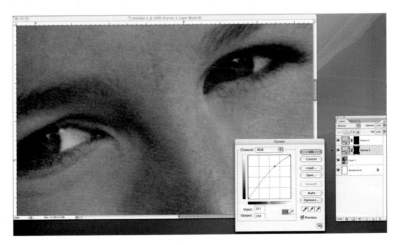

Figure 12-74
Whites of the eyes selected for lightening with curves

The whites of the eyes were lightened, just a little, using that same process

No matter how rested you are, the whites of your eyes can appear bloodshot and too dark. We can help them out, adding a little sparkle to the image.

Figure 12-75
Wrinkles and lines softened, and teeth and whites of eyes brightened

The image is perfectly good now, but if you want to go for the flawless cover-girl look, proceed to the next step.

Figure 12-76
Gaussian Blur applied to a duplicate layer

Duplicate the image
Apply a Gaussian Blur to the copy layer
Move the slider until all blemishes, freckles, etc. are gone
Add a layer mask to bring back detail

Bring back the detail in the eyes, lips, hair, edge of nose, edge of face, etc. This leaves the face blemish-free and flawless. The foliage in the background was already out of focus, and didn't need to be altered.

Figure 12-77
Comparison of original and retouched images

A side-by-side comparison of the close-ups (Figure 12-77) reveals the difference that is possible using retouching techniques.

Figure 12-78
Completed retouching with opacity lessened

You put a blob of yellow here, and another at the further edge of the canvas; straight away a rapport is established between them. Color acts in the way that music does, if you like.
—GEORGES BRAQUE, letter to Dora Viallier, in *The Art of Georges Braque*, by Edwin Mullins (1968)

For my tastes, the image in Figure 12-77 is a bit too flawless, so I lowered the opacity of the Gaussian Blur layer, allowing some of the original to show through. The image in Figure 12-78 appears more natural, albeit improved compared to the original.

Painter Basic Papers

One of the wonderful tools in Painter gives you the ability to simulate various paper textures. These textures can enrich your artwork. Try them out and see what works for your imagery. Figure 12-79 shows a few.

Figure 12-79
Paper textures available in the Painter IX Paper Selector menu

Paper textures vary in different versions of Painter. You can import old textures and create new ones. The paper texture can really affect the look of your artwork, depending on which art medium was used.

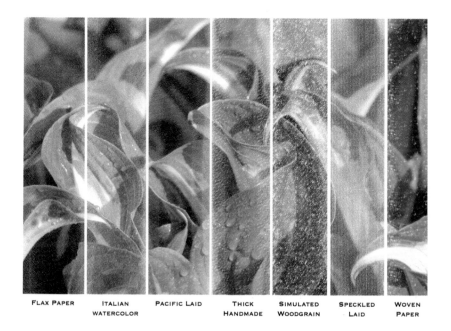

FLAX PAPER   ITALIAN WATERCOLOR   PACIFIC LAID   THICK HANDMADE   SIMULATED WOODGRAIN   SPECKLED LAID   WOVEN PAPER

Figure 12-80
Various paper textures in Painter

Painter Cloning Brushes

Some of the most important tools for a photographer in Painter are the cloner brushes. Each one handles color, saturation, and dispersal of the pigment in a different way. Some cloners increase the color saturation. Some cloners let the pigment actually run. Try them out, vary them—they can be used successfully in combination.

Figure 12-81
Various cloning brushes

Figure 12-81 shows the effects of the following Painter cloning brushes:

A—Coarse Spray Cloner
B—Camel Oil Cloner
C—Impressionist Cloner
D—Watercolor Wash
E—Thick Bristle Cloner
F—Furry Cloner
G—Graffiti Cloner
H—Fiber Cloner
I—Flat Impasto Cloner
J—Straight Cloner
K—Van Gogh Cloner
L—Melt Cloner

H—Soft Cloner
N—Oil Brush Cloner
O—Watercolor Run Cloner
P—Cloner Spray

Cloning Without a Cloning Brush

Although most users of Painter will only use the existing cloner brushes to clone a photo, don't stop there. The painting in Figure 12-85 was achieved with a brush that was not a cloner. You can make other brushes become cloners by selecting the cloning option (looks like a rubber stamp tool) in the color picker. Follow along on the steps that were used to create this painting of geraniums in a windowsill.

Figure 12-82
Clone the photo

File—Clone
Select All—Delete
When working from an existing photo, open the photo in Painter and choose File—Clone. From there, choose Select All and delete the image. This appears to leave a blank page. It seems counterintuitive. Simply

click on the box at the upper right-hand top edge of the image and, voilà, you can see your original image through a faux layer of tissue paper. Another way to achieve this (and it is faster) is to go to File—Quick Clone.

Figure 12-83
Oils—Thick Wet Oils #30 (fat brush)

Select Oils—Wet Oils #30
Select the Cloning option in the color picker palette
Paint the entire canvas with a large, thick brush
A good way to see your composition more clearly is to paint initially with a large, thick brush. This allows you to better visualize the large blocks of color, contrast, and organizational design.

Figure 12-84
Close-up of loose brush work with the Thick Wet Oils brush

A little smaller brush (#16) was used to bring a bit more detail into the piece. Next, a new layer was added and a light application of blue was added to the upper windowpanes with the Oils—Round Glazing Brush set at a very low opacity. This increased the blue color saturation in the upper portions of the window.

Figure 12-85
Completed—"Red Geraniums in the Window"

This painting was deliberately kept loose with its wet oil brush strokes. Many of the Painter brushes will work for you as cloners, if you use the cloner tool in the color picker palette. The options available to you are quite simply staggering.

Figure 12-86 illustrates a composition that was simplified and the nik Burnt Sienna filter was used selectively.

I would suggest picking up a few good books on Painter. Focal Press has two excellent books devoted solely to Painter. They are Martin Addison's *Painter IX for Photographers* and Jeremy Sutton's *Painter IX Creativity*. They are both full of illustrations, step-by-step tutorials, and fine explanations.

This book was not meant to be a primer on the extensive programs available in Photoshop and Painter, but this chapter may by helpful in highlighting the basic skills that will make your task of collaging or digital painting a little easier. As always, I would encourage experimentation. Keep a notebook beside your computer for notes to yourself about tools, brushes, techniques, and more. Become familiar with your options and you will have more artistic avenues to explore.

In closing, it is a joy, as an artist, to have more tools available for making art. The digital tools currently available to us warrant serious consideration as a legitimate art medium, equal to any other being exhibited today. Whether you are a photographer or a conventional artist, the digital art tools demonstrated in this book can add to your repertoire of art mediums to use. As you pursue creating art, brushes loaded with colored pixels can equal those loaded with pigment. It is, after all, all about making meaningful marks. I hope you enjoy exploring the possibilities.

Figure 12-86—*"Hawaiian Surfer Sunset"*

13 *Resources*

. . . .

Suppliers: Equipment, Software, Tools, and Artist Materials

Adobe Systems Incorporated
www.adobe.com
345 Park Avenue
San Jose, CA 95110-2704

Apple Computer, Inc.
www.apple.com
(408) 996-1010
1 Infinite Loop
Cupertino, CA 95014-2084

OPPOSITE PAGE: *"Peonies"*

Auto FX
www.autofx.com
(205) 980-0056
(800) 839-2008
151 Narrows Pkwy, Suite E
Birmingham, AL 35242

Corel Corporation
www.corel.com
FAX (613) 274-6373
1600 Carling Ave.
Ottawa, Ontario, Canada K1Z8R7

Digital Art Supplies
www.digitalartsupplies.com
(877) 534-4278
9596 Chesapeake Dr., Suite B
San Diego, CA 92123
Digital printing supplies

Epson America, Inc.
www.epson.com
(800) 463-7766
3840 Kilroy Airport Way
Long Beach, CA 90806

inkAID
www.inkaid.com
(888) 424-8167
Manufacturer: Ontario Specialty Coatings Corp.
16830 County Route 155
Watertown, NY 13601

Kolo
www.kolo.com
(888) 636-5656
P.O. Box 572
Windsor, CT 06095-0572

Lazertran LLC
www.lazertran.com
(800) 245-7547
1501 West Copans Rd., Suite 100
Pompano Beach, FL 33064
(Manufactured in the UK)

Lineco, Inc.
www.lineco.com
(800) 322-7775
P.O. Box 2604

Holyoke, MA 01041
Flexible hinge binding strips; books-by-hand supplies

National Association of Photoshop Professionals
www.photoshopuser.com
(800) 738-8513
333 Douglas Road East
Oldsmar, FL 34677

nik Color Efex Pro
www.nikmultimedia.com
(619) 725-3150
7580 Metropolitan Drive, Suite 208
San Diego, CA 92108

Paper and Ink Arts
www.paperinkarts.com
(800) 736-7772
3 North Second Street
Woodsboro, MD 21798
Source for Pergamenata (lightweight parchment paper from Italy)

R&F Handmade Paints
www.rfpaints.com
(800) 206-8088
506 Broadway
Kingston, NY 12401

Encaustic supplies
SiteWelder
www.sitewelder.com
(800) 646-7483
10201 Meredith Avenue
Silver Spring, MD 20910
Web site construction for photographers and artists

Wacom Technology Corporation
www.wacom.com
(800) 922-6613
1311 SE Cardinal Court
Vancouver, WA 98683
Wacom tablets

Digital Collage and Painting Web Site

http://www.focalpress.com/companions/digitalcollageandpainting
   This web site contains images used in the tutorials and examples in
Chapter 11 of this book.

Index